A NICKEL AN INCH

ED FITZGERALD

A NICKEL AN INCH

A MEMOIR

ATHENEUM
New York
1985

The lines from "Bridget O'Flynn" (Copyright 1926. Renewed
Shapiro, Bernstein & Co. Inc.) and from "Beautiful Texas"
(Copyright 1933. Renewed Shapiro, Bernstein & Co. Inc.)
are used by permission of Shapiro, Bernstein & Co. Inc.

The lines on pages 42–43 are from "Worner Revisited" in The
Talk of the Town, *The New Yorker*, April 13, 1981. Reprinted
by permission; © 1981 The New Yorker Magazine, Inc.

The extracts reprinted from *Sport* are used by permission.

The excerpt on pages 129–130, "An Appointment in Samarra," is
from *Sheppey*, A Play in 3 Acts, by W. Somerset Maugham.
Copyright 1933 by W. Somerset Maugham; copyright renewed
1961. Reprinted by permission of Doubleday & Company, Inc.

Library of Congress Cataloging-in-Publication Data

Fitzgerald, Ed. ———
    A nickel an inch.

    1. Fitzgerald, Ed. ———. 2. Publishers and
publishing and publishing—United States—Biography.
I. Title.
Z473.F56F57   1985   070.5′092′4 [B]   85-47777
    ISBN 0-689-11590-3

For Liby

who still knows how to ring the night bell

The life so short,
The craft so long to learn.
GEOFFREY CHAUCER

A NICKEL AN INCH

Chapter 1

TH E last night of the war wasn't the worst one, but it was the loudest.

It was the night of June 21, 1945, on Okinawa, an island I'd never heard of in my life until right after we got off Ie Shima, where Ernie Pyle was killed, and Captain Bauer called a few officers and me, the first sergeant, to his cabin on the U.S.S. *Monrovia* and unrolled the maps and the plans for our next landing. But it seemed like we'd been on Okinawa forever, and we had been since April Fools' Day, although, as usual in the Pacific, nobody back home knew there was anybody on the island except the Marines.

Not that it mattered much who had done what. What mattered was that it was almost over now and the ground rolling under our stomachs and the persistent screams of shells over our heads was mostly our artillery going out, not much of theirs coming in. Naha and Shuri Castle had finally been taken and all that the Japanese had left was a few miles of mostly flat ground from the last height on the island, Ara Point, to the East China Sea.

The ground jumped under us so much it made me think of Ingrid Bergman and Gary Cooper in the movies, and the relentlessly increasing noise of the firing behind us and the explosions in front of us sounded like the end of the Fourth of July fireworks when they shoot off everything they've got left to tell you that's all there is, there isn't any more, go home.

The next night we were still on the same hill, right in the same place, but it was a whole lot different. We were out of our holes and we were heating our C rations on Coleman stoves for the first time in four months. I mixed water and a can of meat-and-vegetable stew in my canteen cup and made a thing that tasted like a can of Campbell's vegetable-beef soup. It was delicious, especially with some of the Medical Detachment's whole-grain alcohol mixed with grapefruit juice on the side. Nobody was shooting at us and we guessed nobody was likely to because the word was that the Japanese commander, General Ushijima, had leaned on his dagger and was no more. We would be going down to the beaches in a few days, they said, to load on ship. Cebu, Captain Bauer had heard, for a rest before Japan.

After two years out there, we were pretty good at looking up islands. Cebu was in the Philippines, which we knew about from two beach landings on Leyte, at Tacloban on the west and Ormoc on the east coast.

We didn't have to look up Japan.

What we did was sit around and eat and drink the medical alcohol and talk about what we were going to do after we got home. What we were going to do second, that is. First, for sure, was to see her— in my case Liby, the girl (they were girls then; they had to get older before they became women) with the best legs, the best backhand and the best behind in Gorton High School, Yonkers, New York. Liby had been Mrs. Fitzgerald since June 6, 1942, D-Day minus two years, a twenty-two-year-old bride at the post chapel at Fort Jackson, South Carolina. She was going to come first.

We didn't talk much about our Libys, mostly about what we wanted to do with our lives with them.

John C. ("Desperate") Turner wanted to go right back to driving "the Hound," the Greyhound bus that had made him a good living before the war. Joe Price, the company's song-and-dance man, wanted to go back to being a doorman in an apartment house on the West Side of New York City. "With marble floors," he said proudly. Phil Miller, the company mailman, wanted to go back to being the curator of music at the New York Public Library. (This was the Seventy-seventh Infantry Division, New York's Own, with the Statue of Liberty patch on everybody's arm.) Donald Metzger wanted to go back to West Springfield, Massachusetts, and get into politics. He had no interest in working.

I wanted to go back to writing for a newspaper—not the one I had left in Yonkers, but one of the big ones in New York City. There were a lot of them then—the *Times*, the *Mirror*, the *News*, the *Herald-Tribune*, the *Journal*, the *World-Telegram*, the *Sun*, the *Post* . . . One of them might have a job.

What I didn't know was that they all had two staffs, the one from before the war and the one from during the war. It might have been easier to break into the movies. So I ended up back at the *Herald-Statesman* in Yonkers, city of Otis Elevator and Alexander-Smith Carpets and Habirshaw Cable & Wire and the remnants of Dutch Schultz's ingenious Prohibition pipeline in the city's sewer from his brewery on Chicken Island near City Hall to the docks on the Hudson River waterfront. But that was later.

First, of course, we had to get back home, which, for me, turned out to be even harder than it was for most of the men in the company. After Cebu, where we heard about the atomic bomb while we were celebrating the opening of our just completed bamboo recreation hall, we were sent to an old Japanese officers' academy outside the city of Sapporo on the northern home island of Hokkaido.

Landing day on Hokkaido was an occasion. The major islands, Kyushu, Honshu and Hokkaido, were occupied at once, and the flower and glory of the United States Pacific Fleet escorted us in: destroyer escorts, destroyers, light and heavy cruisers, aircraft carriers and the big battleships themselves. We had been out there for two years and we had had ringside seats at the Battle of Leyte Gulf, but we had never seen an American battleship. At Leyte they were far off in the distance. The only ships that big we'd actually seen were Japanese.

We landed carrying full field equipment—rifles, bayonets, hand grenades, the works—and an hour later we were shopping in down-town Sapporo's biggest department stores with the Occupation Scrip they had given us on the ship. I bought Liby an obi.

The camp wasn't bad. I had an office I could sleep in as well as work in, and the barracks had showers. We could even buy fresh vegetables from the farmers in the neighborhood, although when we ate them the more squeamish among us had to forget that they were fertilized naturally, and at night we could go to the whore-houses in town and buy beer. Good Japanese beer, and cold. They didn't even mind if that was all you bought. You couldn't get the beer anyplace else.

From there we went, a group at a time, to an embarkation station on the Yokohama waterfront, and that seemed closer. But all we did was wait and wait and wait. At least I found out that I could borrow books from a gleaming white hospital ship docked close by. But it was a long wait; I wrote a lot of letters to Liby. Then, one exciting day, the bulletin board showed orders for a dozen first sergeants from the 307th Infantry Regiment, including me, to re-port to a ship that had just arrived in port, and we figured finally we were in. If they wanted a dozen first sergeants, it must be a big ship, maybe even one of the converted passenger liners, and we probably would have to look after work details and loading and billeting and all that. But that turned out to be a fantasy. All we ever were able to figure was that somebody somewhere had it in for first sergeants, because we turned out to be the only passengers on the USS *Samuel Chase*, a Liberty Ship with a cracked piston that had arrived in Japan too late to help the war and was being sent back to the Brooklyn Navy Yard by way of the Panama Canal. The trip took us fifty-six days, relieved only by three or four hours of drink-ing time at Balboa in the Canal Zone.

We didn't suffer on the *Samuel Chase*, we only suffered because we were on it. The food on the ship was good, served, for God's sake, on real china by Filipino messboys, and there was a lot of it, but we drowned in self-pity even when the cook came into the dayroom and asked us what we wanted for dinner tonight, beef, chicken or veal. We weren't consoled even by our three-to-a-cabin sleeping accommodations with adjoining bathrooms, a hell of a long way from personally dug slit trenches and personally dug round holes in the ground. All we knew was that they were taking a long time to get us home. "The only thing afloat slower than this tub," I wrote Liby, "is the Yonkers Ferry."

I had said goodbye to my friend Ricky DelMar in Sapporo with me leaving and him staying and both of us convinced that I had struck gold and he had been screwed, but Captain DelMar took Liby out to dinner in New York a month before I made it to Fort Hamilton in Brooklyn two days before Christmas. And then they wouldn't let our limping *Santa María* dock at the fort because it was loaded with dynamite. It took two hours of arguing and passionate declarations on our part that if they didn't take us in, we would swim in, before the harbormaster relented and let the Army send a small boat for us.

The second lieutenant who met us at the dock said he would give us transportation to Fort Dix but he wasn't authorized to give us home leave for Christmas, even though Christmas was the day after tomorrow. We looked at each other and, in sign language perfected after four years, agreed to take his orders and his money. Then we said we would meet at Dix the day after Christmas and face the firing squad together. I called Liby's office, found out from her that she had a room at the Commodore waiting for us and fled Fort Hamilton in the most beautiful vehicle I'd seen in years, a New York City yellow cab.

Liby was the thinnest I'd ever seen her, but it felt to me like there was a lot of her.

7

Chapter 2

THERE was a spectacular parade in New York on the day I was born, September 10, 1919, but it wasn't for me. General John J. Pershing, commander-in-chief of the American Expeditionary Forces, old Black Jack himself, was in town to lead 25,000 returned veterans down Fifth Avenue from 107th Street to Washington Square. The general had to ride a borrowed horse because his own famous sorrel, Kidron, had been quarantined at Newport News, Virginia, by an unsentimental Department of Agriculture which worried that he might have caught something in France. But Pershing relished every minute of the parade. "I never saw anything like it," the general said, "and I never expect to see anything like it again." His aide, Colonel George C. Marshall, agreed. Only the absence of his beloved horse, which they had let him ride in earlier emotional welcomes in Paris and London, bothered Black Jack. It bothered him enough that he changed mounts in the middle of the march. "Too bad," one parade watcher said, "it's like seeing Grant without Cincinnati or Lee without Traveler."

But the mood of the day was exultant, proud, even boastful. Our boys had gone Over There and they hadn't come back till it was over Over There, and now here they were. The general kissed Miss Kittie Dalton, who gave him a bouquet of American Beauty roses, and he shook hands with little boys and returned a thousand salutes with West Point precision. The crowd loved him, and one of the crowd was my father, Frank Fitzgerald.

My father, an Irish immigrant who had become a naturalized citizen four years before, had worked at the Picatinny Arsenal near Dover, New Jersey, during the war, but now the family lived on West 58th Street and he had a job at Aeolian Hall on 42nd Street, where on a good day he might see John McCormack. Being so close, he went to see the big parade and let my mother take care of having their second child. It's a good thing it was an exciting parade because she never let him forget it. She would remind him of it every time she heard the old Irish ditty:

> Bridget O'Flynn, where have you been, Bridget O'Flynn?
> Sure, it's a fine time for you to come in.
> You've been to see the big parade?
> The big parade me eye.
> Sure, no parade could ever take so long in passin' by.
> Look at your shoes, ain't they a sin?
> Faith, your story and your shoes look mighty thin.
> Now, keep away from them dancin' halls,
> There's nobody there worth while at all,
> 'Twas there I met your father, Bridget darlin'.

It was a full day for the general. Before dinner he hurried to Central Park, where the New York Symphony Orchestra gave a concert for him on the Mall. He did at least have a chance to relax after the dinner. The city fathers took him and his staff to Ziegfeld's *Follies* at the New Amsterdam Theatre.

My remembered life began not on West 58th Street in Manhattan, where we stayed for a year after I was born, but on Oak Street in Yonkers, way up Nodine Hill on the No. 9 trolley line in a poor neighborhood where all the streets were named after trees, Elm, Ash, Linden, Chestnut, Maple, Poplar, Spruce, Cedar, Walnut, Beech and Willow.

Oak Street was high above the Hudson River, an old part of an old city much like an English manufacturing town. A lamplighter used to come around every evening and light the gas lamps in front of the cold-water apartment building we lived in.

Alma Lyon, a widow with two grown children, Al and Evelyn, lived on the first floor of 76 Oak Street and from my earliest years I became her errand boy. If she needed a quart of milk or a newspaper or a pack of cigarettes, I would get it for her.

When my mother and father moved from that old stone-faced tenement, blocks away from the municipal baths on Yonkers Avenue, to Northeast Yonkers, a slightly better part of town, I missed Mrs. Lyon a lot and I used to walk back to The Hill on Sunday morning to see her. Sometimes I even saw Missy, which is what they called Evelyn, in her slip or less as she had her first cup of coffee. She was the first woman I ever saw anything of.

Then one day, a couple of blocks away from our new apartment on Bartholdi Place—I'm one of the few people who has always known who made the Statue of Liberty—I saw Missy again, standing outside her new office. A. J. KIPFER & SONS, ENGINEERING, the sign said. Missy invited me in to talk and I sat with her for a couple of hours while she typed letters. The typewriter fascinated me and I asked her if I could try it. She wanted to show me how to do it right, but I was too impatient for that and I began hitting the keys the way I've been hitting them ever since. Forefinger left hand, forefinger right hand, left thumb for the space bar. The typewriter became my life and I went to Missy's office every day after school to practice.

I also read my head off. I made such a fuss at the Yonkers Public Library that they finally let me into the adult room. I celebrated my victory over authority and the twelve-year age rule by taking home Thomas Wolfe's *Look Homeward, Angel*.

Meanwhile I was doing all kinds of things to make a dollar. My friend Mike Rose, whose grandfather owned a milk company, let me help him with five a.m. deliveries that got me not only a couple of dollars but also an occasional pint of heavy cream for my mother and a bottle of buttermilk for my father, who, inexplicably to me, loved it. I cleaned up Doc Burns' drugstore on Warburton Avenue and sometimes was allowed to make cherry Cokes while he was in the back room dispensing paregoric, Lydia Pinkham's Vegetable Compound and Virginia Dare Wine Tonic. As a special show of confidence, he would even let me make somebody a chocolate malted with milk, chocolate syrup, chocolate ice cream and Horlick's malted-milk powder. I delivered bags of groceries for a fancy fruit-and-vegetable store on South Broadway that catered to people who lived in the elevator apartment buildings from Morris Street to Valentine Lane. The buildings wouldn't let delivery people in the elevators, so I had to lug my paper bags up the back stairs to hand them over in exchange for my nickel tip. I got a lot of dimes, too, and if the lady of the house was a real sweetheart and thought I looked too skinny to be carrying two bags full of everything from potatoes to large fresh eggs, I might even get a quarter. I stayed with that job until I had saved up enough money to buy a Bancroft Super-Winner tennis racquet strung with real gut. Nylon was for the peasants.

My one failure in the job market was my total inability to persuade the manager of the Western Union office in Getty Square to hire me as a messenger. I had a bicycle, which was a prerequisite for the job, a second-hand blue-and-silver Columbia that I had bought from a kid in school for $10, five of which I had borrowed from my mother. But I couldn't convince the manager that I was twelve years old when I wasn't even ten. It broke my heart to have to accept the fact that I was never going to wear one of those olive-drab military uniforms with the Sam Browne belt and the leather riding boots and the visored cap with the Western Union insignia on it. I decided to settle for the blue uniform of the second-rate Postal Telegraph Service, but that manager turned me away, too. No uniform for me.

I probably took my sorrows to the movies. The Model Theatre, at the bottom of the hill on Elm Street, cost a dime and was where all the kids went to see everything from Hoot Gibson and Tom Mix in their latest cowboy epics to Cecil B. DeMille's *The Ten Commandments*. We called the movie house "The Itch," but I'm not sure now what itched. Finally, when I was ten, I got a newspaper route and began making $2.00 or $2.50 a week delivering the

Herald-Statesman every afternoon after school. That, plus Missy's typewriter, is what hooked me.

I had to go to the newspaper plant on Larkin Plaza once a week to meet my district manager and pay my weekly bill for the papers the truck dropped off for me on a street corner at the beginning of my route. The carrier boys were considered "independent contractors" by the management and had to pay for the papers whether their customers paid them or not. In case you have ever stiffed your newspaper boy, it wasn't the paper you stiffed, it was the kid. Red McLaughlin, my boss, who couldn't have been much more than a kid himself, used to give in to my pleas every once in a while and sneak me in to take a look at the city room, where all the reporters were working at their typewriters, and the copy editors, looking terribly solemn and some of them even wearing green eyeshades, sat in judgment over the pieces of paper the reporters handed them to be edited and crumpled into the pneumatic tubes that coughed them up to the printers upstairs. To me it was all strictly Adolphe Menjou and Pat O'Brien in *The Front Page* and I wanted desperately to be Hildy Johnson.

Red also took me downstairs to see the printing presses roll and I never got over either the sight or the smell. There's nothing like the smell of wet ink. Especially, as I learned later, when some of the ink is printing words you wrote. Even Red didn't have the nerve to sneak into the heavily unionized composing room, but I had seen enough. Watching the miraculously folded newspapers clack out of the giant Hoe presses on their way to the trucks waiting by the loading dock upstairs was the finishing touch. I didn't need a guidance counselor to tell me what I wanted to do when I grew up.

Neither, for that matter, does hardly anybody who goes into publishing. Ninety-nine out of a hundred of them never thought about doing anything else.

How I was going to be able to do it, I had no idea. But one day when I was twelve years old and in my second year at Longfellow Junior High School, I decided I ought to go to the second-rate newspaper in town, the Yonkers *Record*, where the standards weren't as high as the awesome *Herald-Statesman*'s, and ask if they'd like to have me cover sports at the schools in my neighborhood, Longfellow and Gorton High School.

"Sure," the old city editor said. Actually, he wasn't the city editor, he was the only editor. "Only we don't pay anything."

"Can I use a typewriter?" I asked him.

"Sure," he said, and went back to his coffee.

That was all I needed. The next day my first piece, a learned assessment of the Longfellow basketball team's prospects for the season coming up, was in the paper with the byline "Edward E. Fitzgerald." I guess I wanted all the space I could get for my name.

My byline, a more modest "Ed Fitzgerald," has been on hundreds of newspaper and magazine articles and mastheads and book covers since then, but nothing has ever been more exciting. There's an old baseball bromide about how it's great to be young and a Yankee, which God knows is true. It's also great to be twelve years old and have your name on a story in the Yonkers *Record*.

I had a few flirtations with the idea of going to college, especially when I wrote away for a Notre Dame catalog, but it was never serious. The *Herald-Statesman* hired Al Lyon as a circulation supervisor and his mother told him to be nice to me or else. He introduced me to Rudy Hoffman, the circulation manager, who introduced me to Ted Worner, the assistant sports editor, and I began covering Gorton High sports for a nickel an inch.

What that meant was that I was allowed to clip everything I wrote that was actually printed in the paper and carry it all in to the city room on Saturday morning. The city editor took out his big steel ruler and measured the columns—no headlines and, even worse, no box scores—and promptly paid me out of the petty cash drawer at the rate of a nickel an inch. That, Liby claims, is why I never write a sentence without at least three adjectives and one qualifying clause. The only way you can pile up a lot of column inches is to write a lot of words.

What I wanted, though, was a job. High school was over and I was sixteen and my friends were either going to college or to work in the carpet shop or Otis Elevator or somewhere. I wanted only to work for the paper, but the paper didn't have a job. Jane Morrissey, a high-school friend, said I ought to talk to her father, who was the general manager of Habirshaw Cable & Wire Company. I did and he gave me a job as a messenger for $12 a week. I had to make two round trips a day between the Glenwood station on the New York Central's Harlem Division and 40 Wall Street, headquarters of Phelps Dodge, the parent company, crossing all the corners where men, many with signs proclaiming that they were unemployed veterans, were selling polished red apples for a nickel apiece.

Once I lost my money and had to borrow a nickel from a cop to get a subway back to Grand Central, from where my commutation ticket would take me safely back to Glenwood.

Finally, one Saturday when I was covering a Gorton game for the paper, Ted Worner found me on the sideline and said he had a job for me and did I want it. "Sure," I said. "Ten bucks a week," he said, and I said, "Okay."

My mother wasn't mad, but she was bewildered. "Why," she asked me, "would you give up twelve dollars a week at a big company like Habirshaw for ten dollars a week at a newspaper?"

"It's what I want to do," I told her, and we never talked about it again until many years later when it was easy to talk about it. By then she knew I would have done it for five dollars a week.

The paper was my college. I learned everything there that mattered to me. I learned how to make a living in publishing. I learned about type.

It's sad for the newspaper or the magazine or the book-publishing company, but even sadder for the editors, that most editors don't know about type. They don't know how it's set, how it's selected, how it's corrected—they don't know anything about it. All they know is that when they read the paper or the magazine or the book and see a typo, they get mad.

Jeff McDonald, a tall, gaunt man, was a senior composing-room foreman at the *Herald-Statesman*. He made up the two sports pages and when Ted was promoted to sports editor and let me go upstairs when he was out, Jeff helped me cut columns to fit and even let me change my mind about headlines if the page didn't look as good to me as I had thought it was going to. Standing on my side of the form, reading the type upside down, I quickly got used to picturing the finished page in my mind as we put it together piece by piece. Or column by column. Jeff, whose younger brother was also called Jeff and was one of the best outfielders in Yonkers semi-pro ball, never let me be afraid of type. He even let me touch it when it was hot, and he wasn't supposed to let me touch it hot or cold. The Big Six typographical union considered that the holiest of all no-nos. We writer and editor types weren't even allowed to touch the scrambled type the printers threw in the hellbox. But Jeff wasn't worried about the union. He wanted me to learn how to be a newspaperman.

My father and I both had to be at work at seven o'clock in the morning, so I always saw him for at least a little while before we left the house. I didn't eat breakfast, a meal I have always thought unnecessary, but I liked to talk to him while he ate his one fried egg over with two pieces of bacon and a single piece of toast. His father had been a schoolteacher in Ballygar, Roscommon, County Galway, and he had a reverence for the written word, so he was proud that I was writing for the newspaper and actually had my name on some of the stories.

But one morning he lectured me. He was the most mild-mannered of men, so a stern lecture from him was like a kindly observation from somebody else. But I could tell the difference. "One of the men at the warehouse," he said, "told me he thought your article yesterday was unfair. He saw the boy's father at the Russian church last night and he was really hurt. So I picked up the paper and I read it over again and I have to agree with him. You can write funny, and it makes good reading, but if it hurts somebody, I don't think you ought to do it. Maybe you're so used to writing that you don't see the difference between talking and writing. But there *is* a difference. If you say it, it goes away. If you write it for the newspaper, it goes all over the city, and if somebody wants to keep it, they can, and it can last forever. I wish you would think about what you write before it gets set in type."

I've tried to, ever since.

I was lucky being in the sports department. The only two people on a daily newspaper like the *Herald-Statesman* who get to do everything from writing through makeup are the sports editor and the women's-page editor. (When I was young, she was the society editor.) I wrote news stories, features and opinion columns, assigned stories, edited staff copy and wire-news copy, rewrote publicity releases, assigned pictures, wrote captions, made up the pages and wrote headlines to fit.

I wrote headlines by counting characters for the width of the head, typing a string of X's across the paper to match the character count, and then writing the words underneath the X's. I'm sure it's not how they teach it in journalism school, but it got the job done.

Except for Liby, the paper was my whole life, and the paper even had a lot to do with my love life. The first time I saw Liby was when I was delivering my older brother Frank's paper route for him. It was a big route, a lot of walking along upper Warburton Avenue and Odell Avenue and North Broadway. One stop was 1178 Warburton Avenue, the last house in Yonkers before Hastings, right at the end of the trolley line. I walked up a cobblestone driveway past a tennis court and stopped to watch a girl in a short white tennis dress hitting balls against the wooden garage wall over a painted white stripe the height of a net. She was wearing short shorts, she had a beautiful backhand and beautiful legs, and the best part was when she bent over to pick up the loose balls on the ground.

Later, after our relationship had survived a lot of suspensions and I had survived a lot of competition, the paper was where we would meet. Liby would ring the night bell at the side door of the building and either the janitor or I would go down and let her in. Waiting around for me to finish the bowling scores or the story about the basketball game or the fight at the County Center in White Plains, she got to know the office as well as I did. If she had nothing better to do, she would sit in the wire room and read the copy coming off the AP and UP machines. She knew exactly what it meant when the bells rang two or three times to signal an especially important story.

The paper even helped us have our first big overnight, away-from-home date. Ted Worner took me on my first visit to the

Empire City racetrack and there I was, with my $10-a-week salary,
itching to bet two dollars on the first race. "Take it easy," Ted said
as we walked in the press gate. "Let's get a program and look at the
horses and bet on the second race."

But I heard the bugle calling the horses to the post and I couldn't
bear to miss it. To reach the clubhouse you had to walk past the
blackboards on which the bookmakers listed the entries and the odds
they were willing to pay. I was afraid I would blow the whole thing,
so I stopped at the second slate—there were no pari-mutuel machines—and I saw there was a horse listed named Scrooge, with oo
after his name. I looked at the name on the board and it said Tim
Mara. I knew that Tim Mara was the famous bookmaker who owned
the New York Football Giants, so I thought I was in safe company.

"What does zero zero mean, Mr. Mara?" I asked him.

"Kid," he said, "that means the least the horse will go off at is a
hundred to one. I'll guarantee you a hundred to one right now. If
the horse wins, you could get more."

As young as I was, I could tell the old man selling me the ticket
thought I was out of my mind. I've never seen the Giants play football since without remembering that the patriarch who bought the
club for nickels and dimes thought I was an idiot but liked my willingness to risk and took the time to tell me how to do it.

Scrooge broke fast and got inside on the rail, stayed ahead all the
way around and paid an unbelievable $228 and change to win. I
couldn't wait to get to the telephone booth and call Liby and tell
her we were rich. "Let's go to the football game at Cornell this
weekend," I said, and she said yes. That sounds like *Ulysses*. Yes I
said yes I will yes.

Ted's press passes allowed us to go into the clubhouse bar, so we
wasted no time having a drink to celebrate. I had already collected
the money—after all, they might run out—so I sprang for the tab
and sat studying the entries for the second race. Orchids Next was
running and the morning line was 10–1. I got right up and bought a
two-dollar ticket on him. Naturally, while we were still working on
our drink, the race went off and Orchids Next won and paid $26.80.

We made Cornell in style, even including a good hotel room for

Liby while I stayed at a boardinghouse. Except for interviewing coaches like Frank Leahy at Notre Dame, Adolph Rupp at Kentucky and Eddie Erdelatz at Annapolis, that was my one brush with college.

The *Herald-Statesman* was my life for most of the six years before the war, but not all of them. They shipped me to New Rochelle to be the sports editor of the *Standard-Star* when I was eighteen years old. Liby was going with somebody else then and it was a lonely time for me. But I was running the sports pages, writing a column, deciding what the paper would cover and earning a big $25 a week. My cup wasn't exactly running over, but it was at least half full.

One night the Police Benevolent Association threw its annual bash at the New Rochelle High School football field and the chief gave me two tickets. I invited my friend Mike Waslenko, who was home from Cornell for the summer, and we went together, dateless. It was a memorable night. The mayor introduced the star act. "Appearing," he said, "in advance of their engagement beginning tomorrow night at the Glen Island Casino, Glenn Miller and his orchestra." Then the man with the glasses stood up with his slide trombone and the band began to play "Moonlight Serenade" and we heard for the first time the music that was going to be part of our lives forever.

My next stop on the Macy-Westchester (now Gannett) railroad was White Plains, where the chain owned the *Dispatch*, had bought the White Plains *Reporter* and was getting ready to launch the *Reporter-Dispatch*. I was going to be the assistant sports editor at $30 a week. Strictly night duty. "You'll have to buy a car," the city editor, Ben Carroll, told me. "You'll have to go out a lot at night to cover things."

I bought a car and I worked six nights a week for five or six months until one or two o'clock in the morning. No column. Lots of bylines and $30 a week, but not much fun. I was a desk man, editing copy, writing heads, making up the sports pages and always, always, sending the bowling scores up to the composing room.

Nobody knows more about six-point type than I do. I missed Yonkers.

But not for long. Ben Carroll called me into his office around ten o'clock one Friday night and told me I was being "let go."

"On account of yesterday?" I asked him. Yesterday I had gone downtown to testify before the National Labor Relations Board. The new Wagner Act forms said we had to be paid overtime if we worked more than forty hours a week. I probably worked somewhere between sixty and seventy hours a week. I had joined the Newspaper Guild and I wanted to support it, so what I had said was simply that the Macy papers had instructed us to fill out the form saying forty hours no matter what.

"Is that why?" I asked Mr. Carroll.

"Of course not," he said.

No matter what, I was out of a job. I owed hundreds of dollars on the car he had said I should buy, I had never been fired before, I didn't know how to do anything except write and edit newspaper stories. I was nineteen years old and hurt.

I didn't do anything for months. It was a big day when I made myself get up and go to the movies. I sold the sleek '37 Dodge convertible I'd bought, a car that was so hot it caught fire under the floorboard once on the Saw Mill River Parkway. I walked or took the trolley wherever I had to go. I never walked near or past the *Herald-Statesman* building.

A great newspaperman, Heywood Broun, once wrote, "I've been fired three times, in the spring, the summer and the early winter. I like summer the best." So I was lucky. I was fired in the summer. But Broun had an edge on me. Walking around broke is more interesting in New York than it is in Yonkers.

From $10 a week in my first job at the *Herald-Statesman*, to $20 and then $25 at the *Standard-Star*, to $30 at the *Reporter-Dispatch*, I was down to nothing. Maybe my mother had been right. Maybe I should have stayed at Habirshaw Cable & Wire. I might have been making $25 a week running the addressograph machine in the payroll department.

At the library I began poring through the Help Wanted pages in *Editor & Publisher*, hoping to find a job somewhere in the metropolitan area. But whenever there was a job advertised that I thought I could handle, for maybe $18 a week, it was always in Northfield, Minnesota, or Eden, North Carolina, or Odessa, Texas. I didn't want to go that far away from Manhattan. I was hooked on the world of Mark Hellinger, Bob Considine, Grantland Rice and Jim Kilgallen. I was young and, despite the pain, I was still optimistic. I not only wanted to be a newspaperman; I wanted to be a New York newspaperman. So far as I was concerned, Westchester was far enough from the *Times* and the *Trib*. There were limits. I gave up reading *Editor & Publisher*.

One day I stopped in front of a magazine stand and studied the titles, wondering if any of them might like to have me cheap. I didn't have any hope for the magazines that got the most prominent displays—*Life* or *Look* or *Collier's* or *Time* or the *Reader's Digest* or the *New Yorker*. I dismissed the women's magazines. They wouldn't be likely to have much use for a man. But I wondered about the movie magazines and about *Argosy* and *True Detective* and all the sports magazines. Why not? For that matter, why not *Motor Boating* or *Popular Aviation*? My friend Mike Rose had taken me out on Peach Lake in an outboard and even a Chris Craft, and I'd seen *Hell's Angels* and *Wings*.

I went to the library to copy down a few names and addresses to write to, and to bring home a few books. I don't remember that any of the magazines ever answered me, but the books helped kill the time and, even if I didn't know it, I learned something from every one, even the bad ones.

I read everything I could lay my hands on. Thank God for Andrew Carnegie. The man who thought multimillionaires were simply trustees of their wealth and had an obligation to use it for the good of all the people, and who endowed some 2,800 public libraries in the United States, did more for me than any man I never met. I read Proust, Steinbeck, Nathanael West, Faulkner, Maugham, Ring Lardner and God knows what else. Many of the books I read then are in my house today. They're part of me.

Especially *Ulysses*. For me, Ulysses was like going to college, sailing to Ireland, going to bed with a passionate woman and getting drunk all at the same time. James Joyce taught me something I've never forgotten. You can do anything with words you have the guts to do.

I read all three books of John Dos Passos' U.S.A.: *The 42nd Parallel, Nineteen Nineteen* and *The Big Money*, and they had an enduring influence on my simmering liberalism. So did Walter Reuther and Paul Robeson and "Joe Hill" and the cops who used nightsticks to club the pickets on the sidewalks during a Habirshaw strike when I was in grammar school. When I was ten, I won a gold medal in an essay contest run by the Yonkers Rotary Club by writing about What America Means To Me, and I've been a little ashamed of myself ever since that I didn't write about the cops breaking up the picket line.

I'd have been better off not winning the medal, anyway, because at the Rotary luncheon where they gave it to me they served a whole cold lobster with potato salad. I didn't have the faintest idea how to go about attacking that lobster, so I ate the potato salad and sat there minding my own business until a sympathetic waiter leaned down and said, "Want some more potato salad?" I had seconds on the potato salad.

My sentence in Purgatory finally ended when my old boss and instructor in the fine art of playing the horses, Ted Worner, called me on our party line at home and said he thought he could persuade Oxie Reichler, the editor of the *Herald-Statesman*, to let me replace Ted's assistant, who was leaving. Oxie saw himself as a crusading liberal and was willing to forgive me for my NLRB indiscretion so long as I promised not to distribute red flags or Guild application blanks in the city room. What interested him the most was whether I would take five dollars a week less than the other man had been making. That put me back to the $25 I had been paid when I left New Rochelle. I wouldn't be inviting Liby to go hear Glenn Miller or the Dorsey Brothers or Glen Gray and his Casa Loma Orchestra at the Hotel Pennsylvania. But I had a job again.

Chapter 3

WHEN I rang the bell and was let in the side door of the *Herald-Statesman* building a few minutes before seven in the morning, the first thing I did was head for the teletype room in the corner behind the city desk and tear off the roll of paper at the end of the last completed story. Then I sat down at the little desk in there, picked up a big pair of scissors and cut off and stacked up every sports story in the overnight file. Back at my own desk, I read them carefully to pick out the ones that seemed worth putting in the paper.

While Ted Worner was still around—which wasn't a whole lot longer, because we stood in the wire room the morning the national draft numbers were drawn and saw his number picked as one of the first to go—I left the yellow sheets I was interested in on his desk and waited for a chance to discuss them with him later. When Ted had become Private Ted Worner, I did my own picking and choosing and wrote heads for the wire stories right then and there to get them out of the way. They came from the Associated Press, the United Press and International News Service, and my goal was to use only the most important ones and the ones with a local angle, no matter how far-fetched the local angle might be. There had to be room enough to cover our local sports in full. We were a local newspaper.

Generally, except on Saturday, we had two pages for sports. My column always ran at the top left of the lefthand page. I didn't have to worry about it in the morning except to proofread it, because I always wrote it the afternoon or the night before, along with everything else I could possibly lay my hands on, especially school sports. I never quit before seven o'clock at night and I didn't worry about the Wagner Act.

Then I had to proofread the goddam bowling scores and any other stories that had gone up to the composing room in the pneumatic tube yesterday afternoon or last night. After that, it was time to look at the wire-service pictures and see if there were any unusually good action pictures or pretty girls to consider. By then our local pictures, the ones I had assigned to our staff photographers, most of whom were named Sarno, would have come in from the lab and I'd hold my breath until I made sure at least one picture from each assignment was usable. For all the pictures, wire or local, I used a ruler and a soft black cropping crayon to determine how many columns wide and inches deep they would run, and wrote captions for them.

Then it was time to begin plaguing the city editor for my page dummies, two 8x11 sheets ruled off in columns with the ads that were going to run on the sports pages marked off by X's. Whatever space wasn't X'd out was mine to fill. Some days it was almost all of it; the sports pages aren't the hottest advertising section in the newspaper. Look at the New York *Times.* Without the television ads, they'd be in a lot of trouble and Punch Sulzberger and Abe Rosenthal would complain even more than they do about the cost of what Red Smith used to call the little boys' pages.

I always enjoyed the next part, laying out the pages. Anything worth a streamer across the top of the whole page? What stories should get two-column heads? The *Herald-Statesman's* standard two-column head was 24-point italic, and I liked to save it for stories of some importance. Otherwise I could use single-column heads with

14, 18 or 24-point Bodoni or boxes of one, two or three columns with either Bodoni or italic heads. It was a point of pride with me to count my characters carefully—*m* and *w*, for instance, are one and a half characters, *t* and *l* and *i* are half a character—and make sure Jeff McDonald didn't have a chance to needle me when the heads ran over and I had to cut them or, even worse, rewrite them. "It wouldn't happen if you'd gone to a good parochial school," he said. "The sisters would have taught you how to count or they'd have busted your knuckles, one or the other."

By then it was time to go downstairs to the diner next door and get my first food of the day. I hardly ever ate at the counter; I almost always brought it back upstairs because the paper went to bed at eleven thirty and I still had a lot to do, including taking a few last-minute stories over the telephone.

My last chore was one of the most important. Jeff or one of his crew would bring down to me two soaking-wet page proofs, my last chance to find something wrong and fix it before the paper went to press. Because it meant so much to me not to have a stupid typo staring at me when I leaned back in my chair to read my copy, one of the first ten or so off the press, I paid attention to what I was doing. Even today, typos in a newspaper or magazine or a book, or even on a sign, jump right up and hit me in the eye.

When I found one, I circled it with a thick blue crayon which was easy to read on the wet paper, and wrote the word or the name correctly in the margin. When I was finished, whether I had found anything or not, I took the pages back to Jeff. And that was that for another day. There was nothing I could do about any of it now.

Sometimes Eddie Schlesinger, who worked on the copy desk, and I walked a few doors up the street to Smitty's and had a couple of ten-cent beers and, like newspapermen everywhere, complained about the Philistinism of the management. I never noticed that the complaining did any good, but the beer tasted fine and, if it was Saturday, it made us brave enough to study the entries in the *Mirror* and walk over to Caesar's cigar store on Wells Avenue next to the police station and get down a couple of two-dollar bets, each one split half and half so we each had two chances to win. Caesar's didn't sell an awful lot of cigars, but the bookmaking business was brisk, including with the cops. Sometimes Mr. Caesar's son, Sid, was working behind the counter and he was always good for a joke and a funny face. Somehow he always seemed funnier when we went back to collect.

After the serious business was taken care of, we would walk to Bickford's for a cheap lunch. The cafeteria was in the heart of Getty Square, where, when I was younger, I used to pick up a pile of Sunday newspapers late Saturday night and sell them all around the stores—W. T. Grant, Genung's, Woolworth's and F. W. Grand, the quarter store. Right next to the newsstand, my friend Larry Christopher's father used to dispatch the trolley cars over the switches on the next leg of their journeys. Trolleys were how you got around in Yonkers. Not that many people had cars. There was no parking problem.

It was a city of ethnic neighborhoods, Russian and Slavic and Polish and Italian and Jewish and Irish, with the Wasps safely tucked away in their one-family homes in North Yonkers. The ethnics, with their redolent foods and their pool halls and their beer and their reverence for their athletic priests and their handsomely steepled churches, lived in places like the Hill and the Hollow and the Flats. Wards, too, were easily identifiable not only by politics but by heritage. The Sixth Ward was the Irish, the Fourth Ward was the Ukrainians, the Fifth Ward was the Slavs. You could tell who lived in the ward by the name of the alderman.

I covered sports all over the city—Industrial Leagues and Twilight Leagues and Sunday School Leagues and every other kind of league—and when I was the editor of the Gorton High School *News* I used to employ our best athletes as reporters so they could earn their National Youth Administration checks after football, basketball or baseball practice. NYA checks weren't quite charity, but they were close to it and they were made more bearable because the guys were supposed to be earning them. The *News* masthead read like a combination roster of the football, basketball and baseball teams. They did the playing and I did the writing. No wonder I learned my trade. Making up the masthead alone was a post-graduate course in spelling ethnic names. But I learned. For years I was the only guy on *Sport* magazine who could spell Wojchiechowicz. And after the war it was hard for me to get into trouble with the Yonkers Police Department because three of my *News* reporters became cops and two of them even made it all the way to captain. I hope they wrote better summonses than they did news stories.

Tom Queally, a skinny, beer-drinking English teacher who liked to celebrate the first days of spring, and sometimes the first days of fall and winter, too, by sneaking over to Lake Avenue with a few of us at lunchtime and having a beer before the afternoon classes, was our NYA advisor and he saw to it that the checks kept coming despite the suspicions of some more straitlaced teachers that the basketball, football and baseball players weren't contributing much to the Gorton *News*. "They're contributing their experience," he would tell the skeptics. He was borrowing from Ring Lardner's " 'Shut up,' he explained."

Queally was never at a loss for a quote or a quip or both at the same time. Giving out the school letters to the members of the successful cross-country team, he said, "You won the city championship and you won the state championship. You just couldn't win the county championship. You must all be Democrats." In heavily Republican Westchester County that made sense.

I never worried about over-emphasizing local sports in the *Herald-Statesman*. Even the New York *Times*, the closest thing we have to a national newspaper, worries about giving in-depth coverage to local news and local controversies and local personalities. If it didn't, a lot of subscribers would become former subscribers. So I never felt too chauvinistic about paying close and continuing attention to our own. But it helped make the paper look less provincial, and more readable, when local sports news got mixed up with national or at least regional news.

Basketball was the sport that helped the most. Yonkers had a history of developing fine players and teams. We were the hometown of Joe Lapchick, center of the Original Celtics, kings of the game, and because of Lapchick's drawing power we saw the Celtics at least once every year, generally against the Yonkers Caseys at the Knights of Columbus Hall, a bandbox arena little larger than a squash court that made your average YMCA gym look like the Brendan Byrne Arena. It was perfectly suited to the kind of half basketball, half wrestling that was the style in the 1930s.

The Celtics were a Basketball Hall of Fame all by themselves. If Lapchick, Nat Holman, Dutch Dehnert (inventor of the pivot play), Nat Hickey, Davey Banks, Pete Barry and Johnny Beckman were all sober on the same night, they were devastating.

We also got to see almost all the recently graduated college stars from the New York area because as soon as their senior seasons were finished they began to play pro ball under names like the Long Island Blackbirds, for Long Island University, the Brooklyn Jewels, for St. John's, and the New York Violets, for NYU. Sometimes we even saw them play under different names when they were still sophomores and juniors. They needed money then, too.

Not that they got a whole bunch of money. Ten dollars a game was a lot for any except the biggest names. But a dollar went a long way in those days. Everybody knows the old story about how you could get a Coke for a nickel, but who had a nickel? These guys would play every night if there was a game. They played the Philadelphia Sphas (South Philadelphia Hebrew Association), the Jersey City Reds, the Brooklyn Visitations, the Harlem Renaissance and the Pittsburgh Crawfords, all members of the loosely drawn and even more loosely controlled American Basketball League, and they played independent teams like the Danbury Big Five and the Caseys. Wherever and whenever they could make a payday.

Yonkers, as the tired old joke goes, is next to the largest city in the world and it was always hard for the local sports promoters to make the fans stay home instead of riding the trolley to 242nd Street and the Woodlawn subway to the city to watch the guys who got their names in the *News* and the *Mirror*. It only cost fifteen cents to get from Getty Square to Yankee Stadium or the Polo Grounds or the old Madison Square Garden. You had to give the trolley conductor a nickel when you got on and then another nickel when you crossed the city line at Riverdale. The subway took you the rest of the way for a third nickel.

If basketball was your game and you wanted to see the awesome teams from the West and the South that came in for a fat Garden check and a chance to spend a few days in the big town, you could have it for very little traveling time. Stanford, Illinois, Wyoming, Utah, Kansas, Temple, Kentucky and Oregon were some of the schools that looked on the Garden as the cathedral of the sport. So for thirty cents round trip and $1.10 for a decent seat in the most famous indoor arena in the United States, you could go big-league. For another quarter you could have a mug of Ruppert's or Rheingold or Piel's in Mickey Walker's place. The Toy Bulldog himself might stop and talk with you for a while, maybe even answer a few questions about his famous fights with Harry Greb, Tiger Flowers, Paul Berlenbach and Jack Sharkey. It was more expensive than the nickel beers at the Savoy in Yonkers, but it was the big time, and if you worked all week in the carpet shop, a taste of the big time could make you forget all the dust and wool you had to eat on the job.

Sometimes it's hard to remember how different things were before television. Now the son of the man for whose favor the Caseys competed with Madison Square Garden knows every move Mark Gastineau or Dan Marino or John Riggins makes in the fall, every shot Bernard King or Larry Bird or Julius Erving takes in the winter, and every hitting or batting or pitching trademark of the boys of summer. He even knows just how Dick Williams spits and Sparky Anderson blows bubble gum. And the beer he asks his wife to get him out of the refrigerator so he won't have to take his eyes off the game is probably an expensive brand, but it's a lot cheaper than what they would charge him out at the old ball park, where it's liable to be two or three dollars for a pale pink hot dog and a beer that's their choice, not yours. It's a different world.

Connie Mack used to keep track of everything with a scorecard and even used the card to move his outfielders around or to tell a base runner when to take a lead. It would be hard for Davey Johnson to do that with his computer. But it would also be hard for the Garden fan to go home with a damp, smelly suit because the high-scoring forward on the visiting team was thrown in his lap by one of his heroes. You get what you pay for.

The solution the Caseys came up with was to mix local talent with the best available name players from the metropolitan area. Tidy Millen and Harry Fitzpatrick were local heroes who had grown up with most of the paying customers and whose every swish of the net with a two-handed set shot and every thread-the-needle pass triggered a roar of approval from the crowd. When Tidy or Fitzie, Sixth Ward boys who had learned the game on the park playgrounds and in the school gyms, threw in a dazzlingly long basket from the middle of the court or drove in for a lay-up like a fullback on an off-tackle play, he did it for them, for the guys he grew up with and drank beer with on Saturday night.

In 1941, my last full year on the job, the hometown boys were supported by Bill McKeever, a few years out of St. John's and a dangerous scoring threat from the pivot; Paulie Adamo, an old Jersey City Red who had seen everything, wasn't surprised by anything and who was the Caseys' quarterback; Jack McGurk, a big Manhattan College center who had played pro ball all over the Northeast; and Matty Begovich, a surprisingly agile blond giant in a day when giants came in smaller sizes than they do now, who had played with Rip Gerson, Mac Kinsbrunner, Allie Schuckman and Max Posnack on the St. John's Wonder Five. They made a good ball club. They weren't the fastest around, but they were smart and they could take care of themselves in the crunches.

There were a lot of crunches; pro basketball then was a lot like hockey. The fights or near-fights kept the fans in a state of partisan frenzy and my old columns don't have much to say about any extraordinary efforts by the promoters or the referees to make the combatants stop shoving and play basketball. The overriding need was to put on a good show and make sure the people came back with their dollar bills next Sunday.

The only student of the game who seemed to be distressed by the emphasis on slaughter over style was the sports editor of the *Herald-Statesman*, a twenty-two-year-old idealist who thought the way they played the game in Ned Irish's college doubleheaders in the

Garden was better. Boxing is boxing, I argued earnestly, and basketball is basketball. I should have taken a lesson from the hockey writers who never criticized the fights except to complain that nobody ever really got hurt in them.

I kvetched: "Wrestling, long since dead and little mourned as a professional sport on its own, plays a large part in pro basketball. A good headlock rates more applause than a graceful pivot shot. . . . A couple of gorillas on the Harlem Yankees never have learned how to shoot fouls but they sure have learned how to commit them. . . . Some day, maybe, some promoter will realize that most fans won't pay to see a basketball game and get a monotonous two hours of pushing and shoving and wrestling and a little half-hearted punching."

You can tell that was a long time ago. You can also tell it was a long time ago because one of my columns said the Caseys' opponent next Sunday would be the New York Colored Whirlwinds. All they needed was to have entertainment provided by Phil Spitalny's All-Girl Orchestra.

It was a paradox that one of our best local angles during the pro basketball season was focused on a visiting ball player, Joe Polcha, our town's finest all-around athlete. Joe was a product of the Yonkers basketball system from the Peewee League through the Sunday School League, on to Roosevelt High School and then semi-pro ball with every team that had a few dollars to give him to entertain the people with his dazzling array of set shots, jump shots, flying lay-ups and twisting corner shots. Joe, who could play baseball well enough to get a contract with Jackson, Mississippi, in the Kitty League, a Red Sox farm club, and pocket billiards well enough to keep himself in spare change, caught on with the Brooklyn Visitations and began earning enough money to make a down payment on a gleaming white Chrysler Imperial convertible with Scotch plaid upholstery and a horn that played "The Campbells are Coming." Joe knew all about being broke; he couldn't wait to find out what it felt like to have money. Born into a beer family, he had a taste for champagne.

The Caseys couldn't afford to pay Joe the kind of money he needed to keep up the payments on his Chrysler Imperial, but some of us would make the effort once in a while to see him play on the Visitations' home court, Prospect Hall in Brooklyn, sometimes known as "The Bucket of Blood." He was the only kid given a chance to play on a team that had famous pros like Willie Scrill, Red Conaty, Rody Cooney, Joe Brennen and Al Kellett, but he was the only one of them who could run all day and he stayed out on the floor while they took turns gasping for air and drinking cold beer out of paper cups on the bench. The Visitations came to Yonkers twice every year to play the Caseys, so we saw Joe then, and sometimes he was asked to fill in when one of the other American League clubs came to town shorthanded and Joe happened to be home that afternoon. Whenever he played, in whatever uniform, not many of the guys from the factories took the trolley and the subway into the city.

College football helped our sports pages, too. Like almost every other city or town in America, we always had at least a couple of kids playing football somewhere. In the early '40s we had two good ones, Joe McCourt at Colgate and Charlie McNulty at Manhattan. When you have hometown college football players or major-league baseball players, you can write about big-league and local sport all at once. Some pretty small papers can make that work for them because football and baseball players can make it to the big time from almost anywhere.

Outside of basketball, though, professional boxing was our best bet in the Westchester towns. The County Center in White Plains was easily accessible not only to all parts of the county but also to the Bronx and Manhattan. The big-city writers who covered the fights themselves instead of sending their probably dollar-an-inch stringers referred to the County Center scornfully as "the only fight club with a canopy over the front door." But the promoter, Joe McKenna, had good connections downtown and came up with his share of interesting shows. They would have been only preliminaries at the Garden, but they were main events at White Plains.

31

Steve Belloise, whose older brother Mike was a good journeyman fighter, became, in the years just before the war, the County Center's biggest single draw. Fighting as a middleweight, he brought the people in with a free-swinging style that was 90 percent offense and 10 percent defense, just about the way the fans like it. He had a likable face that was as open as his stance and there were never many people in the hall except his opponent's immediate family who weren't rooting for Steve to win. That was the essence of club fighting, or anyway of club matchmaking. You had to have a popular house fighter who took on all comers and won more than he lost. Belloise was the County Center's house fighter and when he got a Garden shot at the middleweight champion, Ken Overlin, Westchester's fight buffs squeezed onto the subway by the hundreds and winced at every punch as Overlin outpointed their hero and kept his title. But the loss didn't keep anybody away the next time Belloise, in Navy blue then, showed up at the County Center for a payday.

The clubs were to championship boxing what college football is to pro football. It was where the fighters learned their trade. But it all died with television, beginning in 1949 with Gillette's "Friday Night Fights"—"Look sharp, feel sharp"—keeping the people home. Only the most rabid fans were going to go out of the house and pay to see a fight when they could watch one comfortably at home for nothing.

Aside from the educational merits of the small fight clubs, a certain amount of entertainment value also was lost when television buried them under a deluge of commercials. Consider the good time the folks at ringside had this night at the County Center the winter of 1941:

If ever there was a sure thing in sports, at least as sure as Joe Louis and the Yankees, it was that Patrick Muldoon would beat Joe Taccaro in the main event at the County Center last night. Sure and how could Patrick, wearing his Kelly green trunks with the shamrock on them, do anything but win when he was fighting on St. Patrick's Day in the evening? The great saint who drove the snakes out of Ireland would take care of that.

Patrick is not the most impressive figure of a man who ever climbed through the ropes of a prize ring. Indeed there are finer physiques than Patrick's behind many bars that we know. But underneath Patrick's slipping chest there beats a heart with the incautious courage of an Irishman with a strong right hand and not enough sense to be afraid.

Patrick fought last night pretty much the same as he has in his other White Plains appearances, which is to say not wisely but boldly and optimistically. After feeling each other out in the first round, the antagonists began to swing more freely in Round Two, and that cheered Patrick's supporters because that is his kind of fight. But after a barrage of right hands had been exchanged it was the big behind in the green trunks that was on the canvas, and that wasn't the way the script was supposed to play at all. Bejabbers, Muldoon thought, this is no sight for good Irishmen to see on a holy day, and he lifted himself to his feet, not an easy thing to do when you weigh as much as Patrick does, and went on the attack.

Now, Patrick is not especially agile in the ring. In fact, he frequently experiences difficulty when he tries to get both his feet moving in the same direction. It might not be kind to call Patrick clumsy but it would be over-enthusiastic to call him graceful. But one thing he can do is throw a punch. When he lands a right to the jaw, his opponent generally goes down. Patrick landed his punch, and Taccaro went down and stayed down.

Patrick's fans cheered madly. Everything was right with the world. They settled back and waited for the *pièce de résistance* of a Muldoon fight, his victory speech. Patrick, who murders the language of the hated English with a brogue so thick it can't be understood this side of Galway City, was happily ready to oblige when the New York State Athletic Commission's man at ringside notified announcer Johnny Addie that the commissioners did not want their licensed athletes to practice public speaking at their place of business. Sadly, Patrick was unable to thank his followers and tell them how grand they had all been,

33

but as he headed for his dressing room and a cold bottle of Harp, he had the satisfaction of knowing that he had done his bit to celebrate the feast of St. Patrick.

That kind of ethnic festival would never be countenanced by the MBAs who run television with the help of their Nielsen ratings and their focus panels and their share-of-market statistics. But it had its points. It was homey.

Being so close to the city made it more kosher for me to cover the big-league scene than it might have been if my beat had been farther away. The Yonkers sports fan fought with his friends over the Yankees, Giants and Dodgers just as passionately as if he lived in the Bronx or Harlem or Greenpoint. "He's gonna be better than DiMaggio," the Dodger fan would boast about Pistol Pete Reiser, the phenomenal rookie who hit .343 for Brooklyn in 1941 and never let an outfield fence keep him from catching a soaring fly ball. Which is why Reiser had only two seasons over .300 and why the big-league ball parks now have warning tracks in front of the fences.

You didn't have to live in the Bronx to root for DiMaggio during his batting streak in '41. I wrote a column about one of the close calls, game number thirty-eight; it was an unforgettable afternoon at the Stadium, one I used as an argument years later when Red Smith got on one of his favorite themes, that "Rooting for the New York Yankees is like rooting for United States Steel." Not this day, it wasn't.

Don't ever let anybody tell you that the Yankees, as rich as they are and as loaded as they are with big names, have no sense of team spirit. We saw them get up off the bench en masse in the eighth inning of yesterday's game against the St. Louis Browns and shout encouragement to Joe DiMaggio as their great center-fielder stepped up to the plate for his last whack at the submarine pitches of Eldon Auker. DiMaggio was 0 for 3 and his 37-game hitting streak was on the line.

Joe had hit a long shot to the left-field fence his first time up but Roy Cullenbine caught it. In the fourth, he hit a hard ground ball to short and was safe at first when Johnny Berardino's throw was wide. But the official scorer had an attack of fair play and gave Berardino an error on the throw. In the sixth, Joe was out on an easy ground ball to third. Now, in the eighth, he had one more chance.

Johnny Sturm, the first-baseman and lead-off hitter, was first up, which meant that somebody was going to have to get on base if DiMaggio, batting fourth, was going to get a lick. Sturm popped up to second. One out. But Red Rolfe worked a walk out of Auker, and there was a surge of anticipation in the big ball park. Tommy Henrich, who had already hit a home run to keep alive another Yankee streak, 21 straight games with at least one home run, was the next hitter but manager Joe McCarthy didn't want him to hit. McCarthy wasn't going to risk a double play. Henrich laid one down, Sturm went to second and, with two out, the stage was set for the showdown.

DiMaggio, despite his expressionless face, must have felt the tension, but there wasn't a trace of emotion as he dug in at the plate, raised the bat high over his right shoulder, and waited. Sitting in the press box in the mezzanine behind the plate, I could only catch glimpses of the nervous stirring in the Yankee dugout on the first-base line. I could see Lefty Gomez, Bill Dickey, Art Fletcher and Earle Combs crowding to the front, the better to work on Auker. But the Yankee jockeys didn't have to do anything much. Auker threw one of his patented underhand curves and DiMaggio swung. The solid sound of the bat smacking the ball told you it was a base hit. It flew out to the green grass of the outfield, out of reach of the left-fielder, who had to chase it to the fence, and it easily scored Rolfe. DiMaggio stood poker-faced on second base as the shouting and the applause washed over him. Gomez grabbed a bat and jumped up on top of the dugout and began pounding on the tin roof. Phil Rizzuto, the rookie shortstop, followed him, and Joe Gordon and Charlie Keller and Sturm and Johnny Murphy, the relief pitcher who always finished everything Gomez started. Even in the faraway press box, it sounded like a dozen Gene Krupas down there, waking up the dead.

35

Tennis and golf gave me some good columns, too. The Westchester Country Club in Harrison, which for years had been home to the Eastern Grass Court Championship, was one of the first bastions of the allegedly amateur game to let the professionals show off their world-famous strokes on the club's immaculate grass courts. The crowds weren't quite the same as at Forest Hills, but the tennis was.

Westchester has more golf courses than you can count, so there was always something going on. Winged Foot in Mamaroneck was on everybody's list of the ten best courses in the country.

Tim Mara's New York Football Giants interested our readers, too, although it had taken them a long time to get around to it. When I first worked for the paper, we used to get a brown envelope every week stuffed with free passes to the Giant games and we had a hard time giving them away. Nobody wanted to see pro football. More than 70,000 paying customers had turned out at the Polo Grounds on a fall Sunday in 1925 to see Red Grange make his professional debut with the Chicago Bears against the Giants, but for a long time after that 70,000 was a year's attendance. Things were looking up now, though. The old-timers like Tuffy Leemans, Hank Soar, Ward Cuff and Ken Strong had been joined by young players fresh out of college like Lenny Eshmont, Dom Principe, Marion Pugh and Chet Gladchuck, and the team won eight out of eleven games to win the Eastern Division championship and the right to play the Bears in the National Football League championship game. Which they promptly lost, 37–9. But the game had caught on. Even the legalization of pari-mutuel machines at the New York racetracks didn't worry Mr. Mara. He had a good thing going at the Polo Grounds.

My problem was not that I didn't have anything to write about but that I was running out of time to write it. I still enjoyed the job, but more and more my mind was on the Army. It looked as though I'd be gone soon after the new year began and that had the distinct effect of distracting my concentration on laying out two esthetically pleasing pages a day and writing the best sports column in the city of Yonkers.

I did enjoy putting out our Yonkers Marathon Extra in November 1941. Newspapers still had extras in those days, for presidential
elections and gangland executions and declarations of war. They
were special editions with a new front page laid on top of the regular afternoon paper, and sometimes, if it was a really important
event, with a new page two. The first extra I can remember selling
was the one that announced that Herbert Hoover had beaten Al
Smith in the 1928 presidential election. I sold the extra they put
out in July 1934 when John Dillinger was fingered by the Lady in
Red, Anna Sage, and ambushed outside the Biograph Theatre on
the South Side of Chicago by Melvin Purvis and twenty-two other
FBI men. And I sold a lot of copies of the extra that used the biggest
headlines I'd ever seen to report that Franklin Delano Roosevelt had
defeated Hoover to become the 32nd President of the United States.

But I didn't sell the marathon extra we put out on November 8,
1941. I wrote it. I did the whole thing all by myself and I blush a
little to see that I didn't mind claiming credit for it. My byline was
immodestly splashed all over the front page.

The marathon rated an extra because the AAU had designated it
over the more famous Boston Marathon as the national championship at the 26-mile, 385-yard distance. It was sponsored by the
Yonkers version of Tammany Hall, the Chippewa Club, and its
formidable leader, Thomas A. Brogan. It was no trouble at all for
Tom Brogan, maker of mayors and aldermen and even judges, to
make a marathon. Even Brogan, though, couldn't create a miracle
like the New York City Marathon forty years later. He did manage
to get about 5,000 of the faithful to watch the finish inside the
Empire City Race Track, and there were probably another few
thousand curious spectators along the marathon route. Maybe 8,000
people altogether saw the race, not even half as many as run in Fred
LeBow's Manhattan spectacular, much less watch it.

The winner didn't get anything like $25,000, either. He got an
expensive watch that one of Brogan's henchmen bought at whole-
sale from a local jeweler, all he could eat and drink at the post-race
party at the Chippewa clubhouse on Lake Avenue, and expenses.
Yonkers didn't have a single hotel you would put your worst enemy

37

in, so the name runners stayed in some good Democrat's house.

After the marathon, though, I had progressively less interest in the newspaper and more in squeezing in as many of the things Liby and I liked to do together as we could before the Army exercised its option on my body and soul. We went to some good college football games, NYU vs. Missouri and Passin' Paul Christman at Yankee Stadium, Manhattan with our old high-school friend Charlie McNulty scoring four touchdowns against Marquette under the lights at the Polo Grounds, Columbia vs. Dartmouth at Baker Field. We even took the train to Philadelphia and watched Cornell beat Pennsylvania at Franklin Field while we huddled under a blanket on a frigid Thanksgiving Day and ate hot dogs instead of turkey.

Our choice of a holiday dinner didn't go down too well with Liby's mother, but then, neither did our love affair. She had not raised her daughter to marry a $25-a-week newspaper reporter with no education and no prospects. First she tried to put us on a two-date-a-week basis. When that didn't work, her tactics became more unconventional and bolder. She gave Liby an ocelot coat, perhaps to show her how much warmer a fur coat could be on a winter day than a slender arm around you under a thin blanket. Then she gave in with suspicious ease to our pleas that we be allowed to take a trip to Montgomery, Alabama, to visit Mike Waslenko, who was a flight instructor in the Army Air Corps there. Maybe she thought we'd get it out of our system, as they say. We didn't get anything at all out of our system, but we had a good time.

The time was running out and we filled it greedily. We saw our first Broadway musicals, and we went to a lot of movies. While the weather was still warm, we enjoyed our town's two air-cooled theaters, Loew's and RKO Proctor's, where the cooling consisted of blocks of ice stacked on the roof with big electric fans blowing the cool air over the ice into ducts leading inside the theater. We kept going to Madison Square Garden because I got the tickets for nothing and they gave us free hot dogs and beer along with our seats in the press box.

It didn't make a whole lot of difference where we went or what we did. We always had a good time. Just walking to Hastings along the river or walking on the path on top of the aqueduct that carried New York City's water down from the Catskills was an event. It was, I suppose, the time of your life when even the lyrics in the popular songs make sense.

In our own neighborhood we had Jake Longobardi's place in Tuckahoe. In the afternoon, after tennis, we drank beer there. At night we drank rum-and-Coke with half a fresh lime. Thirty-five cents. On a couple of Sunday afternoons we went to Nick's in Greenwich Village to hear live Dixieland by, among others, Pee Wee Russell on clarinet, Eddie Condon on guitar, Bobby Hackett on trumpet, Jimmy McPartland on trombone and Willie "The Lion" Smith on piano. Nick's was the kind of place where sidemen like Muggsy Spanier, Max Kaminsky, Wild Bill Davison and George Brunis would go for a drink and sit in for a set. They didn't use a whole lot of sheet music at Nick's. What they played was in their heads and in their fingers and in their blood.

We listened to a different kind of music on St. Patrick's night, mostly Bing Crosby singing the standards like "My Wild Irish Rose," "Did Your Mother Come from Ireland?" and "Molly Malone." By then we knew we only had a week left. I had to report on the morning of March 25.

I cleaned out my desk and did some work for tomorrow's paper before Liby rang the night bell and drove us out to Jake's. We stayed up as late as we could stay awake that night. Liby had to go to work in the morning, but she said she would worry about that in the morning. When she said that, it was morning. But we knew we weren't going to see each other again for a long time.

I've always liked the phrase "the sweet disorder of intimacy," and there was a lot of disorder about our intimacy that night. I think what it was was that we were not only in love, we were scared.

Chapter 4

Now that we know we have lived through it, I don't think anybody who was in the war, even if he was one of the ones who were actually shot at, is sorry he had to be. As Winston Churchill said, "Nothing in life is so exhilarating as being shot at without result." Besides, it was the experience of our generation.

I've always been convinced that I would have been less of a writer or editor if I hadn't had those years in the Infantry. I'm even more convinced that I never would have become an editor-in-chief or a company president if it hadn't been for the Army. Being an Infantry first sergeant, especially if you weigh 130 pounds soaking wet, is a learning experience. When you have to tell 175 men, all of them bigger than you are, to get out of bed at five thirty in the morning, you learn how to take charge. You also learn how to reward your friends and punish your enemies. Nobody who gave me a hard time in the middle of the week ever got a pass into town that weekend.

Combat was the ultimate training school. Nobody wanted to dig his slit trench on the outer edge of the company perimeter, but somebody had to, and if it was Tony's turn, I had to make him do it. Nobody wanted to go out and bring back the dead, but somebody had to. Nobody wanted to carry ammunition to the companies and the platoons on the point, but the ammunition had to get there and I had to get people to deliver it. "Never volunteer for anything" is the first law of the Infantry soldier, so the first sergeant does the volunteering for him.

For the first sergeant, the Army also mirrors civilian life in another direction: up. You have to deal with the officers as well as with the guys under you. That was another course in how to make friends and keep them most of the time. Looking back on it, I learned so much from the Army it didn't matter that I wasn't making much money. What I was making, in the beginning, to be exact, was $21 a month. That started right after a swift physical at Camp Upton in which they satisfied themselves that my heart was beating, made sure that my genitals were intact, and half-heartedly asked me to testify that all my sexual desires were directed toward women. With last night alarmingly fresh in my mind, I felt like saying "woman," but I had a feeling this was no time to be a wise guy. A roomful of us took the oath of allegiance and in no time at all I was Private Edward E. Fitzgerald, Army of the United States, Army Serial Number 13232815. The last four numbers were what we stenciled or wrote on all our equipment, so for the next four years I was number 2815.

Putting on the uniform they gave me didn't make me feel like a real soldier, but watching the clothes I'd put on that morning packed into a box to be shipped home made me realize that the world had changed. The barracks they led us to, and the mess hall later, were parts of the new world that I looked at warily. The theater they told us we could go to after dinner was, surprisingly, even worse. The entertainment was so Army, with so many draft jokes and so much nostalgia about World War I when Irving Berlin wrote "Yip, Yip, Yaphank" and "Oh, How I Hate to Get Up in the Morning," that I went away thinking they were trying to tell us we were going to be in the Army for the rest of our natural lives.

It wasn't, I decided, like my high-school friend Whitey Ostrowski signing up for a year in the CCC.

The big excitement of my first whole day in the Army was being asked if I wanted to take the exam for Army Air Corps flight training. They said the interviewer who had done my routine questionnaire yesterday had been impressed by my newspaper experience and thought maybe I was intelligent enough to make a pilot. I can't even read a road map, but they didn't know that. Actually, my interviewer had been impressed not because I was a writer but because I could type sixty words a minute. "Don't worry," he had said, "you'll get a good job somewhere. They can always use somebody who can type."

I hoped so, but I couldn't forget that Ted Worner had always insisted I shouldn't have any trouble getting an easy job like his if I tried. That was the way Ted thought. He was a good-guy Sammy Glick who grew up always looking for the edge. He ended up working for Colonel Oveta Culp Hobby, the commandant of the Women's Army Corps, and after the war one of his new publicity agency's first accounts was the Yonkers Ferry. The things he did to get a story about the ferry in the *Times* were scandalous. Weddings were routine. Impossible passenger applications, like for a circus elephant, were normal.

Ted was something else. The *New Yorker*'s "Talk of the Town" took another look at his "breathless activities" in the fall of 1981 and the reporter couldn't do much except quote the great man: "Did I ever tell you about the time Jackie [Robinson] when he was a big-league star, bet me fifteen dollars he could beat me in a race across a cow pasture—I on a motorcycle and he running backward? He won. It was a bumpy field, and besides, I had to slow down on the curves. Imagine Jackie Robinson risking a broken leg at the height of his career to take fifteen bucks off me!" Teddy shamelessly—everything he does is done shamelessly—got the *New Yorker* man to plug his newest venture, the National Tailgating Association. "I'm trying to organize into it the millions of Americans who picnic on station wagons at football games. Do you know that Yale men hand down Yale Bowl parking spaces from father to son? I'm looking for just the right sponsor for this one—perhaps a food company or a blanket company, I got the idea when I took fifteen thousand cans of my Mott's Clamato juice to a Harvard-Yale game to pass around for making Bloody Caesars, which is what you should call a Bloody Mary when it's got Clamato in it instead of tomato." Teddy closed with a typical Worner rush. "My newest client [is] Ashanti

Gold. It's a cocoa-based liqueur derived, as I understand it, from an ancient tribal recipe in Ghana. I'm going to try to get every black person in the United States to drink Ashanti Gold as a tribute to his brothers in Africa."

It was understandable, back in the early days of the war, that a man who thought like a Broadway Telephone-Booth Indian would take it for granted that he could get me a safe Army job in the Empire State Building or, if I wanted, maybe even a few blocks closer to Liby's office at 386 Fourth Avenue. He did have me go to see him once at Camp Dix and meet the sergeants who ran his outfit, but it was a disaster. Their attitude, I thought, was that I was some kind of a draft dodger trying to get out of the real Army. Considering the nature of their assignment in an office some sixty miles from New York City, I thought they were a little hard on me. But they did manage to discourage me from applying for any other jobs in the army. I decided I would take what I got.

What I got wasn't the Army Air Corps. I passed that exam, as I passed a few Officer Candidate School exams later on, but with that first one I established the pattern that endured: pass the exam, fail the physical. I didn't weigh enough. In fact, nowhere near enough. They could give you a waiver for ten pounds, and three or four months later the Signal Corps stretched it to fifteen pounds, but I was a whole twenty pounds light.

Patrick Muldoon, the rotund fighter who had been in the main event at the County Center on St. Patrick's night, took the exam along with me. He was going for bombardier, a rank he had held in the RAF before he came to the United States, and he passed the exam and passed the physical and got a thirty-day leave to get ready for school. He should have written a funny piece about me.

Our next train ride was a long one. Nobody told us where we were going and we couldn't tell anything by the names of the stations we passed because there were blackout curtains on all the windows. We knew we had got on the train at Penn Station because we had walked through it, but that didn't tell us anything. We could be going west, we could be going south, we could even be going to Boston.

43

Nobody, at least not in our car, guessed the right stop. When they let us off the train, on an appropriately cloudy day, the sign on the station platform said: "COLUMBIA, S.C." That didn't mean anything to us. We were all from New York, New Jersey, Connecticut or Massachusetts and we didn't know that Columbia was the capital of South Carolina or that Fort Jackson was just outside the city. We learned one thing, though. There were a lot of soldiers standing around the station and they all had light blue piping on their overseas caps. "What's the blue stand for?" one of our guys asked. "The Infantry," he was told, and I've never been sure if that information was announced proudly or grimly. I do know that the guy who asked the question said, "Jesus."

We were loaded quickly on trucks and driven to the fort, where we were unloaded on a big drill field facing a platform with a microphone in the center. Standing at it, backed by a row of blue flags with white letters, was a crisply uniformed man who introduced himself as Colonel William H. Craig, the regimental commander. I don't remember him too well because not so long after we acquired our permanent wartime commander, Colonel Stephen S. Hamilton, a big, bony man with the head of a lion, a scraggly gray mustache and silver eagles on his not quite so crisply pressed uniform shirt. Colonel Hamilton was a natural born infantry soldier who made the 307th Infantry Regiment of the 77th Infantry Division his very own.

"It's a regiment with a long and honorable history," Colonel Craig told us that first day. "Maybe you've heard about the Lost Battalion of World War One. Well, the Lost Battalion belonged to this regiment. It wrote one of the bravest chapters of the war. Not because it went and got itself lost, which it did, but because it had the guts to fight its way out of a complete trap. They were surrounded on all sides, but they wouldn't surrender and in the end they fought their way out. That's a pretty good tradition to inherit and we're going to do the right thing by it. Now, let's get going. When your name and company are called, move right up to the company's guidon and just stand there."

It took a long time, but I finally heard, "Private Edward Fitzgerald, Service Company."

"You're lucky," somebody next to me said. "At least it's not one of the rifle companies." I didn't know exactly what he meant, but I understood that the word "service" didn't sound too threatening. I waited until a tall, lean man with an appalling number of stripes— three on top and three on the bottom, with a diamond in the middle— on his sleeves told us to pick up our bags and follow him.

The next week was a blur. The men in our company were gradually assigned to the Regimental Personnel Section, the Regimental Supply Section, the Motor Pool, where all the trucks and jeeps and drivers and maintenance people were, the Regimental Post Office or Company Headquarters. I drew Company Headquarters, which had some specific jobs like company supply sergeant and company clerk and company mail clerk and chaplain's assistant, but mostly staffed the regimental sections. It was weeks before I got a job of my own. In the meantime I hung around the Orderly Room and did some typing and whatever else I could for the first sergeant.

First Sergeant William E. Hunt was a field soldier, a Regular Army man who relished his new rank after years of being a corporal, but who hated being a nursemaid to all us goddam civilians. He also hated being confined inside the Orderly Room. If he couldn't be out in the field, preferably "under canvas," as he called living in a tent, he preferred inspecting the barracks and raising hell about badly made bunks, or terrorizing the cooks and the KPs in the mess hall and drinking a cup of hot coffee while they made him a ham sandwich. You didn't, I learned fast, have to be an officer to know that rank has its privileges. Being a first sergeant, it was clear, would do nicely.

I typed and filed and learned how to make out the Morning Report and kept the office running while Willie did what he liked to do. And finally I got my reward. Willie told me to report to Regimental Headquarters and tell the sergeant major, who ran the office, that I was the clerk who was supposed to work for Colonel Manuel.

Lieutenant Colonel Thomas B. Manuel was the executive officer of the regiment. He was, to Colonel Hamilton's occasional despair, the number-two man. Colonel Manuel was as fat as Colonel Hamilton was lean. He was as soft as Colonel Hamilton was tough. Fresh from running the Florida State Highways Commission and giving out millions of dollars' worth of paving contracts every month, he didn't know what the hell he was doing on active service with an Infantry regiment except that he had made the mistake of belonging to a very social National Guard outfit and achieving the rank of lieutenant colonel. The last thing he had expected to hit him was a war.

I couldn't help Colonel Manuel with tactics—nobody could—but I did my best to see that every piece of paper that went out of his office made him look like the very model of a modern lieutenant colonel. One day, the day that affected my years in the 307th all through the war, I tried to help him by arguing with him. He had asked me to write a memo on "preventative maintenance of motor vehicles," and I wrote the phrase as "preventive maintenance."

The colonel couldn't have been friendlier about it. "Son," he said, "you've got this word here wrong, and it's the most important word in the memo, so we'd better get it right. It's 'preventative,' not 'preventive.'"

"Sir," the former sports editor of the *Herald-Statesman* said, "it's 'preventive,' honest."

The colonel wasn't used to having privates tell him what was right and what was wrong, but he was still in a good mood. "I'm sorry, son," he said patiently, "but I've been around motor pools and vehicles"—he pronounced it the Southern way, "ve*hic*les"—"a whole bunch, and it's 'preventative.'"

I figured talking wasn't going to do any good, so I got out the office Webster and showed him that "preventive" is the word for anticipating and preventing a problem, and that "preventative" is the word for something you use to solve a problem, especially medicinal. There was a moment when I was afraid I had offended the colonel, but then he turned even more Southern. "I got to hand it to you, son," he said. "You saved me from lookin' like a jackass, and, between you and me, Colonel Hamilton makes me feel like a jackass often enough as it is."

Fifteen years later I wrote a less than successful novel about a professional baseball player and I had him enlist in the Army after

Pearl Harbor and I put him in the Seventy-seventh Division. (Everybody says you should write about what you know.) My ballplayer was patterned after a combination of Sid Luckman and Lou Boudreau—his father had gone to jail and died there, as Luckman's father did, and he had become a player-manager at twenty-four, as Boudreau did—and I dreamed up a ball game in Hawaii between the Seventh Air Force team, with Joe DiMaggio playing center field, as he really did, and the Honolulu Wanderers, with my ball player playing center field for them because the commanding general of the Seventy-seventh wanted him to and had made a bet on the Wanderers. I'm ashamed to say my hero won the game, or saved it, by making a spectacular catch off DiMaggio, and made the general very happy. It doesn't hurt, I wrote, when you're a private in the Army, to have the general as your friend. I found out that it didn't hurt to have a colonel as your friend, either.

It didn't hurt when he railroaded through a promotion for me to the three stripes and a T of a sergeant technician, which meant a big $78 a month. "I'm not going to have a private running my office," he said sensibly.

It didn't hurt when I asked Liby to come down to Fort Jackson and marry me, and she said yes, and I wanted to go home on a three-day pass and work out the arrangements with her. The company commander, Captain Ballschmider, a cocky little man who acted as though he had gone to West Point and wished he had, said no. Like the civilian I was, I asked Colonel Manuel if he would give me a pass, and he did. Which made Captain Ballbreaker blow his top and put out a company order reducing me in grade to private. Back to $38 a month, a private's pay under the new scale.

Colonel Manuel hadn't been a politician for nothing. He took the trouble to call Ballbreaker and tell him it was all his fault, he had acted without thinking and he apologized, but he knew the captain would agree that Sergeant Fitzgerald shouldn't have to suffer for his transgression. There wasn't a whole lot the captain could say. I stayed a sergeant and I went home for three days and settled our wedding date with Liby. June 6 it was going to be, June 6, 1942, a date that was going to be as easy to remember as Pearl Harbor Day.

Liby could have used a Colonel Manuel at her end. Her mother hadn't thought much of her marrying an underpaid newspaperman and she thought even less of her marrying a soldier. She invited Liby to leave the house. So, with nobody to run interference for her, my intended packed some necessaries in a suitcase and moved into the YWCA, an act of defiance which probably surprised her mother but shouldn't have.

With my mother riding along to show family interest and to carry the plain gold wedding band my father had bought for us for $7.50 in downtown Yonkers, Liby sat up all night on the Seaboard Air Line's Silver Meteor to arrive in Columbia on the morning of her wedding day. She and my mother checked into the new Wade Hampton hotel across the street from the capitol building, and we were married at the post chapel by Father John S. Chester, the Catholic chaplain of the 307th. Mike Waslenko had flown his little one-engine trainer over from Montgomery, but Father Chester wouldn't let him be our best man because he wasn't a Catholic, so George Scales, a Service Company man from Johnson City, New York, took on the job.

I think about George almost every Memorial Day. He had been married when he was drafted, and his wife had twin daughters while we were at Fort Jackson. He was killed on one of the last days on Okinawa. Branch Rickey used to say, about baseball teams, that luck is the residue of design. In a shooting war, luck is just plain luck. Bad luck is getting hit; good luck is not getting hit. George was unlucky: I was lucky.

I never felt luckier than I did the afternoon of June 6, 1942. Or the night of June 6, 1942. I remember waking up early in the morning of the seventh and looking at Liby sleeping next to me and thinking about how many years I had spent dreaming about this moment. Now, here it was. From now on we would never have to wonder what it would be like.

The only trouble with our little corner of paradise was that it couldn't last, because Liby couldn't stay away from her job forever. She went back home and back to work and I went back to living in the barracks.

48

Our luck hadn't run out yet, though. When it seemed pretty clear to Colonel Manuel that the Seventy-seventh was going to stay at Fort Jackson for at least a few more months, Liby quit her job and came to Columbia and got another one working for an insurance agency. Her Katie Gibbs credentials wowed them in South Carolina and they agreed right away to pay her at the rate of sixty cents an hour. That was $24 for a forty-hour week and, along with my $78 a month, it made it possible for us to take on the $50-a-month rent for an extraordinary find in semi-suburban Five Points, well on the way out toward the post. An ad in the Columbia *Record* sent us to what turned out to be a private house that the owners had cut up to make a separate apartment for their son, who had just been drafted and wouldn't be using it for a while. We had a separate entrance off the front porch, a combination living room and kitchen, a tile bathroom and one of the original bedrooms. Mostly, we had each other almost every night and almost every weekend. Working for Colonel Manuel had its compensations, and so did Sergeant Hunt's reliance on me to keep his Morning Report and his office in order. The only times I had to leave Liby to sleep alone were when we were on an overnight or weekend tactical problem. Once we were in the woods for a week, but even then I managed to ride shotgun on a couple of truck trips into the city to pick up stores at the railroad station. Our house was on the way to the station, so it made sense to stop there twice, once on the way in and once on the way back.

The time in Five Points was the longest and best we had together until the war was over. Liby had brought our tennis racquets and some tennis clothes with her and we were allowed to play on the courts at the University of South Carolina, a short walk from our house. We also had the new movies at the Fort Jackson Theatre, where a special section was roped off for officers and enlisted men with their wives. And when we rode the bus home, it wasn't like riding the trolley home in Yonkers. We could be together all night.

It all ended when the War Department decided we ought to get ready for Africa by learning how to live and fight a war in the desert. That got us a long train trip across the country to Phoenix,

Arizona, and then a jolting ride in a convoy of two-and-a-half-ton trucks to a bleak tent camp in a Godforsaken place called Hyder, Arizona, which wasn't a place at all; Hyder was simply a name for that particular piece of desert.

Our training experience was supposed to be exquisitely realistic, so with our meals we had a choice of iced coffee or tea or Kool-Aid, all without ice. We spent a lot of time out on the floor of the desert, where it wasn't unusual for the temperature to hit 125 degrees in the afternoon. We learned to dig slit trenches in the rocky sand and learned that if you were tired enough you could even sleep in them. We learned that most snakes won't kill you and that even a kid from New York can recognize a rattlesnake. We learned to eat K rations—cheese and oily crackers—and cold C rations because we weren't allowed to make fires. "When they leave here," the Desert Training Center commander said, "they can stand anything."

We did get cold beer at the PX tent on Saturday and Sunday nights and once a month we got a weekend pass. I went to Phoenix once, to Tucson once and to Hollywood once. We were sorry we went to Hollywood. Instead of traveling the 108 miles to Phoenix, or the maybe 150 miles to Tucson, and then spending the rest of the weekend living like civilians in an air-conditioned hotel, we spent two thirds of the time riding trains and the rest of it looking for a hotel room. We didn't see any movie stars. In fact, the only movie stars we did see were at beautiful downtown Hyder when Linda Darnell and Constance Moore came to the desert with a USO show and had their pictures taken eating lunch with Colonel Hamilton and Colonel Manuel. Miss Moore even put on an Army shirt with the Statue of Liberty on the sleeve. Miss Darnell didn't, probably for the sensible reason that it would have obscured her most famous attributes.

Aside from the visit by the movie queens and our three weekend trips, the guys in our Company Headquarters group didn't have much to look forward to except the mail and the weekend beer. In that order. Not even beer was as important as mail from home.

I got the biggest break of my time in the Army when Sergeant Hunt was picked to join a cadre that was going to organize and train a new division. Our new company commander, Captain Charles W. Bauer, a Philadelphia gentleman who became my closest friend on the little worlds of Guam, Leyte, Ie Shima and Okinawa, and on Cebu and Hokkaido, for that matter, decided he wanted me to take Hunt's job. To celebrate my promotion, he gave me a furlough to go see Liby in New York before the division was shipped back east to Indiantown Gap outside Harrisburg, Pennsylvania. I could report back to Indiantown Gap after my few days with Liby.

After three nights on the train I showed up at her office wearing wrinkled khakis, GI shoes and three or four pounds of sand. My new stripes were in my pocket for Liby to sew on. She got me out of the office and into a couple of ice-cold daiquiris in a matter of minutes.

Then, when I got to the Gap, Liby used up a lot of her gas ration stamps to drive down and spend what was supposed to be a week with me at the Penn-Harris Hotel in Harrisburg, only a couple of blocks from the state capitol. We decided, over an Italian dinner and red wine one night, that we had a thing for state capitols. The one week stretched into two when Liby's boss gave in gracefully to her telephone plea and let her stay on. Unhappily, that second week was the week Service Company had to qualify on the rifle range, so those of us whose wives were in town had to meet in front of the hotel every morning at three a.m. and drive in Liby's 1939 Buick out to the post in time for a bleary three-thirty formation. We were probably in bed every night at nine. But we had learned that you have to take every day you can get, even if it's only part of a day.

Our next adventure was amphibious training at Norfolk, where we practiced climbing cargo nets, huge rope ladders, up and down the sides of troopships into and out of landing craft. We also practiced running out of the beached LCVPs (landing craft, vehicle, personnel) in full field equipment the way we would have to do it if we ended up in the Pacific, which was the latest word. The only thing we didn't practice was the one thing we should have: how to keep from getting seasick.

Mountain training in West Virginia was next for what we were beginning to think was going to be one of the most versatile divisions in the whole United States Army. It was about twelve degrees above zero most of the time we were in the mountains, a nice change from the months in the desert. If the Germans or the Japanese didn't kill us, we figured, the Army would. But the mountain maneuvers ended happily for me, late in December, when I got a Christmas pass to New York before meeting the company at Camp Pickett, Virginia, which was to be our staging area for overseas.

I felt guilty leaving Charlie Bauer to accomplish the move without my invaluable professional help, but not so guilty that I didn't do it.

Liby got us a room at the Commodore, which led to one of our funnier wartime stories. When I got off the train at Penn Station, which always looked to me like a movie set with dozens of couples holding each other in goodbye embraces until the man in uniform broke away and raced for his train, I took a cab to the hotel. Liby was supposed to be there, but they told me she hadn't checked in yet. The best way to tell what happened is to quote the letter I wrote the hotel manager when I got a bill from him demanding payment for an overdue bill even though we had paid our bill when we checked out and headed home to Yonkers for the holiday. I was pretty mad at them:

Mr. C. E. Copeland
Credit Manager
Hotel Commodore
New York, New York
DEAR MR. COPELAND:

I am in receipt of an invoice from your office, billing me for $6.50 for room rent and telephone service December 21–22, 1943. Your invoice is in error and I hope you will bear with me through the somewhat lengthy explanation.

The morning of December 21st, I was to meet my wife in your hotel, she having procured a reservation for a double room well in advance. I arrived at about 6:55 and went to the desk to inquire if my wife was registered. The answer was no. I inquired if there was a reservation for us. The answer was no. I was, however, offered a room and signed your register for myself and my wife, and was shown to a room.

I waited several hours for my wife but she failed to appear. I called our home and was informed she had spent the night at your hotel and was still there waiting for me. Naturally, I checked back with the desk. The desk remained adamant. The answer was still no. I called my wife's office. One of her co-workers had left my wife at your hotel the night before. I tried the desk again. No soap. Now, a soldier's pass contains only so many hours and I must confess I was pretty mad about the way my hours were flying by with my wife still somewhere else. I see her all too seldom. I was unhappy.

I called my wife's mother then and was told that my wife just had called her from your hotel. The chase seemed to be growing hotter. Back to the room clerk, determined not to be put off easily, I went. The room clerk, I suspect, was more than a little weary of me by now and probably thought I was working some new crackpot game on him. However, his face was much pinker when a thorough check of the records revealed that the Commodore had been keeping my wife in a room six doors away from mine, on the same floor. Apologies were profuse. Of course, they were no help in bringing back the lost hours but being an easy-going type, even though I am a First Sergeant, I did not become too angry at your hotel's error. Just saddened.

Your invoice, however, places matters in a different light. This is placing injury upon injury. I was instructed to leave that desolate room of mine and join my wife in her room and simply pay the bill for hers. I did that. I have before me the receipted bill which I shall save, now that you have brought up the matter. Perhaps I should bill you for the telephone calls you forced me to make. Certainly I see no reason why I should pay you for the privilege of being arbitrarily separated from my wife for many precious hours of a short pass. I concede that I owe you $0.44 for phone calls. One of the phone calls listed on your invoice also appears on the one you had me pay

already so I guess you had the two room records together.
Don't you gentlemen ever question the unusual?

Yours very truly

EDW. FITZGERALD
1st Sergeant, Service Co.

Camp Pickett was our last stop in the United States, except for
Oakland, California, where we shipped out. Pickett was near a little
town called Blackstone, which had the virtue of possessing a state
liquor store, and not far from Petersburg, a gentle old Civil War
city that made Liby and me very happy for seven straight weekends.

There was no secret about the fact that when we left Camp
Pickett we would be heading overseas. Where, nobody knew, not
even Captain Bauer, but because we were on the East Coast the
logical guess was that we would be on our way to Europe. So much
for logic. When we finally got on the blacked-out train, they told
us we were going to California to board a ship heading for some
place in the Pacific. Before that happened, though, we had a lot of
work to do and nobody knew how many weeks to do it in. That got
me on the telephone to Liby, and to the room clerk at the Petersburg
Hotel, setting up the first of what turned out to be seven breathless
but memorable weekends with my travel-weary but brave bride.

Liby would arrive in Petersburg late Saturday carrying a small
case with everything she needed for the weekend—her toilet articles,
a nightgown in case the temperature fell below freezing in our
room, a bottle of Bacardi silver-label rum, two fresh limes and a
sharp knife. We ate in the handsome dining room on the first floor
of the hotel with its gleaming white tablecloths, white-jacketed
black waiters and Southern specialties like corn bread and home-
fried chicken, and we could get Cokes from room service, so we
hardly had to go outside the hotel. On Sunday night we turned into
pumpkins and walked down the hill past the ancient brick Farmers
Market, across the street to the handsome wood-and-marble railroad
station, and waited quietly for the train that would take Liby to
Washington, where she would get a sleeper for New York in time

to show up for work Monday morning. We had usually had about twenty-eight hours together.

We couldn't always get a room at the Petersburg, which was the Waldorf-Astoria of the town, but we always managed to get something. Once we were settling into a dormitory room at a girls' college when one of our Company Headquarters gang, Donald Metzger, the Springfield, Massachusetts, politician, took pity on us and gave us a room he had reserved at the Petersburg. I always suspected he was curious about the possibilities that might go with the room at the girls' college, but if he was rewarded for his unselfishness, he never mentioned it.

Those were our last times together for a long time, but they weren't bittersweet, they were joyous. We made a lot of love and, like Scarlett O'Hara, we were willing to worry about tomorrow tomorrow.

We finally ran out of weekends. I knew it when I kept her from getting dressed as long as I dared, I knew it when I walked her to the railroad station for the last time, I knew it when I kissed her on the platform and gave her a letter to read on the train, I knew it when I watched her settle into a seat and wave at me, and I knew it when I saw the last of the back of her head as the train pulled out. But when I went back to the loneliest barracks I'd slept in since Camp Upton, I was grateful for what we had had.

Sitting around on the long train ride to Oakland, I heard some of the guys talking about how they had made what our intellectual sergeant major, Tom Healey, called "emotional wills" with their wives. What that meant was that they had told their wives to get married again if they didn't come back. Liby and I hadn't done that. We hadn't even talked about it much. We chose to take it for granted that I would come back.

We got off the train at Camp Stoneman, California, but we never saw the camp. The trucks they put us on took us right to the dock, where, in long lines, with our brutally heavy duffel bags hoisted awkwardly on our shoulders, the straps of our overstuffed field packs digging into our backs, rifles banging against our legs, we walked the long walk down the side of a darkened ship to a narrow gangplank. A loading like that was generally a noisy affair with a lot of needling and joking, but this one was quiet. Every man had his own thoughts and kept them to himself. The whole scene—the darkness, the massive steelwork of the pier, the shadowy bulk of the blacked-out ship, the Red Cross women moving quietly along the lines filling paper cups with coffee from aluminum tanks strapped to their backs—smelled of war. Nobody saw anything funny about it.

There wasn't anything funny about the seven-day voyage to Hawaii, either. We slipped out beneath the Golden Gate Bridge under an ominously red sky and sailed right into an endless storm that churned up waves that smashed relentlessly against the ship and threatened to bury its bow in boiling white water. By the second day we didn't risk venturing out on deck. By the third day we had stopped going to the mess hall. Nobody wanted to eat; nobody even wanted to climb out of his bunk, at least not until the floors began to run with vomit and the stench forced all of us first sergeants to recruit every man who could manage to stand on his feet into mop squads. Actually, hoses did the job better than mops, and by the fourth and fifth days we weren't above turning the hoses on the worst cases, just to get the smell down.

I was lucky. I never threw up on that first boat ride of the war, although I skipped a lot of meals, and the experience gave me enough confidence to endure the countless hours we spent pitching offshore Guam and Leyte and Ie Shima and Okinawa in the flat-bottomed landing craft that were as much a part of the infantryman's war in the Pacific as the mud we lived in onshore.

Hawaii was pretty and it was more of a vacation than we'd had since we stood the formation on the drill field at Fort Jackson. We were stationed in a tent camp near the little town of Kahuku at the northern point of Oahu and it took only a few minues in a jeep to get to a beach that was as private as if we owned it. It was May and the sun was benevolently warm. We made it into Honolulu once a week or so, driving over the mountains through the breathtaking Pali pass, and stared enviously at the Army and Navy and Marine personnel who were permanently stationed there. The Pineapple Army, we called them. There were drinks at the bars at the Royal

Hawaiian and at the Moana next door. We didn't even mind that
the beach beyond the Moana was a jungle of barbed wire stretched
out fiendishly on tall iron posts. For me, there also was the chance
to browse and buy some books in the best bookstores I'd seen since
New York. My big acquisition was *Finnegans Wake*, which I read
off and on for the rest of the war and haven't really read yet. It
became my security blanket. As long as I had *Finnegans Wake* in
my duffel bag, I had something to read.

For someone with a reading vice like mine, being the first sergeant
was better than being the company commander. I got first shot at
each new shipment of the paperbound Armed Forces Reading Editions that the book publishers of America sent us every month. They
really piled up when we were incommunicado for a couple of months
or more, and I went through them like a wolf, making a huge stack
of the junk for the less discriminating men, a smaller stack for the
serious readers, and a very small stack for me—to be shared later
with the serious readers. I was a smoker then, and I also got first shot
at the good cigarettes—somebody else got the Tareytons—but the
books were my biggest fringe benefit. All of my life I've been willing to kill for a good book to read.

I tried to be fair. When some of our sergeants wanted to hit the
Honolulu night life, including the places like the New Congress
Hotel that James Jones wrote about in *From Here to Eternity*, and
a reliable charge of quarters was hard to find, I manned the Orderly
Room, wrote a long letter to Liby and read myself to sleep.

One weekend I got together with my Yonkers friend Joe Polcha,
the basketball and baseball player. He'd been on the island since
long before Pearl Harbor Day and he knew everything. I watched
him play a game in Honolulu Stadium with the Wanderers, the
game I used years later as the model for the game Vinnie Burns
played for the general in *The Ballplayer*. We had a good weekend—
lots of drinking, lots of eating and lots of talking. We didn't talk
much about Liby; he had been one of my principal rivals, so mostly
we talked about sports and who had heard what from the guys we
used to know back home.

June 6 was coming up and I wrote Liby that I had arranged to call

her long-distance at eleven o'clock in the morning that day to celebrate our second anniversary. You had to book a call like that a
couple of weeks in advance, but they said okay and they assigned
me to a public phone booth outside the shimmering white Mormon
Temple at Laie, just a few miles down the road from Kahuku.
"Bring ten dollars' worth of quarters with you," the long-distance
operator said. "There won't be anybody from the phone company
there. You'll have to drop the quarters in yourself."

The quarters were easy. I got them at the PX tent. The crisis exploded when I got out of bed in the morning and found out that the
long-awaited D-Day had finally happened. Eisenhower had landed
in force on the beaches of Normandy and the battle for *Festung
Europa* was on. The only thing I thought was: Oh, Jesus Christ,
there goes my telephone call. Which was, I found out when I talked
to her, exactly what Liby had thought when she heard the news.
But the phone company didn't cancel the call, the Army didn't im-
pose any restrictions on personal calls and I shattered the stillness
around the Mormon Temple with the clatter of dozens of quarters
and then, miraculously, got some excited person at the switchboard
of the Platt, Forbes advertising agency in Manhattan who put the
anniversary girl on the line. Not everybody has such a big fuss made
of their wedding anniversary. As I said, it's never been possible since
to forget it. Every newspaper and magazine and radio and television
station in the country reminds us every year that it's coming. The
day we got married had for us forevermore become D-Day minus
two.

There wasn't any way that telephone call could be topped. Not
even a Honolulu haircut by the first woman barber I'd ever encountered could do it. Not even an overnight stay at the Moana with my
friend Al Barraclough, the insurance man from Hartford, who'd
taught us how to drink Southern Comfort and used to lend us $5 at
the end of every month to keep our Five Points establishment running until payday, could do it. The only thing that could was shipping out, and that's what we did. With the last vehicle waterproofed
and, as the standing joke went, our shoes dubbed so we could walk
through the water to the beach, we headed for the real war.

Chapter 5

S PIRO Agnew, a loser if there ever was one, once said, "If you've seen one slum, you've seen them all," and that's just as untrue of slums as it was of D-Day landings. Every one was different, and for us in the Seventy-seventh, Guam was the most different. To begin with, it was our first one. Second, we had to spend endless queasy hours circling offshore before we were sent in. Third, we had to go in over what is generally considered the greatest barrier reef in the Pacific. Our landing craft couldn't go over it, so we had to walk over it. We lost a lot of men before we ever got close enough for the Japanese to shoot at us. Some of them were too seasick to keep themselves upright, some of them stepped into holes in the reef and just disappeared from sight. The average Infantryman that day, according to the U.S. War Department, was loaded down with rifle, gas mask, bayonet, grenade launcher, two bandoleers of ammunition, field pack and a pouch of hand grenades. A bulletin Charlie Bauer and I saw later on in the war claimed that some 46,000 grenades had been thrown at the Japanese on Guam, and even though I couldn't figure out how the hell they knew that, I was prepared to believe it. The damn things were going off all the time. It was the first time in combat for almost everybody, and there was a beautiful sense of security attached to lobbing a couple of grenades into a suspicious-looking hole or ditch.

D-Day, July 21, 1944, began in the dark. We got up early and
we hurried up and waited in the best Army tradition. We repeated
all the jokes about the right way and the Army way. We tugged at
our combat boots to make sure they were as tight as we could make
them. We'd been warned that we'd have to walk a long way in the
water.

The noise overhead from big guns firing and airplanes screeching
in long dives made us even edgier because we were kept below decks
so long. When they finally told us to move up topside, we watched
the shelling and the bombing in awe. They told us there were four
battleships and three heavy cruisers out there where we couldn't
see them relentlessly firing broadsides of shells ranging from five
inches to sixteen inches. We could see a long line of slender, graceful, quick-turning destroyers patrolling a steady beat to protect the
big ships and turning spitefully every once in a while to fire their
own guns at the island. Agat Bay and Agat Village stood in plain
view. Clouds of black smoke and leaping sheets of red flame showed
the ferocity of the attack on the Japanese defense positions. "There
won't be anything left alive on that island by the time you guys get
there," a sailor standing near me said admiringly.

That's what *he* thought. It was our first lesson in the exaggerated
confidence the Navy had in the effectiveness of offshore shelling.
What we found out was that when it started, the Japanese went
into their elaborate caves, and when it stopped, they came out and
started shooting. They fired their rifles and lobbed their mortars
down on us from the high ground and even opened up with artillery
pieces that they had made room for in the same caves they hid in
themselves. It wasn't that our side didn't get the mail through. It was
just that the Japanese weren't out walking on the beaches or on the
streets of Agat where they could be picked off. They were inside,
deep inside, behind walls of natural rock and coral.

When we moved into one hastily abandoned position on the day
after the landing, we found three wooden cases of Japanese-made
Bee Brand red wine sitting in a corner of a big cave that looked like
some kind of headquarters, and not one of the bottles was even

cracked. We split them up and drank them in our slit trenches every night for a week.

The climb down the cargo net into the landing craft was a bad moment for all of us. It felt final. Three years later, when I made my first airplane flight to interview Bob Feller in California, I had the same feeling when they closed the door of the DC-3 at La Guardia and said, "We're cleared for takeoff." You knew you couldn't get out now, you had to go whether you liked it or not. "I'd really rather not do this," I said to Donald Metzger, and he said, "You know, West Springfield wasn't so bad."

The first worry we had, in the boats and after we got out of them, was that our own planes would aim short and hit us. They were coming in right over our heads. But when we saw the first guys go down in the water without a sound and we reached for them and they weren't there, we realized that our biggest worry was just making it to the beach without drowning.

"Tell them to move off the beach as fast as they can," Charlie said. "Go inland as straight as they can and as far as they can. Tell them to guess about five hundred feet past the beach line and stop, dig a foxhole and wait. We'll look for each other later."

We had practiced digging foxholes, round and deep, for temporary shelter, and slit trenches, long and just deep enough to keep our heads and behinds below the ground, for all night.

I learned another lesson that first night. Some people could stay in their holes, but some of us had to move around the company area and deliver messages and the orders that the colonel gave the captain to give the lieutenants and me. That's what Charlie's two silver bars and the bars our lieutenants, Morris Shulman and Ricky DelMar and Tex Wood, wore and my six stripes were for.

In four years I had only one man refuse an order, and that was in Louisiana, on maneuvers. Nobody ever did in the Pacific. Everybody wanted desperately to live through it and we made a lot of jokes about it, but we trusted each other.

The Infantry's kind of war is hard to explain. We did a little bit of everything. We joined the Navy, we walked, we rode on trucks,

we dug holes in the ground, we laid out perimeters at night to pre-
vent suicidal Japanese from jumping into our holes and we walked
and walked and walked.

If there is one picture of the war engraved in my head, it's of a
long, uneven line of men who hadn't shaved in weeks, wearing
fatigues covered with sand and drenched in sweat, walking slowly
but steadily from the place where they had been to the place where
somebody would tell them to stop.

Guam was our high school. Everything before that was kinder-
garten or grammar school, or, if you want to give weight to things
like the obstacle course and the infiltration course and amphibious
training, junior high school.

On Guam we learned that the big thing wasn't getting mail or
something hot to eat, but staying alive. Charlie and I stood on a hill
above Agat on the second day ashore, talking to a warrant officer
whose name was Warren Pepple, when the first Japanese planes hit
us. They were the first Japanese planes we'd ever seen and all of a
sudden they were right over our heads. It was the old joke, "Hey,
they're trying to kill me!" Machine-gun bullets came first and then
shells, digging deep, angry holes in the dirt all around us. We threw
ourselves down, but Pepple got hit in his behind by a shell burst.
"Don't worry," I told him, "you're only bleeding on the side of
your ass." Charlie called for an aid man while I gave Pepple a
drink of water and rubbed some of the water on his sweaty face.
"He needs help," Charlie told the medic. "No, he doesn't," the
medic said after a minute of working on him, "he's dead."

Joe Podraza, who had been our mess sergeant and then had gone
to a rifle company, was the next one I knew to get it. Joe was always
out scavenging for food. He was convinced you could, as he said, do
good just picking up what the Marines and the Seabees threw away.
But one day he went too far and he got hit and some of our guys
went out and brought him back wrapped up in his poncho. When
they loaded him on a three-quarter-ton truck, all I could see was his
shoes. That bothered me a lot. I'd seen him put them on many a
morning and all I wanted to do was take them off. I've always hated
shoes. I take them off as soon as I get home. Sometimes I took them

off under my desk as soon as I got to the office. Joe's shoes sticking
out from under his poncho said plainly they weren't only trying to
kill us, they were killing us.

But Guam ended on August 8, 1944, or August 10, or whatever
"the island is secure" date you want to accept. It didn't matter to
any of us except the fifty-two GIs who became casualties between
August 8 and the time we left the island.

Once the island was secure and we could put up tents and get in
out of the rain, the biggest problem we had was getting our company radio to work. For a company with a full complement of
mechanics and even a couple of electricians, we had very little success. Even if somebody got it to work for a while, it produced more
static than sound. Morris Shulman, the captain who ran the Motor
Pool, finally came through, but even he couldn't fix it so we could
get the Voice of America or Armed Forces Radio. We had to settle
for one of the numerous Japanese stations. They played good music,
though. "If you American fighting men want real home-style music," the announcer would say in perfect English, "music with the
real U.S.A. label, just keep listening to this station." Then we would
get Harry James or Benny Goodman or Glen Gray or Tommy
Tucker, followed by a silken feminine voice asking, "Wouldn't you
like to be home with your girlfriend now?" That was followed
immediately by an appropriate piece of musical propaganda like
"Somebody Stole My Gal" or "I Wonder Who's Kissing Her Now."

Partly because the radio was an uncertain source of entertainment, I began writing magazine articles while we were on Guam.
The first one was on the ferocity with which the American soldier
hunted souvenirs. Any piece of Japanese military equipment would
do, but flags were precious and the ultimate souvenir was a samurai
sword. No dead Japanese was ever buried still wearing or carrying
anything that an American GI thought was worth something as a
souvenir. Even if you already had one just like it, you could trade it
to a sailor or a Seabee for something really useful, like a few cold
beers.

Liby acted as my agent, sending the pieces out to every magazine
she could think of, and she made three sales during the months I

spent in the Pacific. She scored with the *New York Times Magazine*, with the Sunday supplement *This Week* and, the biggest hit of all, with *Esquire*. A telegram I got on June 9, 1944, told me that my story "I Will Be the One" had earned $250 of *Esquire*'s money.

My appearances in print once got me an acknowledgment from Colonel Hamilton when he made a surprise visit to our makeshift camp on the beach at Leyte. "So you're the famous Sergeant Fitz-gerald," he said. "Not very famous, sir," I said. "I don't know about that," the colonel said pleasantly enough. "Tenth Army asked General Bruce about you, and he asked me. That's pretty famous. Anyway, I liked that last piece of yours. Keep it up."

I kept it up, even when my agent and I got discouraged by the pile of rejection slips she accumulated. I was convinced that the only way to learn how to write was to write, and I kept at it.

When we loaded on ship again and they told us we were going to Noumea, I asked Charlie, "Where the hell is Noumea?"

"It's on New Caledonia," he said.

"Thanks."

"Well," he said, "on the map it looks like it isn't all that far off Australia. It's a big island, and Noumea is a good-sized town, maybe more than fifty thousand people. It ought to be a good place to take it easy for a while. Garrison life."

It might have been a good place, but we never got there. We came close. But one night after dinner the General Quarters horn beeped and the loudspeaker came on: "Now hear this. This is the captain speaking. We have orders from Admiral Nimitz to turn around and proceed with all deliberate speed to Leyte. We are heading for the Philippines."

Even the trip home from Yokohama didn't add up to as many continuous days on shipboard as the voyage from Guam to almost Noumea to Leyte. As much as I love beans, even I had stopped eating them for breakfast before we finally landed at Tacloban. For lunch, maybe, but not for breakfast. But it was wonderful to be clean every day, to wear dry clothes and to sleep dry. Then we hit Tacloban and were back in the mud.

Our biggest and most frightening adventure on Leyte was one of

MacArthur's best ideas. I was no MacArthur fan. I disliked his imperial manner, his fried-egg cap, his royal "we" and, even worse, his
"my Infantry," or "my Navy" or "my Air Force." I didn't like
George Patton, either, for the same kind of showiness, for his pearl-
handled pistols and his contemptuous treatment of the slobs who
had to go where he sent them. I liked Joe Stilwell and Omar Bradley; I liked my generals low-key. I liked them to be aware that people got killed in the war. But my dislike of MacArthur didn't keep
me from admiring the general's boldness in pulling off his end run
at Ormoc on the other side of the island from Tacloban. The Japanese had been pouring reinforcements ashore on the beaches of
Ormoc Bay; more than 100,000 of them had landed there and were
moving rapidly to back up the reduced armies facing the Americans
pushing inland from the east. MacArthur decided to hit them from
behind.

The end run was mounted so quickly we didn't even take all of
our people with us on the operation. We took only the people who
were essential. We left personnel people and mail people and all
kinds of support people behind. Those of us who went got on a
shiny new LST that gleamed like a new car fresh from the show-
room, and we thought it was great. Eating in the mess hall was like
eating in Horn & Hardart's. One day the captain, who was a young
lieutenant who looked barely twenty-one, dropped the ramp and
let us jump off and swim in the beautiful blue water, and after that
we thought *he* was great. He was no Mister Roberts, though. When
we got to the beach at Ormoc the morning of December 7 and he
shoved that ramp onto the shore and let us off, a flight of Japanese
airplanes raced in like a swarm of angry bees trying to get even with
us for poking a stick in their nest. The kid didn't like the looks of
things. We were just beginning to lug off our ammunition and food
when he began to back off the beach.

"Where the hell are you going?" a bunch of us screamed at him.

"Listen, you dumb bastards," he yelled back, opening up the
water between us and our stuff and leaving us standing up to our
asses in the water, "don't you know these fucking things cost five
million bucks?"

That was the maddest I ever was during the war.

Ormoc also gave me my biggest scare of the war. We were only fifty or sixty yards in from the beach that night, wriggling uneasily in our slit trenches, trying to duck the maddeningly random mortar fire coming from just a few hundred yards ahead of us, when a Japanese version of the LST plowed up on the beach behind us and dropped its ramp just about where Captain Courageous had abandoned us.

"Don't let them get ashore!" Charlie Bauer hollered loud enough so everybody around us could hear him. My liking for Charlie had always been coupled with respect, but this was the most aggressively military I'd ever seen my gentle Philadelphia friend. "Get them on the ramp! Watch the side of the ship! Get them if they jump!"

Months later I wrote a piece about that night and called it "When the Infantry Went to General Quarters." Except for the night two Japanese tried to jump into our double-bed slit trench on Okinawa and we scared them off with Charlie's .45 and my carbine, it was the closest thing to hand-to-hand combat we ever knew. But we kept our beachhead and the Japanese were finished on the island.

Leyte was a big part of our war. We cast absentee ballots for Roosevelt there, we had a hot turkey Thanksgiving dinner *al fresco* there, we had upper-balcony seats for the Battle of Leyte Gulf that decimated the Japanese Navy, we ate Christmas dinner there, and when it was safe we did a lot of swimming in the Pacific Ocean while we read letters from home and wrote letters back. Liby sent me an ingenious Christmas present of a loaf of rock-hard bread that had a bottle of Southern Comfort inside it. One of our chaplain's assistants who, thank God, didn't drink got a package from his mother which had two factory-processed and labeled cans of Campbell's vegetable soup in it. One was full of bourbon and the other rye.

After the fighting was over, the little regimental band that lived and traveled and even worked with us got its chance to entertain. They put on a couple of shows that everybody loved. Joe Price, the New York doorman, did soft-shoe dances and sang songs like "Down on the Corner of Thoity-Thoid and Thoid." Dick Skehan, an Irishman from Boston, put on his finest brogue and let the people have

all of his St. Patrick's Day favorites, even "You're as Welcome as
the Flowers in May to Dear Old Donegal," finishing up with his
guaranteed George M. Cohan show-stopper, "What did Robinson
Crusoe Do with Friday on Saturday Night?" Price came back with
a New York ditty I've seen printed but never heard sung since:

> "Tammany Hall's a patriotic outfit,
> Tammany Hall's a credit to the community.
> On the Fourth of July we always wave the flag, boys,
> But we never waive immunity.
>
> Tammany Hall, like Robin Hood, professes
> To rob the rich and give it to the poor,
> But Tammany Hall, like us, makes mistakes sometimes.
> They rob from all and give to Tammany Hall."

The *pièce de résistance* of those impromptu gigs was a public
clamor for Lieutenant Harold E. Wood, "Tex" to officer and enlisted man alike, to lead the regiment in a rousing rendition of
"Beautiful, Beautiful Texas." First, Tex had to be coaxed. Then he
had to be yelled at. Then somebody had to give him a fresh cold
beer and finally he would get up on the bandstand with the head-
lights of a dozen six-by-sixes on him and, with his iron-gray hair
shaking in the island night and his red face getting redder, yell
fiercely, "All right, you sons-of-bitches, get up on your feet like
men!" and he would lead the charge:

> "In beautiful, beautiful Texas,
> Where the beautiful bluebonnets grow,
> We're proud of our forefathers
> Who fought at the Alamo.
> You can live on the plains or the mountains
> Or down where the sea breezes blow,
> But you still will be in Texas,
> The most beautiful state that I know."

Repeat choruses of this hallowed hymn were available upon request, especially if the request was accompanied by another beer.

Then everybody walked off to sleep, maybe to dream of home. It didn't have to be Texas. It could be Philadelphia or Boston or New York. Everybody had someplace and somebody waiting for him.

Then we got on another boat and had that meeting in Charlie's cabin and looked at the map of Okinawa. "What do you think?" Charlie asked me.

"I don't know," I said. "It's another island. A big one. Pretty close to Japan, isn't it?"

"The Navy people say if you're on a destroyer you can make it overnight," he said. "That's pretty close."

I decided to worry about that when I had time. Right now I was busy being comfortable. The ship's captain had put all of us first and master sergeants in with his chief petty officers, two to a room. It was like a double room at the Commodore, only the person in the other bed was a he. We had a private day room, a separate mess, no standing on line to eat or even to go to the bathroom. Heaven. It's terrible how fast you can get used to the British notion of "I'm all right, Jack."

One night we paid back our hosts by sneaking into the hold and searching for an hour until we found Service Company's jeeps and uncovered six contraband cases of Budweiser. The Navy boys had ice ready in big buckets when we got the beer, prudently wrapped in white Navy blankets, safely upstairs. As I said, Heaven.

The bad news about that luxury cruise to Okinawa was that the Japanese had brought out their desperation weapon, the Kamikazes, pilots willing to crash-dive their airplanes smack into the decks and the bridges of U.S. warships and troopships. Kamikaze means "divine wind," but what it really meant was that the pilots were willing to fly themselves straight into what they knew would be places in Heaven by making themselves into human torpedoes and taking an American ship out of the war along with them. They went to last rites for themselves, wrapped white cloths around their heads to show that they were already dead and sent their most precious effects home before they took off.

We saw one Kamikaze hit a destroyer making speed past us on our port side. We saw another burned-out shell of a destroyer trying to limp back to find help. We watched as a Kamikaze dived into the midships of the troopship carrying the 305th Infantry, one of our two sister regiments, killing or wounding most of the regimental command staff, including Major Winthrop Rockefeller, who later became Governor of Arkansas. Finally, we saw two or three of them zoom in contemptuously on our own ship until one of them finally struck it right in the middle of the top deck. A lot of our men got hit in that one. I was below decks, but I'll never forget the way it sounded and felt when that Japanese plane exploded into the steel plates of the deck over our heads.

Later we read that the Kamikazes hit more than thirty American ships and caused almost 10,000 casualties. A carrier strike force could hardly have hoped to accomplish as much.

D-Day on Okinawa was set for Easter Sunday morning, April 1, 1945, but we didn't make the parade. We were sent instead to Kerama Retto, a group of small offshore islands which Admiral Nimitz wanted as bases for radar and bombers. Nimitz, much to General MacArthur's displeasure, still commanded the area in which Lieutenant General Simon Bolivar Buckner's Tenth Army, which included us, was operating. The most important island, Ie Shima, with three airstrips long enough to accommodate four-engine planes, was where our company ended up as part of a battalion attack force. "A walkover," they told us at the shipboard briefing the night before the April 16 landing, and Joe Price never forgave me for talking him into going along when he could have stayed on the ship. "You missed Ormoc," I told him. "At least you'll pick up a D-Day arrowhead, and maybe you'll see something interesting."

Joe's misgivings were wiser than my optimism. We didn't dare lift our heads above the rim of our slit trench all night, and by morning every bush anywhere near us had been sliced to little pieces. The hills on the tiny island's high point, Mount Iegusugu, were a honeycomb of caves. We were willing to swear, every one of the four nights we were on the island, that they had every military weapon you could imagine in those caves except maybe long-range bombers. Our officers called for air and sea support in a hurry, and the Navy gave us the most devastating bombing and shelling we'd seen yet. But the Japanese still came out every night and gave us hell until the dawn. The only way we got them in the end was with flame-throwers. Grenades, too, and rockets, but mostly flame-throwers. We literally burned them out.

They took a lot of our men with them, more than 2,000 casualties that left our attack teams badly in need of reinforcements. They also took, less than a week after President Roosevelt died on April 12, another one of America's secret weapons, Ernie Pyle, the incomparable war correspondent who wrote so feelingly about the GI's war. Pyle was riding in a jeep with Lieutenant Colonel Joseph B. Coolidge, the commander of the First Battalion of the 306th Infantry, when a Japanese machine gun that had been passed safely by dozens of other jeeps and riflemen suddenly opened fire. Colonel Coolidge and Pyle jumped into a ditch, but Pyle's helmet was pierced by a bullet that killed him instantly. He was buried by a detail that put up a hand-lettered sign:

AT THIS SPOT
THE 77TH INFANTRY DIVISION
LOST A BUDDY
ERNIE PYLE
18 APRIL 1945

Losing Roosevelt, the hero of every Depression kid, gave us the feeling that something would never be the same. God wasn't in his Heaven any more. But losing Pyle, and on our own dirty little island, was like a death in the family.

When we finally got back to the ship, Charlie Bauer said I had to meet him in his cabin right away for a briefing on our landing on Okinawa, which, he had been told, would be either tomorrow or the day after. "Shit," I said. But when I got to Charlie's place, there were no maps, nobody there except him and on the table a bottle of Scotch and a bowl of ice cubes. I have never liked Scotch, I don't like it now and I didn't like it then, but I drank it. I also took a hot shower and ate some hot food and slept all night without pushing my head deeper into the dirt.

Okinawa was easy in the beginning. It had been easy for the

D-Day landings and easy for the Marine and Army divisions that widened the landing breach from Kadena to Yontan. Ernie Pyle had been with them when they first went ashore and he wrote, "Never before had I seen an invasion beach like Okinawa. There wasn't a dead or wounded man on our whole sector of it." He went to Ie Shima with us before the fighting on Okinawa got tough, so he never saw what happened after the honeymoon ended.

Everything was still nice and easy when we followed the D-Day troops ashore, but by the time we were fully committed to the assault the Japanese commander had made clear his intention to defend the southern part of the island literally to the death. His headquarters was in Shuri Castle, a fifteenth-century stone monument that once was home and fortress to feudal kings and princes. The names of the places General Ushijima chose to defend—Shuri, the Kakazu Ridge, Ishimmi, Yonabura, Naha and, worst of all, the Escarpment at Urasoe-Mura, a jagged limestone cliff 500 feet high that guarded the final approaches to Shuri Castle and that became the 307th's personal assignment—have stayed in my head.

Desmond Doss, our Medical Detachment's conscientious non-combatant who wouldn't touch a gun but who won the Medal of Honor for saving the lives of seventy-five men at the Escarpment and who was still alive to go to a regimental reunion at Valley Forge, Pennsylvania, in 1983, will never forget the terrible struggle to get to the top of and past the forbidding obstacle of Sawtooth Ridge. Neither will anybody else who was there. "The north face of the cliff was too steep to climb," the War Department said later, "even with 50-foot high scaling ladders, so the 307th borrowed cargo nets from the Navy, managed to hang them from the top of the cliff and climbed up them at night."

I used that in my novel about the ball-player soldier. He was alone in a cave they were using as Company Headquarters when a captain from Battalion Headquarters came looking for a detail to carry ammunition, food and water to the first squads that had made it to the top. "Now," the captain said, "we need it now." He got it. The first squads that got up there never came back down. They went down the other side.

With Shuri and Naha gone, the Escarpment behind us and only flat land and the ocean in front of us, the battle for Okinawa didn't have much left. Enough, though, to kill General Buckner, who was hit by shell pieces while he stood on a hill on the southwestern tip of the island and watched the fighting. General Buckner was the highest-ranking officer killed in the Pacific war.

What was left was the stubbornness of the Japanese, their willingness to die, their profligate artillery bombardments and ours in kind. Then there was that last night when the ground shook unbelievably and the shells rocketing over our heads were mostly ours going out and Ushijima made up his mind to die.

The Japanese historians tell us that on the night of June 20 General Ushijima and his chief of staff ate an elaborate dinner the commander had painstakingly ordered. There was fish, rice, potatoes, cabbage, pineapples for dessert and a lot of sake. In the morning the two generals buried their ceremonial knives in their bellies and had their heads sliced off by sweeping swings of a Samurai sword wielded by one of their staff officers.

That was the night we made our first fires and ate our first hot C rations and talked about what we were going to do when the war was over. It had to be over soon. The Russians were coming to help us, the divisions from Europe were coming, the Navy would have new ships and new airplanes and it couldn't last long, could it?

On Cebu it was hard to believe we were going to have to go back to it again. But in our hearts we knew it would be worse than anything yet. If they had fought that hard for Leyte and Okinawa, not to mention Tarawa and Guadalcanal and Iwo Jima and all the other islands, and in all the sea battles and air battles, surely they would fight even harder for their home islands. We read our letters from home and answered them and drank beer and ate real food and slept dry. All a man could do was hope.

Then we dropped the Bomb.

I was more or less detached from Service Company a week after we set up camp on Cebu. I was given my pick of a couple of dozen men, including noncoms, to build a recreation hall for the regiment. We were allowed to hire native laborers, too, especially for the intricate business of twisting bamboo fronds into thatch for the roof and the sides. The structure itself was made of thick bamboo tree trunks. It looked pretty good when it was finished, and we decided to have a dance as the grand opening. We picked August 6 as the date. Ricky DelMar, who seemed to have established the best connections short of Regimental Headquarters with the officials in Tabogon, the nearest town, arranged to have a convoy of trucks pick up a hundred or so girls who had said they would be willing to go to the dance, along with as many of their mothers and fathers and town officials as wanted to come.

It was a good party. The boys in the band, Don Stanton, Burt Tobias, Bernie Campbell, Louie Vadala and Bernie Saber, had never sounded better. The girls were wearing the best white dresses their mothers had been able to save during the years of the Occupation, and they looked beautiful. There was enough beer and Coke for everybody and the regiment's mess sergeants had knocked themselves out to provide a buffet table that looked like a catered affair in Great Neck, Long Island. The Filipino girls danced with everybody who asked them, and their parents beamed with pride. Everybody told us over and over again how bad it had been with the Japanese there and how good it was to have the Americans back. The night would have been a night to remember anyway, but there was a blockbuster of a surprise coming that we didn't know anything about.

Our dance had been going on for a couple of hours when a young lieutenant I'd never seen before, probably a replacement who had so little clout that he had been stuck with the duty officer's job at headquarters while everybody else at least looked in on the party, hurried into our bamboo Roseland and stopped the band in the middle of a song. He got up on the stand and waved his arm for attention. "We've dropped an atom bomb on Japan," he said breathlessly. "There's never been anything like it. It's the most powerful bomb in the history of the world."

"What's an atom bomb?" everybody who could get near him asked him. But he didn't know any more than we did. All he knew was that a big Japanese city had been blown to hell by one bomb and didn't it make sense that if we had a bomb that could do that, the Japanese would have to surrender?

Three days later there was Nagasaki. That was a plutonium bomb, a different, less powerful type than the uranium bomb used on Hiroshima.

Six days after the second bomb had fallen, at four p.m. on Wednesday, August 15, Emperor Hirohito ordered an end to all hostilities. "We must," he said solemnly, "endure the unendurable and suffer the insufferable." It was the first time in history that a Japanese emperor had spoken to his people over the radio. He had told them to stop fighting and to cooperate fully with the occupying forces and that is what they would do, because the emperor is divine.

The war was, at last, over.

One of the observers at the surrender ceremony on the battleship *Missouri* was General Joseph W. Stilwell, outside of MacArthur the highest-ranking Army officer on the scene. Stilwell had accepted from MacArthur the command of the U.S. Tenth Army after General Buckner was killed on Okinawa. "Will you do it?" MacArthur had asked the unemployed general who had left China after a series of bitter disagreements with Chiang Kai-shek. MacArthur meant would he take a three-star general's job even though President Roosevelt had bestowed four stars on him to give him a chance to stand up against the Chinese dictator. "I'd take a division if I could be back with troops," Stilwell is reported to have told him. And he took the job and began to plan the part the Tenth Army would play in the invasion of the Japanese home islands. That part, Army historians say, would have begun with a landing on the Tokyo plain itself.

Now the general who liked to walk with the foot soldiers, who never wore ribbons on his chest and who swore like the best of his troopers, wouldn't have to make that landing. Neither would we.

Forty years later we don't think much of nuclear weapons or even nuclear power. But when we dropped that first one, the only emotion I felt was pure elation. It meant going home.

Chapter 6

Home for Christmas. It was hard to believe. Liby's childhood bedroom on the top floor of her family's house had a little fireplace that we used every night, even though we couldn't keep it from smoking up the room. The smoke smelled wonderful to us. We could carry everything we needed up there when we made our excuses for the night—we always kept some rum in the room and it wasn't hard to carry the necessary ice and fresh limes.

In a way New Year's was even better than Christmas because by then I was a civilian and we could begin to make plans. The Army had made it pretty easy for our platoon of first sergeants to go through the formalities at Fort Dix. They sent us home with the clothes on our backs, our uncollected pay, less allotments, and $50 in separation pay. They gave me a blue leather box with my Bronze Star medal from Okinawa, my Combat Infantryman's Badge and assorted ribbons and tiny D-Day arrowheads. Most important of all, they assembled us in a group to hear a thank-you speech from an over-age lieutenant colonel who then gave us a handshake and the discharge papers we had signed half an hour ago. From March 25, 1942, to January 1, 1946, it had taken almost as long as going to college.

75

The first surprise Liby had for me when I got home was that we were rich. Well, rich for two kids who hadn't had a dime when they got married. My Czechoslovakian wife had out-thrifted the thriftiest of her ancestors and put together a bank account of more than $3,000. It surprised me. There must have been a lot of fifteen-cent lunches in those 108 pounds she was carrying so easily. We both wanted to spend some of it on a trip, and we decided to begin with New York City. Hotel space was scarce in those days, and we were glad to settle for three days at the Gramercy Park Hotel, complete with walks in the private park that you could get into only after you had borrowed a key at the front desk, and then five days at the Hotel Duane on Madison Avenue. (Six dollars a night at each hotel.) We saw some good shows. Then we took off for Baltimore because we wanted to take time to ride to a different city, Baltimore wasn't too far and we had had some good times there during the war. The Lord Baltimore Hotel was every bit as warm and as comfortable as we remembered it from a few overnights (and only cost fifty cents a night more than the New York hotels) and we had time alone to talk and catch up and try to figure out what we wanted to do with our lives.

We agreed we wanted to stay in or near New York—"the city," which is all we've ever called it. For one thing, Liby's mother had had a bad stroke while I was overseas and Liby couldn't move far away. For another, the kind of work I wanted to do was in New York. I knew that Boston and Philadelphia and San Francisco and other cities also published newspapers and even magazines and books, but I didn't know there was any city to work in besides New York.

When we got back home, I began writing letters in earnest. I talked to Paul Sann, city editor of the New York *Post*, who was willing to see me because one of his reporters, Betsy Luce, an old friend of ours, had asked him to. "You're the only veteran I'll push on him," Betsy told me. But it didn't do any good. There was no place to put me.

Not even the January issue of *Esquire*, with my story "I Will Be the One," about Benny, the Filipino guerilla, could get me a job in New York. At least, though, it had paid for a lot of our $6 hotel nights and had given us a lot of pleasure when we saw it on news-stands in New York and Baltimore.

After a while I got tired of spending the money Liby had worked so hard to put in the bank, and I didn't want her to have to go back to work any more than she wanted to, so I went back to the *Herald-Statesman*. They had a new sports editor, so they put me on the city desk. Instead of the $30 a week I'd been making when I left, they paid me $45. Except that I didn't get to do much writing, I liked the work. I edited copy, wrote heads, did telephone rewrites on late-breaking stories and went out on assignments whenever Bill Seely, the city editor, thought one up.

Like the story about the Yonkers man, Henry Trefflich, who owned a pet store on Fulton Street in the city, and whose assistant let a hundred monkeys escape from a cage and out of the store into the crowded Manhattan street. "The monkeys caused a tremendous amount of chaos when they made their bold bid for liberty," I reported.

> They climbed happily on the walls of office buildings. They dashed swiftly into stores and restaurants. In one bar some mid-morning customers took one look at a troop of them rushing in and left without even paying their checks. Three monkeys were captured by choirboys practicing in Trinity Mission House. Three others ended their brief fling in the lavatory of a nearby fire house. About forty of the smartest beasts, all of which were newly arrived from India, camped out in the L. J. Callanan grocery store on Vesey Street, scrambling in through an open window. One unfortunate monkey forgot how tall the build-ings are in New York. He tried to jump from one ledge to another on the twelfth floor of a building on the corner of Vesey and Greenwich Streets and didn't quite make it. He was very dead after he reached the sidewalk.

Mr. Trefflich was even good for a follow-up story a week later when a New York judge dismissed a police charge that he had com-mitted a public nuisance by allowing the monkeys to escape. The publicity got him a lot of new business. And he told me a trap he had set in the back of the grocery store had been empty for four days, so he thought the whole thing was over. The owner of the grocery store, he said, had put his bananas in the refrigerator for the duration.

I also got a story out of the fact that May 1, the second busiest day of the year for moving men (October 1 is the busiest), was a dud in 1946. Nobody was moving because there wasn't anyplace to move to. If a moving van did pull up to an apartment house in those days, it was the signal for a concerted rush on the superintendent's door. "Wistfully, the moving men remembered better days," I wrote. "The good old days when people swapped apartments all over the place. The days when you'd up and move if Johnny couldn't get along with the kid next door or if the landlord wouldn't paint over those bad spots on the wall. Now you just tell him, 'Oh, don't worry about it. I'll paint it myself.' The moving men have to move the furniture around in their own offices just to keep in shape."

Bill Seely, a wispy little man with a bony, sharp-featured face, thin gray hair and blue eyes that saw everything but kept their own counsel (unless he got mad, which he did frequently but with great eloquence and elegance), had been my journalism professor before the war and he picked up right where he had left off. There wasn't anything he didn't know about putting out a newspaper or constructing an English sentence. He held all of us to the strictest standards—his. Since I worked for Bill, I have never once confused "imply" with "infer." "I imply," he told me sternly, "you infer." It's as good a way to remember it as any. I've never said somebody presented someone with an award. I learned from Bill that you just present an award. A Phi Beta Kappa graduate of Cornell and a former high-school principal, he never let me write that somebody graduated from high school or college. "Say he was graduated," Bill commanded. "It may be a little more trouble, but it's the right way." Once I committed the sin of writing that last night's dinner of the Italian-American Society at Columbus Hall was the most heavily attended affair in the organization's history. He was outraged. "Edward," he said in his formal style of exaggerated patience, "an affair is something between a man and a woman. You mean event." It's been "event" ever since. I learned from Bill that you are eager to do something you want to do, anxious about something that makes you apprehensive.

Bill gave me a real present when he sent me to the North Broadway mansion of Colonel John B. Stilwell, where General Joe was his brother's guest on a visit from his San Francisco headquarters as commander of the Sixth Army in charge of the Western Defense Command.

The general, wearing comfortable trousers, a woolen shirt open at the neck and a sweater, received me with informal warmth. I had been ready for a severe military type, but that wasn't what I got. Sitting down with me in the library, he said he had been told that I'd been in the Army and he wanted to know with what outfit and where I'd been. When he found out I'd been in the infantry, and in the Pacific, I was home free. He was especially pleased that I'd been in the Seventy-seventh because it was part of the Tenth Army that MacArthur had given to him and the Bomb had taken away. But he made it clear that he was glad the Bomb had ended the war. I got the feeling that if there was a war on, he wanted to be fighting it, not moving papers around, but that he didn't have to have a war to be happy.

For me, it was a doubly rewarding assignment. I got to talk to one of my two Infantry general heroes and I was in the paper again as a writer and not just as an editor. I was so eager to write that story that I did what I've done ever since I first wrote for the Yonkers *Record* and the *Gorton News*. I wrote it fast. I think a lot before I write, but when I sit down at the typewriter, I just write. Everybody who is interested in writing knows that Red Smith said it was very hard work and that he stared at the blank piece of paper for a long time and only began to type when he saw the first drop of blood on the page. I've never had that feeling. When I see a piece of paper in the typewriter, I want to write on it. I write what I have to say fast.

The piece about General Stilwell sticks in my head still as one of the luckiest assignments I've ever been given. The general looked older than his years and was plainly tired, but he was still full of energy and he wasn't short of opinions. Chiang Kai-shek, whom he scornfully called "The Peanut," was a man who always had "a lot of fancy charts and dirty intentions." The way Stilwell saw him, "The Gimo had to have his fingers in the pie" all the time. Vinegar Joe hated that; he had nothing good to say about the man he felt had sold out China and the Chinese.

Stilwell didn't like Madame Chiang, either. But his dislike of her fancy manners and fancier clothes was tolerance compared with the way he felt about her husband. His biographer, Barbara Tuchman, says that when President Roosevelt instructed him to present a Legion of Merit to the generalissimo, he wrote in his diary: "Peanut was half an hour late. . . . Everyone anywhere near him turned to stone. . . . When I grabbed his coat and pinned it on, he jumped as if he was afraid I was going to stab him."

That was my last important story for the *Herald-Statesman*. I still treasure the goodbye handshake I got from the general. He took me to the door and said he hoped he had given me what I wanted. I said he had and he said, "Well, goodbye, Sergeant."

My job and the ready access it gave me to the composing room helped us solve our apartment problem and got us out of the one room we'd been living in. Ever since we'd decided to look hard for an apartment, I'd made it a habit to stand by the classified pages while they were being made up and do my upside-down-reading number on the "Apartments, Unfurnished" columns just in case there might be something interesting in them. Mostly there wasn't, because nobody had to waste money advertising a vacant apartment. All you had to do was tell a few people about it. But one day I spotted one, wrote down the telephone number and told Liby to call right away. The paper wouldn't be out for a couple of hours yet, so she would have a good head start. Even the people in the rest of the newspaper offices wouldn't see it for a while yet.

Liby got the apartment. Amazingly, it was much like the one we'd had in Columbia, and for the same reason. The owners of a two-story house near the Empire City race track had made a separate apartment on the first floor for a married son who had moved away. We got the original kitchen with its own back-porch entrance, a bedroom and a living room which had been the master bedroom. In no time at all we were in it, surrounded by brand-new furniture and a Royal portable typewriter that I expected to use to help pay for everything.

Pretty soon I had to. The $45 a week I had thought was so satisfactory turned out to be pretty skimpy. The furniture had destroyed our bank account, and the things I wanted to do, like going to the theater and buying books and seeing Liby dressed well, cost money. I got busy sending outlines to magazine editors. I wanted to write and I wanted to make money.

Then I became serendipitous again. Bill Seely picked up the telephone on the desk one morning, talked earnestly for a minute, then held the phone to his cheek and asked, "Does anybody here have a car with him?" I said I did. I usually took the trolley to the office because it was so convenient and it only cost a nickel, but that morning Liby wanted to stay home and had suggested I drive to work.

"There's a big jewelry robbery in Bronxville," Bill said. There were always big jewelry robberies in Bronxville because that was where the jewelry was. Bronxville was Westchester's most affluent village. It was where our correspondent, Jerry Conway, rang the bell of the Joseph P. Kennedy residence one morning and got a skinny kid who said, "My father isn't home. I'm Teddy. Can I help you?" It was also the home of Sarah Lawrence College, which we at the *Herald-Statesman* liked to say was where the presidents of United States Steel sent their daughters to learn how to be Socialists. Bronxville was money.

"Go meet Chief Brennan at Police Headquarters," Bill said. "You know where it is, don't you?" I knew where it was. Liby and I used to go to Bronxville once in a while to drink or eat when we could afford it.

The chief was an amiable Irishman who wasn't upset about having his name in the paper even when some of his town's jewelry had been carried off to a New York fence, and after I phoned in the story he took a bottle of whisky out of his desk drawer and poured us a drink. "I remember your sports column," he said. "How come you're not writing it anymore?" I explained that when I got out of the Army there was another sports editor on the job and the paper had put me on the city desk. "But I'd still like to get back into writing sports," I said. "I've been writing some letters. I'm trying to find a place somewhere."

"Maybe I can help you," the chief said. "One of my best friends is Art Flynn of the *Sporting News*. He takes me to the Baseball Writers' dinner every year."

"No kidding?" I said. "I just wrote him a letter the other day and asked him for a job."

"Have you heard from him?"

"Not yet," I said. "But it's pretty soon."

"Wait a minute. I'll call him. You never know."

So the police chief of Bronxville, New York, called Arthur Flynn at the *Sporting News* in New York City and told him he had this fine Irish boy in his office who had written Arthur a letter and wanted to see him and why didn't Arthur make a date right now? Arthur did, for ten o'clock on the morning of March 18, a date which carried no special significance for me then but did when I saw a very hungover Arthur Flynn at ten o'clock in the morning on the day after St. Patrick's Day. He was drinking a Bloody Mary that was barely pink. "What can I do for you?" he asked bravely.

When I told him that I had worked for six years for the papers in Westchester and knew how to write and read copy and write headlines and make up pages and just about everything you had to do to get out a newspaper, he said he'd heard somebody say at a meeting the other day that the *Sporting News* was looking for an editor to replace a man who had retired. "I'll call the boss," he said. Not only did he call J. G. Taylor Spink, the awesome editor and proprietor of the paper, but he gave him a two-minute speech that made me sound like a cross between Grantland Rice and Paul Gallico. Still holding on to the phone, he looked across the desk at me and said, "Okay, they can use you. How about sixty-five a week?" Sixty-five a week? That was twenty more than I was making and it was the big league and what more could I want? "Sure," I said. "Tell him thanks."

"He wants to know when you can start."

"Any time. The paper knows I'm only there while I'm looking for a job. They won't mind when I leave. How about next week, Monday?"

Arthur Flynn looked puzzled and he was still holding on to the phone. "Didn't you tell me you were married?" he said. "How can you get all packed and move to St. Louis by Sunday night?"

"Who," I asked, "said anything about St. Louis?"

"Well, that's where the *Sporting News* is."

There wasn't much I could do except thank him and tell him to thank Mr. Spink but I really didn't want to go to St. Louis. I got something out of it, though. As I was leaving, he said, "The only thing I've heard about lately that might interest you is that Macfadden is starting a new sports magazine, a monthly. Why don't you go see them?"

I did. I saw the editor, Ernest V. Heyn, the former editor of *True Story* and *Photoplay*, just back to work after a war in the Signal Corps, and he was encouraging. He didn't have a job for me on his magazine *Sport*, but he gave me an assignment to write a piece on Army's All-America tackle, DeWitt Coulter. Liby drove me up to the Point and we both interviewed Tex, as everybody called him, in the visitors' room. It was the first time in my life I'd ever been called "Sir" at the beginning and end of every sentence. The magazine decided against using the piece, but did pay me $250 for it and did, after a couple of months, hire me as an associate editor. The New York Giants hired Tex Coulter.

I'm sure Tex did better, but Ernie said the best *Sport* could do was $50 a week. I said that wasn't enough, my commutation ticket would cost $12.50 a month and there would be lunches to pay for and, besides, I ought to be making more money working in New York, not less. Ernie settled the problem by offering to pay me $50 a month out of the editorial budget for editing (and, it turned out, sometimes writing) the "Letters to the Editor" column. So I made $50 a week and $50 a month in a separate check, and we survived.

Chapter 7

I was the last person hired to work on *Sport* and the only one who knew anything about type. That wasn't important until the galleys of the first issue came back from the printer along with a dummy from the production department showing where the ads were scheduled to run in the back of the book. The runover columns from the stories that opened in the display section had to be cut, or stretched, to fit into the space allotted to us in the back. Nobody else knew how to accomplish this miracle, so I got my first big break. "Let me have the whole thing," I said, taking the pile of dummies and galleys into my cubicle. "Go away and leave me alone. I'll do it."

I'd like to say that got me a raise. It didn't. But it got me out of the crowd and into a place of my own on the staff. The "Letters" didn't hurt, either. When we didn't have any provocative ones, I wrote them. There also was a kind of "Talk of the Town" feature of short takes in the front of the book that was always hungry for material and I wrote more pieces for it than anybody else. I'd get to the office every morning with my pockets stuffed with clips I'd torn out of the *Times* and the *News*. Al Perkins, the managing editor, who had come to Macfadden from *Look* by way of the Walt Disney studios in Hollywood, knew that whenever he needed half a dozen items for "SPORTalk," he could get them from me. There was nothing too small or too big for me to say yes to.

When they needed somebody to ghost a piece every month for Grantland Rice, I got the assignment. He could still get to talk to anybody he wanted to talk to, but he couldn't sit down at the typewriter and make sense out of it anymore. "Sure," I said, "I can do that." So I got to have lunch with Granny once a month, two martinis straight up at the bar and one sitting down at the table in the dining room, a little conversation about the subject he'd chosen for the month, and then back to the office and the typewriter. It was a good thing the Army had got me in shape. I didn't get any credit for the pieces because you could hardly advertise that you were using a ghost writer for the most famous sportswriter in the United States, but I got credit inside the office and I kept getting more work.

That's how I got the job of writing a 10,000-word *Sport* Special, the lead piece in the magazine, on Bobby Riggs, the tennis pro. Riggs was going to get $1,000 for talking to me and I was going to get $250 for writing the piece. But I'd get a joint byline, "By Bobby Riggs as told to Ed Fitzgerald," and it was going to be in the November issue, only the third issue of the magazine, so I wasn't going to argue about money. Maybe it wasn't better than interviewing General Stilwell, but it was better than editing wire copy and writing two-column heads on the city desk of the *Herald-Statesman*.

Anyway, what I wanted was all the work I could get. By the time the Riggs piece came out, Liby knew we were going to have a baby. It became even more important for us to find an extra check in the mailbox every once in a while.

There were pieces to ghost for non-writing broadcasters like Harry Wismer, Don Dunphy and Bill Stern, and rewrites to do for some of the old-timers whose stuff was so bad we had to rewrite it or else deal with the embarrassment of sending it back and telling the famous old guy to do it over until he got it right. We didn't want to risk losing them, so it was easier and probably wiser to do it in the office. Doing it in the office meant me. My reward was a big chance that came out of somebody else's bad luck.

The magazine had scheduled a *Sport* Special on Baseball Commissioner Happy Chandler for the June 1947 issue, but we decided to call it off when Happy confounded the baseball world by suspending Leo Durocher from his job as manager of the Dodgers for a year because of his "continuous associations with unsavory characters detrimental to the best interests of baseball." That left the June issue with a great big hole. We had to find a subject strong enough to carry the cover and 10,000 words inside and a writer who could do it in a week, including travel and interview time. Sticking to my policy, I said I could do it and we should do it on Bob Feller.

Ernie Heyn wasn't sure. "It's Tuesday now," he said, "and the story has to go to the printer next Monday. Ten thousand words." He was frowning. "The Indians are in California, somebody said, so you can't take a train out, you'd have to fly. Then you'd have to fly back and write it over the weekend and give it to us on Monday morning. I don't see how you can do it."

"I can do it," I said firmly. "Tell the girls to get me a ticket on the first plane tomorrow. I'll call the Indians right now and get them to set it up with Feller. I'll follow him around all day Thursday and Friday and fly home Friday night or Saturday morning and write it over the weekend." Everybody quit arguing. I told them to buy me every magazine back issue they could find with a Feller piece in it, and I called a guy I knew at the *News* and told him I had to borrow the paper's morgue file on Feller for the weekend. He told me he'd get killed if they found out he'd loaned it out, and I said, "I'll give you twenty bucks." "So okay," he said, "I'll get killed."

Even Feller thought I was crazy when I met him while he was having breakfast at the hotel in Los Angeles early Thursday morning. I was dead tired from sitting up all night on a twin-engine DC-3 from La Guardia Airport in New York non-stop to Los Angeles except for a refueling stop in Tulsa, Oklahoma. Thirteen and a half hours in the air, cold sandwiches to eat and coffee or tea in paper cups to drink. But I couldn't waste time sleeping. I didn't want to miss the team bus to the Bakersfield ball park, where the Indians had an exhibition game against the White Sox that afternoon. Feller agreed to let me ride with him on the bus and talk with him whenever we could get together at the ball park. "That won't be hard," he said reassuringly, "they don't make me do much when I'm not pitching." He generously agreed to have dinner with me that night if I'd pick up the tab for him and one of his impoverished rookie friends and let him pick the restaurant.

I called my pregnant wife in Yonkers before we took a cab to the Brown Derby on the Sunset Strip, where, I found out, the hors d'oeuvres cost more than the steaks did in the restaurants I was used to. Liby was glad to know I was still alive, and when I told her about the airplane flight, she wasn't even jealous about where I was going to eat. With whom was different. Liby was beginning to be a baseball fan.

Feller brought along Felix Mackiewicz, a young outfielder from Purdue who looked at the menu and moaned. "I couldn't eat a sandwich in here on that twenty-five-bucks-a-week meal money they give us for spring training," he said. Feller wasn't impressed. "That's why they're signing all you college football players," he said. "You guys are used to that kind of money."

I began writing in longhand on the flight back, and I had a pretty good idea of how I was going to organize the piece by the time we landed at La Guardia. Working on that flight was better than sitting there thinking about it. I let the magazine treat me to a cab ride home and got to work. The title I was using, "Bob Feller Incorporated," also provided a lot of the approach I planned to take. Feller was one of the first athletes to incorporate himself as a business and go after every dollar of subsidiary income he could add to his baseball salary. It kept him busy. "What a life," he said, leaning out of his hotel-room window and breathing in the soft spring-night air. "Tomorrow I have to cut two records, meet a couple of writers for interviews, sign two side-deal contracts and see some business people about maybe setting up a partnership in an aviation corporation. That's the business to be in these days." He stood up and stretched. "Oh, yeah," he said with that Midwestern farm-boy grin, "if I find the time, I think I'm supposed to pitch a game of ball, too."

It was obvious that one reason Bob was so busy was that he had never hired a business manager. "If I had one," he said, "I'd have to spend all my time watching him." I thought about that years later when I sat with Sugar Ray Robinson in his Harlem restaurant and listened to him tell me how his business manager, a man he had known and trusted for years, had run off with all the money Ray thought had been squirreled away in investments for him. "He was squirreling it away, all right," Ray said bitterly, "but not for me." Maybe Feller wasn't so dumb to do it all himself.

The Feller story got me promoted to assistant managing editor, with a raise that helped when our daughter Eileen was born in July. The doctor charged us $250 for the delivery, and I made $300 selling a short story I wrote while I sat in the waiting room. The Feller piece also got me another *Sport* assignment, this one on the genius who ran the Brooklyn Dodgers, Branch Rickey, the inventor of the farm system and possessor of one of the most sophisticated and complicated minds ever to devote itself to what Red Smith called the game of rounders. That one ran in the November 1947 issue, exactly a year after my Riggs piece. It contributed a lot to my education, if only because I had to stretch my vocabulary and my understanding of innuendo and allusion—detractors of Mr. Rickey, like the *Mirror*'s Dan Parker, who called Rickey "a man of many facets, all turned on," would say illusion—to the fullest to understand what he was talking about. Even when he was talking about something simple, like why he had hired Jackie Robinson. (To win, naturally.) Which reminds me of the night *Sport* prevailed on Rickey to give the principal speech at a dinner for 1,200 at the Hotel Astor at which we gave the Top Performer of the Year awards to the stars of 1948. In an effort to get our young magazine some much needed publicity, we had splurged and invited virtually every living ex-champion to come to the dinner as a special guest. Jack Dempsey was there, and Walter Hagen, who ran up a $3,000 hotel bill on us at the Astor. Nat Holman. Babe Didrikson. Joe DiMaggio. Red Grange. Frankie Frisch. Sugar Ray Robinson. Tris Speaker, Frank Leahy, Willie Hoppe, Marion Motley, Lester Patrick, Willie Shoemaker and Jackie Robinson were there. Hank Greenberg and Otto Graham were there. O. J. Elder, president of Macfadden Publications and a sports buff from childhood, wasn't making any money on the magazine yet, and this night wasn't going to help the balance sheet any, but he had the time of his life. He even enjoyed Mr. Rickey's speech, which had given everybody a lot to think about.

Tom Henrich was sitting next to me on the dais. When Rickey finished, Tom leaned close to me and said quietly, "It was a hell of a speech. I bet there wasn't a man in the room who understood it."

One man in the room who either didn't understand it at all or understood it too well caused us a lot of embarrassment. The *News* had him all over the paper the next morning because he had rushed up to Rickey in the lobby after the dinner and tried to punch him in the mouth. "You ruined the whole night!" he yelled in a loud and lubricated voice. The cops grabbed him before he could do any damage to Rickey, but not before a reporter from the *News* found out that he was one of our advertising salesmen.

Not all of my article assignments were important only because they earned an extra check or got me the chance to know somebody I'd read about for years. When Granny Rice arranged for us to do Bill Klem, "The Old Arbitrator," dean of all the umpires in both leagues, Klem told me to meet him at Dinty Moore's restaurant on West 46th Street. I'd never been there, but over the years my family, my friends and I ate more meals in Moore's than in any other restaurant in Manhattan. The doors were dark wood, heavily varnished, and so was the long bar that lined the left side of the room. The railings were polished brass. The women who ran the cloakroom wore white aprons over their black dresses and looked and talked as if they had just got off the boat from the old country. The waiters were all men, Irish men, and once everybody got to know you, it was like eating at home. Until they were in their late teens, Eileen and Kevin, our son, who was born just after Christmas in 1949, had to submit to being stood against the cloakroom wall and having their height checked against the mark from the last time.

Jim Moore, who was "Dinty" only on the menu and to out-of-towners, was still there when I had my first lunches with Klem. Jim would buy the first two rounds of martinis and let Klem buy the next two. It was many years later that John Sargent, president of Doubleday, told me, "Fitz, it's a drinking business. Drink or get out." But there is no doubt that, what with the likes of Grantland Rice and Bill Klem, I got off to a fast start. I'd sit there happily listening to Klem tell me how he used to tame John McGraw and I would wonder how anybody could bear to work in any other business. Eventually, Jim's daughter Dolores, in a sweeping black dress but conspicuously no apron, would force us to look at a menu and order some food. Dolores, who ran the restaurant for many years after Jim died, clearly was running it then but didn't have the heart to interrupt her father when he was having such a good time.

"Did you tell Mr. Klem what you're going to put up on the wall over the bar?" she asked him one time. "Oh, no," the old man said, "but I'm glad you reminded me. William," he said with the curious formality of the very old to a dear friend, "I've still got that cap you gave me that you wore in your last game. I put it on every night when I get in the car for the ride home through the park. But I've decided what I'm going to do with it is hang it up there over the bar on top of your picture, and underneath I'm going to put a sign saying 'The only boss McGraw ever had.' "

Dolores wasn't quite so gentle with me one night, five or six years later, when Al Perkins had become managing editor of *American* magazine and gave me the job of doing a piece on a typical Rehearsal Club member. The Rehearsal Club, in an old townhouse on West 53rd Street, provided low-cost housing and meals to young women who were trying to make it on Broadway. A friend of Al's had suggested the magazine piece should focus on Larri Thomas, one of the current residents, who, he assured Al, was typical. I guess she was typical of the beautiful young women trying to get on the Broadway stage, but she sure wasn't typically typical. Larri was tall, close to six feet, big and blonde and beautiful. She would stop traffic if she walked down the street in a Salvation Army uniform carrying a tambourine. Naturally, when I arrived punctually at the Rehearsal Club for our dinner date, she was still upstairs getting dressed. Men weren't allowed above the first floor of the club, so I waited in the lounge until she dazzled it with her abundant presence. "Hi," she said brightly. "I'm Larri Thomas, and you must be Ed Fitzgerald." I agreed that I was and we shook hands. "Where are we going?" she asked. "I mean, do I look all right?" She was wearing a light blue summer dress that admitted bravely that she had everything she was supposed to have. As Liby has always said, "Them that has them wears them." Larri had them and Larri was wearing them.

"I thought we'd go to Dinty Moore's," I said and I promptly gained twenty points. "Wonderful," she said. "Somebody took me there once and I loved it. I guess this dress will be all right, then." I wasn't sure if she meant all right because it was dressy enough or all right because it wasn't too dressy, but I wasn't going to ask.

Moore's always had half a dozen tables set up behind the main dining room, in the front half of the big kitchen, where some of the regulars liked to sit, and it was to one of those that Dolores led us imperiously. She looked disapprovingly at Larri's cleavage and asked grimly, not "What would you like to drink?" but "And where is Mrs. Fitzgerald?"

After "Two Guys Named Ted Williams" in April 1948, a piece that had more influence on my life as an editor than as a writer, there was a good *Sport* Special to do in the summer of 1948 on Lou Boudreau, the shortstop and manager of the Cleveland Indians. "The Last of the Boy Managers," I called him. But by then I had another career going, not so much with my left hand as with my evening and weekend hours. I had begun to write books.

One way or another, the magazine was entirely responsible for my getting into the book business. The first way was my favorite: by accident. Naomi Burton, head of the book department at the Curtis Brown agency, had asked our freelance star Jack Sher to write a series of juvenile baseball novels that A. S. Barnes, the sports publishing house, wanted. But Jack was ambitious to go to Hollywood, where his brother-in-law, Howard Fast, was beginning to find out that a nickel an inch in New York can easily turn into $100 a line in the movie business (and also into blacklists) and he suggested that Naomi talk to me. I didn't know Naomi, but Jack was represented by Edith Haggard, who ran Curtis Brown's magazine department, and I knew her. It wasn't hard for Naomi and me to get together on a deal for me to write the baseball book with an option to do two more if the first one didn't drown.

I invented Marty Ferris, a baseball player for White Plains High School who wanted desperately to play for the Yankees and who had a beautiful blonde girlfriend, Jean Turner, who wanted whatever he wanted. *The Turning Point* (1948) took him through the end of his high-school career and his decision not to accept a minor-league contract offered him by a Yankee scout but to go to college first. *College Slugger* (1950) took him through Fordham and the NCAA championships. In *Yankee Rookie* (1951) he finally made it to the ball club of his dreams even though, like Mickey Mantle that year, he was sent back down once. Joe DiMaggio, who was never sent back down, graciously posed with me upstairs at Toots Shor's looking at the book with the kid in Yankee pinstripes on the cover.

Naomi, who was a sports buff herself and spent some of her spare time making the spots around town with the Rangers' silver-haired star Neil Colville, thought there ought to be a lot of books in my magazine work, and they piled up satisfactorily. Dick Simon, one of the Simon & Schuster partners, and his editor Peter Schwed were tennis players as well as publishers, and they thought a Bobby Riggs book based on our piece in *Sport* would be a good idea. Since Bobby wanted almost all of the money and they didn't want to pay him and a high-priced tennis expert, too, they took Naomi's advice and settled for me. I had a lot of the material already, I got along well with Riggs and his wife, Kay, and I would come cheap. I got the job and made $1,000 putting together a 245-page book out of my *Sport* piece, the material in my notebook that I hadn't used and a few more interviews in various hotel rooms when I could persuade Bobby to take some time away from whichever twenty-one-year-old groupie he was bedding that day.

Once I went to Grossinger's in the Catskills with Bobby and Kay, who hasn't been what Bobby refers to as "my present wife" for a few wives now. "I worry about him in this place," Kay said after we had left the dining room after lunch on Saturday and were watching Bobby clown around with Pancho Segura on a practice court. "Too much food?" I asked, thinking about the endless courses I'd just watched Robert demolish. Kay looked at all the pretty young things in short shorts standing alongside the fence and shrieking appropriately as the great man showed off for them. "It's not the food I'm worried about," Kay said thoughtfully.

Tennis gave me two more friends but only one more book. You don't get a book out of every friend. I was disappointed that Mr. Rickey didn't ask me to do a book with him and even more disappointed that Jackie Robinson didn't. But Rickey had his executive assistant, Arthur Mann, a sportswriter of extensive experience, to do the job, and Jackie decided on Carl Rowan, a distinguished black journalist, foreign correspondent and State Department official who had been Ambassador to Finland in the 1960s. My non-book tennis friend was Gussie Moran, the tall, dark-haired, green-eyed young woman from Santa Monica who never quite made it in tennis but became more famous than a lot of women who did. Gussie caught the magazine's attention when she made the Wimbledon semi-finals in 1947. The magazine was always interested in good-looking women athletes. Magazines still are, even in these days when "chauvinism" is a dirty word. I called her up and asked her to meet me for an interview whenever she was in New York next. She said, "Sure, all right," and one day she called me and we met for lunch.

Gussie showed up wearing California tennis player's clothes, nothing glamorous, drank something like a screwdriver, ate a lot of serious food—"I always weigh a hundred and twenty-six," she told me confessionally, "never more, never less. So I eat whatever looks good." This was three years before Teddy Tinling designed lace panties for her to wear at Wimbledon, so she wasn't a household word yet, but she had a magnetism that made people look at her. I got a good story out of the magazine's $18 investment (this was 1948) in the lunch. I called the story "Glamour Girl Named Gussie," which I thought was an interesting contradiction.

"I got stuck on a fellow," Gussie said, explaining why she was a late starter in big-time tennis at twenty-four. "I didn't want to get big muscles. Then he went away, and I didn't care about the muscles anymore. So I started to play hard again. I did all right in the Nationals and better at Wimbledon, and now I think maybe I can make it in 1949."

Gussie didn't take herself too seriously. She wanted to play tennis well, she wanted to be a good daughter to her mother, whose husband and son were dead, she wanted to write, she wanted to love somebody and be loved back. But she laughed her way through everything and was always surprised when somebody behaved toward her as though she was somebody. She preferred to make jokes, like the one about her T-shirts. Somebody had written that she bought her T-shirts two sizes too small. "That's ridiculous," Gussie said. "I wouldn't do that. They just shrink."

"Her name," I wrote at the end of the piece, "is Gertrude Augusta Moran, and you can call her Gussie."

Actually, Gussie spells it Gussy. So does just about everybody else. I spell it my way.

Hazel Wightman, the Queen Dowager of tennis, once took the trouble to use Gussie as a role model for what young women tennis players shouldn't do. Mrs. Wightman had just got through saying that her ideal woman tennis player would have Helen Wills' concentration, Alice Marble's dash, Sarah Palfrey's grace, Louise Brough's determination and Margaret du Pont's innate sportsmanship. "I think I'd throw in Suzanne Lenglen's shots," Mrs. Wightman added. "They might come in handy if she was having an off day." Asked what she thought about Gussie wearing a pair of black shorts in a tournament in Cairo (on a State Department tour on which the Maharajah of Cooch-Behar became her new best friend), Mrs. Wightman said, "I don't think there was really any need for it. Didn't Gussie say she had to wear those black shorts in the semifinals because she had only one pair of whites left and she had to save them for the finals? Well, there was no reason in the world why she couldn't have worn the whites in the semi-finals, washed and ironed them after the match, and had them ready for the next day." Mrs. Wightman did not know Gussie.

The woman who met the real Gussie was the woman who approached her after she had lost badly to Pauline Betz at Madison

Square Garden in the opening match of their cross-country tour and offered Gussie a glass of brandy. "Thanks," Gussie said. "Why didn't you give it to me before the match?"

My next tennis friend, who helped me do the best book I've ever written, was Althea Gibson, whom I never saw play. I not only saw Bobby Riggs and Gussie play, I even played against Gussie. She took me to Forest Hills one day and beat me 6–1, 6–2, 6–3, 6–4. In my own defense, I never looked at the ball once. I had blisters on my feet for a week. But I never played with Althea Gibson. All I did was write her life story, a book that I think is more of a race book and a book about aspiration than it is a tennis book. Which is why it still sells.

I had to work the Althea book through her coach and advisor, Sydney Llewellyn, a New York taxi driver. It was hard to put together all of the details, but I've always been glad I did. I was fascinated by the incredible story Althea had to tell and the artless way she told it. If Cicely Tyson played Althea on television now, it would seem made up. From a shabby apartment on West 143rd Street in Harlem to the champion of Wimbledon and the United States in both 1957 and 1958, from stealing sweet potatoes out of a barrel in front of a Lenox Avenue grocery store and roasting them over a wood fire in a vacant lot to getting ready for a pre-tournament dance in India by straightening her hair with a curling iron dipped in a can of red-hot Dixie Peach Pomade, to cutting her own album of torch songs like "A Cottage for Sale," Althea was an original. She spent weekends at our house while we were working on the book and they were memorable. She drank very dry Gibsons before dinner and told us cheerfully they were named after her. She played football with the high-school boys and could throw the ball the length of four full backyards. She carried our sick daughter's breakfast up to her one morning and told her, "This may be the only time in your life you'll ever be served breakfast in bed by the Wimbledon champion." She never said a word about where I took her to eat when we met for working dinners in the city, although she knew perfectly well that some places I liked wouldn't have let her in. She didn't talk about race much except to say she was no Jackie Robinson, she didn't see herself as a crusader, just as an individual. "I'm not a racially conscious person," she told me. "I can't help or change my color in any way, so why should I make a big deal out of it? I'm a tennis player, not a Negro tennis player.

"Somebody," Althea said, "once wrote that the difference between Jackie and me is that he thrived on his role as a Negro battling for equality where I shy away from it. That man read me correctly. I shy away from it because it would be dishonest for me to pretend to a feeling I don't possess."

Writing a life story with somebody, which I have done often enough to qualify as a minor authority on the job, depends not only on the candor of the subject but on the attitude of the subject's wife, husband, lover or Svengali. Althea didn't have any of those attachments, although Sydney Llewellyn liked to cast himself in the Svengali role, so she just did it her way. It was all Althea, not glamorized, not bowdlerized, not a cop-out. She didn't even mind giving credit where credit was due: to Buddy Walker, the Harlem playground supervisor who gave her her first chance to play; to Sugar Ray Robinson, who gave her money and support; to Alice Marble, who took on the USLTA in her behalf and shamed the stuffed shirts of the game into letting her play with the white women. "It's time," Marble wrote in the July 1950 issue of *American Lawn Tennis*, "we faced a few facts. . . . It's time we acted a little more like gentlepeople and less like sanctimonious hypocrites. . . . If Althea Gibson represents a challenge to the present crop of women players, it's only fair that they should meet that challenge on the courts, where tennis is played. . . . She has a much better chance on the courts than in the inner sanctums of the committee, where a different kind of game is played."

So Althea got her chance and always gave credit to everybody who helped her get it. She even accepted full responsibility for the way I ended the book: "I think I've already got the main thing I always wanted, which is to be somebody, to have identity. I'm Althea Gibson, the tennis champion. I hope it makes me happy."

I was glad she liked it enough to claim she wrote it. Anyway, even when your name is a credit on the cover of the book, a ghost is still a ghost.

It's a whole lot less fun being a ghost when somebody won't let you write what you know ought to be written. Yogi Berra and I could have written a good book. Yogi was willing to talk and he had a lot to say. What he had to say was objective, never boastful, warmly nostalgic and filled with passion for the game of baseball. Yogi grew up in a tiny house on what he calls Dago Hill in St. Louis. His best friend, Joey Garagiola, grew up right across the street. Yogi's father, his mother, and Joey's father, who worked with Papa Berra at the Laclede-Christy Clay Works, talked to me without making any fuss. The men took me to their neighborhood bar, with the Italian trademark, a boccie court, in back. We walked down the street past the immaculately tended lawns, the stained-glass windows in the front doors and the statues of the Virgin Mary in the frontyards, and talked about their famous sons. Sometimes it seemed to me that they talked about them in a puzzled sort of way, as though they knew they were famous but couldn't exactly understand why. They used to hit them in the face because they came home too late after playing ball all day, and now because they were playing ball their pictures were in *Life* magazine and even in the St. Louis *Post-Dispatch*. They were friendly and they were helpful. Papa Berra was even funny. He had gone to New York for Berra Day at the end of the 1959 season and he was still making the joke about "They give him everything, a car, a new swim pool, jewelry, good stuff for the house. But all for him. Nothin' for me."

But Yogi and I didn't write as good a book as we could have because Carmen Berra wouldn't let us. I've looked at a few reviews of *Yogi* and found myself reminded of the Casey Stengel anecdote about showing Mickey Mantle how to play the caroms off the right-field wall at Ebbets Field before Mickey's first World Series game there. The old man, who had played the outfield at Ebbets Field for all three New York ball clubs, the Dodgers, the Giants and the Yankees, patiently showed his nineteen-year-old rookie how the ball might bounce depending on where and how it struck the wall.

Mickey wasn't interested. He could barely bother to pay attention to what Casey was doing, throwing the ball against the wall. He obviously thought it was like a schoolyard game. "Jesus," Casey said when he came back to the dugout sweating, "that kid thinks I was born sixty-five years old and the manager of the New York Yankees." Carmen wanted everybody to think she was born the wife of the Yankees' All-Star catcher, the mistress of their beautiful house in Montclair, New Jersey, and the mother of their three sons. Anything and everything from before their marriage was off limits. She wouldn't even let me tell the story about how Yogi spotted her when she was waiting on tables at Stan Musial's (and Biggie Garagnani's) restaurant in St. Louis and—egged on by Garagiola, who couldn't believe that Yogi was finally showing some real interest in a girl—got Musial to introduce him to pretty Carmen Short.

Carmen likes the way it turned out, but when I wrote about the way it began, she took it out of the book. She didn't want her Montclair friends to know she was a waitress when she met Yogi. Most women would be proud of it because there isn't any question that Yogi was as much in love with her, and as proud of her, in 1960 as he was when he met and married her in 1948. The All-Star Game was in St. Louis the summer of '48 and Carm, which is what Yogi calls her, got her ring at a family dinner at the Berra house the night before the game. "I was trying to figure out how to give Carm the ring," Yogi told me, "and it was worrying me because I didn't know the first thing about how you were supposed to ask a girl if she would marry you. . . . Actually, she wasn't the first girl I had ever asked out, she was the third. . . . Then I figured, well, all I had to do was give her the ring, and if she took it, that was that. I wouldn't have to say anything. So when we sat down at the table, and when Carm turned her head to talk to my brother Tony, I put the box with the ring in it on her plate. You should have seen the expression on her face. She didn't say anything, but she put it right on her finger, and it fit."

I never understood why Carmen wouldn't even leave in the story about the St. Louis announcer Harry Caray asking Yogi if the girls on the Hill weren't sore at him for marrying somebody who wasn't one of them. "Too bad," Yogi said, "they had their chance."

Joey Garagiola thought my book wasn't complete anyway—and because he had told me a lot of the stories Carmen took out, he knew exactly how much damage she had done. When I got back from Florida that spring of 1960, Joe wrote me a letter about his manuscript, *Baseball Is a Funny Game*, which we'd talked about while we were talking about Yogi, and which was going to be excerpted in *Sport*. Trying to figure out how to get both Yogi and Elston Howard in the lineup at the same time, Casey had tried Yogi at third base in a couple of exhibition games. "After watching Yogi play third base," Joe wrote, "I think you missed the most thrilling part of his life because he really took it in his hands. It was really something."

Yogi and the other guys thought so, too. Ellie Howard got in first with his: "Oh, boy, I'm gonna drag those bunts down there." Moose Skowron shook his head. "Not me," he said, "I'm pullin'." Yogi explained that. "The Moose is a right-handed hitter. He meant he was going to aim right at me." But Yogi didn't concede anything. "You'll never hit me," he told them. "Once I played third against the A's in a regular game, back in '54, and they got fifteen hits and never even came close to me. They were trying, too. I bet every guy on the club tried to measure me. You'd think they were giving a kewpie doll to the first guy that hit me." Pete Sheehy, the clubhouse man—you can't call him a boy because he used to take care of Babe Ruth and Lou Gehrig—had the last word, and Pete didn't talk much. "You ought to wear a mask down there," Pete said. "And a protector, too."

Doing the Berra book was a course in how writers give in to the temptation to make up stories about a man who can be matter-of-factly funny in his natural responses but never in the world would think up some of the complicated stories they spin around his public personality. The real Yogi is the homesick kid who was sitting in the lobby of the Hotel Edison, half a block from Broadway, when the Yankees finally got back to New York after Yogi's first spring training in 1947. They played their way back on the train in those days, stopping overnight and playing profitable exhibition games in minor-league towns all the way north. Jimmy Cannon was on his way out to dinner the first night back in New York when he saw the kid turning the pages of a magazine. "What's the matter, Yog?" Jimmy asked him, "no place to go?" "Nah," Yogi said, putting down his magazine. "What's there to do in this town anyway?"

The real Yogi also is the man who had dinner with me every night in St. Petersburg while we were working on the book and who listened to me order filet of sole one night and said, "Listen, I'm gonna eat half of it anyway. Order the steak."

Maybe the real Yogi also is the man who took me to the St. Pete dog track night after night and amazed me by always having the winner in race after race. "Sure, he always has the winner," Max Lanier, the old Cardinal pitcher who was selling tickets at one of the windows, told me, "he bets on every dog in the race."

Phil Silvers swore he was telling the truth when he claimed he saw Yogi at the bar at Shor's after the opening of *High Button Shoes* and, when he asked him how he had liked the show, got the whispered answer, "Phil, I pissed in my pants." But Yogi never said, as CBS Radio said he did, "It's like déjà vu all over again."

Sometimes it isn't easy to find out if a story is true or not, even when you go to the horse's mouth. Yogi said he didn't remember it, but he probably did say back there in '47 that Bill Dickey was learning him all his experience. But he doubts that he ever told Bucky Harris, his first Yankee manager, what he's supposed to have said when the manager told him to stop swinging at so many bad pitches. "You have to think up there," Bucky told him. "Aah," the storybook Berra said, "how can you think and hit at the same time?" He did indeed say, and sometimes still says, "It ain't over until it's over." And 50,000 people know he said, "Thank you for making this day necessary," in his speech on Berra Day.

Some things he knows. He knows he has played in more World Series games (14) than any other ball player in history, made more World Series hits than any other player and played on more world-championship teams (10) than any other player. He knows that his erratic play behind the plate in his first Series in '47, especially his wild throws to second, led Connie Mack, an old catcher himself, to say, "Never in my life have I seen worse ketchin'." But he also knows he hit the first pinch-hit home run in Series history that year. He knows that he hit 358 home runs during his regular seasons and 12 more in World Series games. He knows he has a lot to be proud of, including the fact that he began the 1985 season as the only major-league manager in history besides Connie Mack (who owned his own ball club and could do whatever he wanted) to open the season with one of his sons playing for him.

It's his friend Joey who makes his money getting laughs. Yogi has always made his winning baseball games. This is how we ended his book:

I've been with this ball club a long time now, I've been with them longer than any other ballplayer they've got, and maybe I still don't look like a Yankee but I like to think I've been a good one. Anyway, I've noticed that Yankees, just like sports-writers and bartenders and cab drivers, come in all different shapes and sizes. Some of them look like Joe DiMaggio and some like Tommy Henrich and some like Mickey Mantle and some like Elston Howard. Yankees can be as big as Moose Skowron and as small as Phil Rizzuto. All that matters is that, as Casey always liked to say, they can execute. I hope I have executed well enough to be able to say that a Yankee can look like Mickey Mantle but he can look like Yogi Berra, too.

Chapter 8

THERE was a publication party for Susan Brownmiller's book *Against Our Will* in early 1975, and because it was a Book-of-the-Month Club selection, a number of us who were officers of the company were invited. I walked to it with Axel Rosin, the Club's chairman, and Al Silverman, our editorial director. Jack Newcombe, editor of the *BOMC News*, was already there when Axel, Al and I came in and shook hands with Irv Goodman, president of the Viking Press. We were all old friends and we stood together talking until it suddenly hit me that this was one of the most singular groups I'd ever been with at a book party. "Do you know," I said as we accepted our drinks, "that four of the five of us used to be editors of *Sport* magazine?"

It was true. Through most of 1951 and 1952, until Al became the first defector by leaving for brief hitches at *True* and *Argosy* magazines before locking himself up at home to write magazine pieces and books, the masthead of *Sport* listed me as the editor, Jack Newcombe as the managing editor and Al Silverman and Irv Goodman as associate editors. We were living proof of the old maxim that the book business is nothing if not clannish.

The time when Al and Irv and Jack and I worked together was a good time for me not only because we all got along well but also because the magazine and the company were changing dramatically and suddenly there were more opportunities for younger people. O. J. Elder, the dignified president of Macfadden Publications, was sitting in his office one morning when his secretary told him a man named Irving S. Manheimer wanted to see him. Elder thought he had heard of Manheimer, but couldn't place him and told his secretary to ask what he wanted to see him about. "Tell him," Irving said with the full force of his five feet four inches, "I've just bought his company."

He had, too, and it was never the same again. Irving Manheimer was the president and controlling owner of a newsstand distribution company, Publishers Distributing Company, which handled a list of magazines heavily weighted toward the schlock, and he was a loose cannon. PDC put out a lot of confession magazines, detective magazines and movie magazines, not much that might be called serious. One of his publisher clients was Bob Harrison, who became famous and rich as the man behind *Confidential*, one of the first of the brazen gossip magazines, which attracted lawsuits by the dozen and circulation in the millions. Irving was not interested in literature; he was interested in making money. He was raised on Hester Street on the Lower East Side and he knew about buying cheap and selling dear. He had seen a good opportunity in Macfadden, which published *True Story*, *Photoplay*, *Radio Mirror*, *True Romance*, *True Experience* and *True Love Story* in its Women's Group and *Sport*, the adventure magazines *Saga* and *Climax* and the detective magazines *True Detective* and *Master Detective* in its Men's Group. The magazines made most of their money on newsstand sales. Only *True Story* was a successful advertising medium. But Irving, who was a childhood friend and a lifelong rival of Henry Garfinkle, owner of the powerful Union News Company, and who would have given his shirt to elbow past Garfinkle as a major force in national magazine publishing, thought he saw a chance to shake up Macfadden and go places with it. He began to buy stock on the open market and in block sales, using street names and hiding his identity and his intentions, until he had accumulated enough to take control of the company and organize his own board of directors. That was the day he walked into Elder's office.

At twelve thirty that day, a couple of hours after Manheimer made his unannounced appearance, *Sport* gave a luncheon at "21" for Phil Rizzuto, its Top Performer in Baseball for 1950. O.J. was on our guest list along with George Weiss, the general manager of the Yankees, Tommy Henrich and Jackie Farrell, the tiny publicity director of the ball club. O.J. was strangely quiet and he drank a lot, so much that Tommy and I had to help him downstairs to his car before the lunch was over. I didn't find out why until the next day when he called a meeting in his office to tell everybody what had happened. "I won't be here much longer," he said somberly at the end of the meeting. "Mr. Manheimer plans to move his office here and run the company himself." Actually, O.J. left early that afternoon for his home in Short Hills, New Jersey, and never came back.

A lot of other people left soon. Irving had done a lot of homework and he didn't waste any time getting rid of people, especially people with high salaries. Ernie Heyn was the first to go because he made the most money. Fred Sammis, who later joined Jerry Mason to launch a pair of book-publishing houses, Ridge Press and Rutledge Books, became editor-in-chief of the company. I was asked if I could run *Sport* with just Newcombe, Silverman and Goodman, and I said sure, so Al Perkins, the managing editor, and Johnny Winkin, the assistant editor, who didn't edit or write but scouted sports for the magazine, both went. Money was being saved all over the place. My salary as editor was put at $22,500, but Manheimer's bargain stipulated that I wouldn't be paid extra for anything I wrote for the magazine as I had been in the past. Furthermore, I had to write at least five 10,000-word *Sport* Specials a year, free. Irving was determined to get his money's worth. But I didn't mind. I was only thirty-one years old, we had two kids, a house and a mortgage, and I was getting my chance.

That was a wild spring for Liby and me. I was in Florida when I got the word that I'd been made the editor of *Sport*. Ernie had awarded himself a trip to spring training, something he hadn't done since he'd gone with O.J. in the magazine's first spring, 1947, and because Ernie didn't know how to travel any way except first class, he had booked two adjoining bedrooms for himself and his wife on the Silver Meteor to Florida. When the Manheimer explosion happened, Ernie decided he'd better stay home and see the hurricane through. He invited me to take Liby with me and use his train and hotel reservations. I had planned to go by myself in a few weeks to do a Special on Peewee Reese, so my conscience was only a little bit fractured. Anyway, I not only wanted to take Liby on such an appealing junket, I also thought it was a good idea to get out of New York while the new broom started to sweep. Ernie and I had had a few lunches to talk about what was likely to happen, and he had no illusions about his chances of staying on. "I'll be the first to go," he said, "and they're going to need you to run *Sport*, so you may as well go and enjoy yourself. You'll have plenty of headaches when you come back."

We didn't have any headaches on the trip. Between us we had the two bedrooms, two doors, four beds, two bathrooms and two separate buttons to push to ask waiters to bring us rum-and-Cokes or sandwiches and cold beers or whatever. We forced ourselves to walk to the dining car for dinner. We were in bed when the Meteor stopped at Columbia, South Carolina, but we pushed up our shades and, warm in bed, looked out at the world Liby had first seen getting off the same train on her wedding day ten years ago after having sat up in a parlor-car chair all night. We went back to sleep satisfied with the way the world was treating us.

That wasn't the only spring training that was made warm and exciting and entirely special for us because we spent so much of our time with Red Smith and his wife, Kay, Frank Graham and his wife, Lillian, and Grantland Rice, but it was the first and probably the one we remember the most. Maybe because we were learning a new world and were loving it. Granny was Granny, a unique figure in the business, and we found out why Tom Meany said, when Red and Frank walked into Toots Shor's together, "Here come 1 and 1-A." They were an entry. Nobody but Red could have told the story about Frank bumming a ride to Florida with him a few years before and looking pained when Red pulled up by a Manhattan cigarette shop on the way out of town and said, "If a cop bothers you, Frank, drive around the block and pick me up back here." "Red," Frank said, "I can't drive."

We know, because Red and Frank told the same stories beautifully over and over again, that Frank had used his clout to get Granny into a World Series game one day when Granny had left his tickets back at the hotel. Granny was going to go back to the hotel to get them, but Frank stopped him. "Don't worry," he said, "we'll get in." He began to explain the problem to a gatekeeper who didn't even listen to him. "Mr. Rice," he said, "I've always wanted to meet you. Can I do anything for you?" "It was wonderful," Granny always said later, "Frank took care of everything." Just the way he did the night we went to a popular St. Pete restaurant for dinner and were late getting there because Liby had met John Lardner and Walt Kelly outside the hotel and they had said we should all have drinks before dinner. We did, and Walt and John and Granny and Red and Frank talked, and by the time we got to the restaurant our table was long gone. Red, who could talk pretty good, as the athletes say, had a story all ready, but he didn't have to say a word. The *maître d'* took one look at Granny and said, "Mr. Rice, this way, please."

That was a Saturday night, and because our dinner had got under way so late, it was very late ending. By the time we got back to the hotel it was Sunday morning, and on Sunday not even Grantland Rice could get a nightcap in St. Petersburg. But Red was equal to the emergency. He unlocked the trunk of his convertible, rummaged around among the blankets and came up with a bottle carefully labeled "The Grantland Rice Memorial Bottle." We had a good-night drink before we all went off to bed. Granny felt extra good because he had stolen one piece from the giant jigsaw puzzle on the table in the lobby.

You couldn't help but feel good around Red Smith. Effortlessly charming, he was the world's greatest raconteur. You never noticed whether the food was good, bad or mediocre when you were eating with Red. Even driving with him was a pleasure. He was taking us over the skyway between St. Petersburg and Sarasota one day when he looked out the window at the birds and said, "Liby, did anybody ever tell you you should leave no tern unstoned?"

Red did all the packing for himself and his wife, Kay. "How the hell do you pack a crinoline, Liby?" he asked her one afternoon. "Have you got a silk stocking?" Liby asked him. "Sure," the distinguished columnist said, and came back with one. Liby picked up the crinoline he'd been wrestling with, rolled it tightly and stuffed it into the silk stocking the way you would push a rolled calendar into a cardboard tube. Red never got over admiring that engineering feat. Kay was only mildly interested. She had Red to do her packing.

Kay was, however, intensely interested when we were cooling off in a Sarasota bar after a ball game and Arthur Daley, the gentleman from the *Times*, came in looking for Red. Arthur declined a drink on the ground that he had given it up because he couldn't drink and handle "the unremitting tension" of the job, too. Nobody said anything. Red and Frank Graham, daily columnists of some reputation, held tightly to their gin-and-tonics as though they were afraid Arthur might take them away. It was a relief when the conversation turned to kids. Frankie Graham, Jr., was working in publicity for the Brooklyn Dodgers and wanted to be a writer; Terence Smith was still in school but was already talking about wanting to be a reporter. "Bob," Arthur said of his son, "wants to be a writer, too, but he's determined to be a real writer. He doesn't want to write the kind of tripe we do."

Mrs. Smith lifted herself halfway up from her chaise-longue, careful not to spill her gin-and-tonic. "Speak for yourself, Arthur," she said mildly.

A year later Liby and I went to Phoenix, Arizona, to watch the Giants in spring training. It was 1951, the year of Willie Mays. Tommy Henrich, an old friend, was a coach for the Giants that season and a Yonkers ball player, Steve Ridzik, whom I had known since he was in high school, was a long relief man. We had dinner one night with the two of them and another coach, Bucky Walters, the old Cincinnati third baseman who had managed the Reds in '48 and '49. The dinner ended up in a long discussion about how much difference a manager could make in a tight ball game. "Not much," Bucky said. Tommy disagreed, so they argued about Durocher and Dressen and Stengel and the other managers who were supposed to be the smartest. Tommy remembered Charlie Dressen's old battle cry in the dugout when his Dodgers were losing badly. "Just hold them for a couple of innings," Dressen used to say, "I'll think of something." But Walters wasn't buying it. "Bullshit," he said. "Managers look good when pitchers pitch and hitters hit. They can help keep the ball players in line, all right, but strategy is bullshit. If the game was all that fuckin' complicated, a lot of us country boys would never have been able to play it, much less manage."

When we got back to the hotel, there was a telegram in our mailbox, an ominous sight when you have a couple of young kids back home. But all it said was "TRIPE, EH? LOVE, KAY SMITH." In the morning, when we looked at the New York *Times* with breakfast, we found out that Arthur Daley had won the Pulitzer Prize for a series of columns on Casey Stengel.

One night when Red was in our house, Eileen was caught sitting at the top of the stairs at an outrageously late hour listening quietly to the talk in the living room. "I am not going to bed," she protested grimly, "while Mr. Smith is still talking."

There are so many great Red Smith stories it's a waste of time to single one out, but my favorite is the one about the old Dodger pitcher Van Lingle Mungo, who was so good he won more than a hundred games for the stumblebum Dodgers of the '30s. "Van," Red said, "had a lady friend in Brooklyn during the season. His wife stayed home in Pageland, South Carolina, with the kids. It went fine for a couple of years, the girl in Brooklyn, the wife home, everybody happy. But the third year the girl in Brooklyn missed him so much she began writing him letters, and it was only a matter of time before Mama found one of them, a real doozy. 'I miss you so much, Van, I can't sleep without you here next to me.' Stuff like that, not calculated to make a wife happy. But when Van's wife confronted him with it, he denied the whole thing. He was as cool as a cucumber.

" 'I was just throwing it away,' he said calmly. 'It ain't for me.'

" 'What the hell do you mean it ain't for you?' Mama demanded in a rage. 'Look at the damn thing. It's got your name all over it.'

"Van examined the envelope judiciously. 'Honey,' he said finally, 'it must have been some other Van Lingle Mungo.' "

Nobody but Red could have better summed up the furor over the announcement that the Dodgers were going to move to California. "To make everybody happy," Red said, "they ought to send O'Malley to L.A. and keep the Dodgers here."

The last time we saw him was at a dinner at our house to celebrate the completion and the near-publication of *To Absent Friends*, a book I had urged him for two years to let Pat Knopf and me put together out of all the wonderful columns he had written about great sports heroes and just plain friends who had died. "Nobody," he grumbled, "wants to read a book of obits." But we persisted. "Red," I argued once, "they aren't obituaries. They're memories." Finally, he gave in, the book was put together over many hard months and we celebrated with a party. It was an unusual if not unique party. There was the hardcover publisher Pat Knopf and his wife, Alice, the paperback publisher Herb Schnall and his wife, Ann, the book-club publisher and his wife, and the author and his second wife, Phyllis. The title of the book came from Red's favorite toast; whenever he picked up a glass, he would say solemnly, "To absent friends." We repeated it at the dinner table that night. The next absent friend was Walter Wellesley Smith, the only sportswriter, his old boss Stanley Woodward used to say, named after three women's colleges. You could look it up.

One of the eulogists at Red's funeral mass was Tom Seaver, who summed it up for everybody. "I was standing out by the batting cage one day this summer," Tom said, "and one of the kids on the ball club saw Red standing by the batting cage talking to Greg Luzinski. 'Who's that little old guy with the white hair talking to Greg?' he asked me. I looked. 'That's Red Smith,' I said. 'No kidding?' the kid said. 'The famous sportswriter?' I suppose I shook my head sadly, but I know I said, 'Take it from me, in his league that little old guy is the MVP.' "

I made a good start on my commitment to write a lot for the

magazine by going to Miami to interview Sugar Ray Robinson for a four-part series on the man they said was "pound for pound, the greatest fighter of them all." Ray was staying at a small house he had bought for his mother in Miami, and when I called him from our hotel, he invited us to come right on over. The doorman got us a cab and off we went to interview the middleweight champion of the world. When we got to his mother's little frame house in what was obviously one of the city's all-black neighborhoods, I asked the driver for a card so we could call a cab when we were ready to leave. He looked a little dubious when he gave me the card, and we found out later, when nobody showed up after we called, that the white drivers weren't about to go into that district. We had to walk out. After that we rented a car for our daily trips and drove ourselves.

Ray was lying on top of a bed wearing jockey shorts and nothing else when we were shown in to meet him. Surely one of the most beautiful male animals in the world, sleek black flesh rippling over graceful muscles, eyes laughing in his handsome, confident face, he sat up and stuck out his hand and said, "Glad to see you again, Ed." Then, looking at Liby, "Gee, it sure was nice of the magazine to send you and your girlfriend all the way down here to see me." Liby has rarely, she says, felt more complimented. She didn't even mind the long walk back to where the cabs were.

Ray gave us enough material to make four good pieces and I think he was pretty open with me. He even complained with good humor about the criticism he'd taken over the Charley Fusari fight a few months back. "They all said I took it easy on him just to make sure the fight went fifteen rounds and some people won some money betting it would. Took it easy? You realize how hard I had to work? I had to fight fifteen rounds for me and fifteen rounds for him."

He was particularly good on his middleweight title fight with Jake LaMotta at Chicago in February. Ray, the welterweight champion, had beaten Jake four times in five fights and, understandably but much to Ray's chagrin, Jake wouldn't have anything to do with

him after Jake won the middleweight championship from Marcel
Cerdan in 1949. "Between the pressure he was getting from everybody and the plain fact that he could make a lot of money out of it,"
Ray said, "He finally signed to fight me. He was getting forty-five
per cent of the gate and I was only going to get fifteen percent. He
also wanted ten percent of whatever I made as long as I was champion, but I wouldn't go for that and he finally agreed. I signed in a
hurry before he could change his mind. . . . I trained hard for that
fight. I didn't have to worry about making the weight. Jake could
worry about that. He had to get down to one sixty. I knew I
wouldn't weigh more than one fifty-five if I ate six meals a day."
Ray's confidence was justified. He took the title with an eleventh-
round technical knockout and now he was the champion of two
divisions.

The Sugar Ray series helped me show Irving Manheimer that he
had made a good deal. I followed it in the rest of the year's issues
with Specials on Ewell Blackwell, Yogi Berra, Otto Graham and
Johnny Lujack, with a story on the Giants' rookie centerfielder,
Willie Mays, thrown in for good measure. Willie, who was twenty
then, came to the *Sport* office with a friend and sat around for three
or four hours. We called downstairs to the drugstore for sandwiches and Cokes for lunch and talked about Willie's life as a
boarder in a Harlem apartment, his stickball games with the kids
on the street and how he felt about his chances of making it. He
was confident. "I ain't worried," he said, biting into his hamburger,
" 'cause when I ain't hitting I don't hit nobody, but when I'm hittin'
I hit everybody."

The Berra story, which came in handy when I got the job to do
the book with him in 1960, gave me a good chance to do what all of
us on *Sport* believed in: to write a fact story with the sense of place
and the informality that make fiction work. We wanted to get away
from formal interviews. We wanted to show the man or woman
without artificial touches and we wanted to describe the place where
the work was done so that the reader felt he had been there himself.
The Berra piece began this way:

It was only half past 11 and a bunch of the Yankees were taking it easy in the comfortable lounge that adjoins their dressing room. Batting practice wouldn't begin for an hour yet.

Billy Martin tuned in a disk-jockey show on the table radio and leaned back in his armchair, tapping his feet to the rhythm of the music. "Bewitched, Bothered and Bewildered Am I." The slow but insistent beat filled the room and a few more ballplayers wandered through the doorway.

Joe DiMaggio, sitting in his underwear across the room from Martin, looked up briefly. "King Cole?" he asked. Martin nodded without speaking. DiMaggio said nothing more.

Phil Rizzuto held up a letter from a pile of mail he was busy answering at the writing desk in the corner. "Hey, look at this one," he laughed. "It's got URGENT marked all over it and it's postmarked three weeks ago."

Jackie Farrell, the road secretary, came in and showed the boys a handsome wrist watch. "I got it for doing the Guy LeBow television show," he said. "It was an easy deal, too. I took McDougald with me and LeBow wants to know if any of you other guys want to do it sometimes."

"I'm always eligible," Jackie Jensen said amiably, looking over the watch carefully.

Yogi Berra was sitting on the couch talking to a writer. "Hey," Rizzuto said to him, "did you see that column about you this morning?"

"Yeah," the stocky catcher said, "I read it."

"What did you think about it?"

Yogi shrugged. "I don't know," he said. "Lopat said it was okay except for the crazy way he had me talkin'."

"He made you sound like a meathead," Rizzuto said indignantly.

Yogi laughed softly. It was plain that Yogi wasn't going to lose any sleep over what any sportswriter said about him. "What the hell," he said without bitterness. "They been doin' that for five years, haven't they?"

Nothing I might have written about Yogi's reaction to his publicity could have been as expressive.

All four of us who were going to end up in the book business wrote in virtually every issue of the magazine. There might be a piece on the Green Bay Packers by our resident football expert, Jack Newcombe; a piece on Wimbledon champion Dick Savitt by Al Silverman; a piece by me on Ewell Blackwell, the man who threw his sidearm pitches for the Cincinnati Reds from somewhere behind third base; and a piece by Irv Goodman on Lew Alcindor, the high-school basketball phenomenon from Philadelphia whose paychecks have been made out for years to Kareem Abdul Jabbar. We were all young and hungry and we didn't need as much sleep as we do now.

Irving was so happy about our low-budget operation that he promoted me to editorial director of the Men's Group, giving me the adventure magazines, *Saga* and *Climax*, and the two detective magazines to run in addition to *Sport*.

That led to one of the more memorable evenings in our family history. For Liby, not the kids. I made a lot of cameo and sometimes longer appearances on television, giving away cars and talking about sports on panel shows, and Liby usually wanted to watch me, but the kids didn't. They wanted to watch something else. "But it's your father," Liby would protest. "Come on," they would say, "we see him every day. We want to watch *our* show." So only Liby saw me give the 1956 Corvette for the Most Valuable Player in the World Series to Mickey Mantle on the six-o'clock evening news and on the eleven-o'clock news make bail at the Nassau County Jail for a pretty young woman who had been locked up as a material witness in a murder case involving her dead husband and her lover. She had agreed to tell her story in *True Detective*.

The next piece of excitement was Irving telling me that I was going to spend the next year as a Fellow at the Harvard Business School, with my salary paid by the company. "Jim Linen from *Time* called me," he said proudly, "and they want to have somebody in the program who's from one of the second-tier publishing companies. He asked me to nominate somebody and he said if I nominated him he was in. So you're it." "No, I'm not it," I told Irving. "That's a graduate program and I don't even have a degree." He thought I was wrong and that Jim could make it all happen, but we both found out that I was right and I stayed at Macfadden working for Irving as not only editor-in-chief but his personal assistant.

Anyway, Irving was happy with me and I think he even gave me a raise. I'm sure he declared a celebration and I know that to celebrate he took me in his chauffeured limousine to Katz's famous restaurant on Houston Street, where we both ate kosher hot dogs and he drank a bottle of Dr. Brown's celery tonic and I had a Coke. I love Katz's, although I was a little embarrassed when we walked out of this landmark eating place—nobody dines in Katz's—where most people ate standing up, and got into the limo. At least Irving's chauffeur didn't hold the door open for us. Irving didn't like show.

Chapter 9

WHAT Irving didn't like the most was spending money. We had to beat our brains out week after week trying to figure out how to put out the kind of magazine we wanted to with the kind of money he was willing to give us. The biggest arguments I had with him were over my occasional fits of hunger for a big-name writer to use for a major cover story that would make our newsstand sales jump. "The people don't give a damn about writers," Irving insisted. "It's the story that counts."

"But you've got to have writers to write the stories," I argued.

"Sure," he agreed. "But not expensive ones. You'll never get your money back. Just think up the story and get somebody cheap to write it. You'll sell just as many copies. Look, when I was a kid, everybody I knew read all the Horatio Alger stories and I'll bet not one of them had any idea who wrote them." How could I argue with a man like that?

Mostly, my young, hungry writers and my even hungrier editors—you'd better believe they made less money than the writers did—and I lived on ideas. We read as many newspapers and magazines as we could get through, we listened to the radio and watched television and we didn't think any idea was out of bounds. We were firm believers in the right of the public domain. One thing we had in abundance was chutzpah. We knew we had to invent our own successes because we couldn't afford to buy them, so we never let up looking.

I learned that it's a good policy never to trust an idea to stay in your head. It's safer to write it down on a pad on your night table, even if your bed partner isn't crazy about being awakened at half past three in the morning, or to scribble it in whatever you carry on your person in the way of a notebook, or to tear the clipping that made you think of it out of the newspaper or magazine you're reading, no matter how much noise it makes on the train or the plane. You may think your idea is so good you'll never forget it, but the chances are a few hours later all you'll remember is that you had a hell of a good idea and now it's gone.

Way back in the '50s my kids, like the rest of the kids in America, went wild over the television series on Davy Crockett. We had just sent to the printer a Daniel Boone frontiersman cover for *Saga*, and after watching and listening to the kids in our living room I wrote down an obvious idea. As soon as I got to the office in the morning, I called everybody together and told them "We're changing the *Saga* cover to Davy Crockett. Let's get Jack Pearl to do a Crockett story to go with the cover, change the fur hat to a coonskin and put a new blurb on the cover. We're going to sell Crockett and the Alamo." Patriotism, pure and simple.

One day I read a piece in which Jimmy Cannon, the sentimental sportswriter who lived in a room in the Hotel Edison on 46th Street near Broadway looking out across the street to Dinty Moore's, said that his two favorite people in sports were Joe Louis and Joe Di-Maggio. "It's a dead heat," he said. "They're both my friends and you can't explain friendship." I thought it would be a great idea to publish in *Sport* two 10,000-word pieces by Cannon, one "I Remember Joe Louis" and the other "I Remember Joe DiMaggio." But I knew I would never get Jimmy to sit down at his typewriter and pound out 20,000 words even about his best friends, so I figured I'd get clips of every column Jimmy had ever written about either of them for the New York *Post* and put the best material into short pieces which could be separated by asterisks. It would be easy to do it chronologically, and that, I figured, would take care of the lack of transitional material.

The two pieces turned out even better than I had hoped. Here is Cannon on Louis:

I believe Louis was the greatest fighter who ever lived the night he took Max Schmeling apart. But I'm concerned with the soft evening I spent with him the night before the fight. I had gone to Pompton Lakes after I had written my piece. We had dinner together and sat on the porch of the old farmhouse he lived in.

"You make a pick?" he asked.

"Yes," I said.

"Knockout?" Louis asked.

"Six rounds," I said.

"No," Louis said. "One." He held up a big finger. "It go one," he said.

That's all it went.

*   *   *

There was a hot day at Yankee Stadium when the Red Sox were playing the Yankees. I came upon Louis sitting behind third base.

"You know Ted Williams?" he asked.

I said I did.

"A good hitter," Louis said.

"Would you like to meet him?"

"Yeah," he said.

I took Louis back to the Boston dressing room. Williams was in his underwear, standing before his locker. They looked at one another and Louis spoke first. He didn't wait to be introduced.

"My," he said, "you skinny."

*   *   *

Frankie Harmon, whose father, Paddy, built the Chicago Stadium, promoted an exhibition match between Louis and

Billy Conn when both were finished with fighting. Louis dropped by Harmon's office before the fight and asked him:

"What percentage Billy getting?"

Harmon told him.

"Take five percent off my end," Joe said. "Put it on Billy's."

He never told Conn that.

* * *

There was a season when Louis toured with a softball team and played first base.

"What did you hit?" I asked him.

" 'Round .200," he said.

We talked awhile about other matters. Louis returned to the subject of softball. "You don't have to put my average in the paper?" he asked.

"I do," I said.

He thought about it a while. "You're a bad hitter," he said, "I guess you're a bad hitter."

And this is Cannon on DiMaggio:

Joe had trouble getting started in the Spring of '47. On the night he finally came up over .300, I walked down Broadway with him. Strangers followed him down the side street to his hotel and some stopped him and explained how happy they were that he was hitting again. They nagged him for his signature and asked him absurd questions. They appointed themselves partners in his success and they enjoyed his presence on the street even though they just shouted his name out of a taxicab as he went by. It was a flattering tribute by the people of the town where he played and there was more in it than people trying to break the pattern of their obscurity by associating themselves with a celebrity. They realized that something wonderful had happened to a guy whom they admired from the distances of the grandstand and in some mysterious way it touched them beyond the rude adulation such people usually bestow on the famous.

"I better keep hitting," Joe said. "I forgot how nice this is."

* * *

There was a man on second and two were out in the fifth when Berra came up to hit against Bob Feller. They decided to walk Yogi on purpose and pitch to DiMaggio. It must have infuriated him because, until this season, DiMaggio had hit Feller with destructive consistency. In the circle where the next hitter kneels, DiMaggio leaned on his bat. At no other time had this posture of genuflection seemed so significant to me. Before this multitude, a reputation unmatched in baseball was being defaced with contempt.

. . . The first pitch was a strike, the second a ball. The next one was a slider. The sound identified it as a base hit. It fled on a true line and the cries of the crowd billowed out from the stands, thick as the cigarette smoke. The ball bounced in deep left-center field. It rolled past Larry Doby and reached the fence. Two runs scored and DiMaggio, running with that long-gaited stride, pulled up at third. The hit journeyed 457 feet from the bat to the base of the bleacher wall.

There was a stack of telegrams on the stool at DiMaggio's locker after the game. The big guy looked them over and grinned ruefully. "When I get a hit now," he said, "they send me telegrams."

* * *

DiMaggio was sipping sallow coffee from a cardboard container.

"Made up your mind yet?" I asked him. We were sitting on stools in front of his locker in the Stadium clubhouse after the Red Sox beat the Yanks, 4–2, on a mild September night in 1951. It wasn't necessary for me to explain the question. In the spring of the year DiMaggio had told the ball reporters this might be his last season.

"I still feel the same way," he said. "I don't know."

Eddie Lopat came over and asked him to autograph a baseball for a kid. "You were really cutting the pie out there to-night," Lopat said. "You were like a young buck taking your cuts."

"Cool weather," DiMaggio said, "a clean uniform, a shave and a haircut."

* * *

He avoided crowds and was embarrassed by mass adulation. He wasn't rude to strangers but he took side doors to get away from them. He liked to eat in the corners of restaurants and he avoided ringside tables in night clubs. And then he got married to Marilyn Monroe, one of the most famous women of her time.

When DiMaggio's romance with Miss Monroe was first reported, a guy who knew him slightly seemed troubled.

"Is this good for DiMag?" the guy asked a sportswriter.

"It's better," the sportswriter said, "than rooming with Joe Page."

Jimmy liked the pieces. The only thing he didn't like was that the treasurer of Dolly Schiff's New York *Post* made me send the checks to him and he deducted 50 percent for the *Post*'s take before he sent the rest on to Cannon. Dolly, one of the richest women in New York, probably needed a new dress from Mollie Parnis.

I wanted to do a big piece on Rogers Hornsby, supposedly the toughest interview in the major leagues, and Frank Graham fixed it up for me with a phone call to his old friend, once again out of a job after being fired by the St. Louis Browns and the Cincinnati Reds. I took the Twentieth Century to Chicago and a taxi to the Edgewater Beach Hotel in Evanston, the WCTU town, and found the greatest right-handed hitter in baseball history sitting in the lobby. "You'll find him in the lobby," Frank had said. "He never goes out." Hornsby must have liked Frank a lot because he treated me like a member of the family and he opened up freely on every subject I asked him about. Like the 1,165 shares of stock he owned

in the Cardinals when Sam Breadon traded him to the Giants for
Frank Frisch after the 1926 season, which ended with Hornsby's
Cardinals beating the Yankees in the World Series when Grover
Cleveland Alexander, drunk or hungover or whatever, came out of
the bullpen to strike out Tony Lazzeri with the bases loaded in the
last of the ninth. "I paid $45 a share for it," Hornsby told me, and
you could see he was still mad about it, "and after all the success the
Cardinals had had, I wanted $120 for it. Breadon said it wasn't
worth anything like that and he wouldn't pay it. So I still owned it
when I went to spring training with the Giants. Now, there was no
way Judge Landis could let me open the season playing second base
for the Giants when I was the second biggest stockholder in the
Cardinals, so when we were in Washington for our last exhibition
game with the Senators, the Judge called me to a meeting at the
Wardman Park Hotel. Not only was the Judge there, and Mr.
Breadon, and John Heydler, the president of the National League,
but all the other National League club owners were there, too. The
Judge wasted no time. He got from Breadon the top price he was
willing to pay me for the stock and he got from me the lowest price
I would take. Then he calmly suggested to the seven other owners
that they make up the difference. I wouldn't say they were enthusiastic, but nobody had a better idea, so they did it."

Hornsby, who turned thirty-one that spring, got over the frus-
trations of the protracted war of wills sufficiently to play all 155
games for the Giants and hit .361 with 26 home runs and 125 runs
batted in.

The Rajah provided an interesting perspective on the times then
and now when he said, with more sadness than bitterness, that
Breadon had refused to declare a dividend on the stock as long as
Hornsby held it, but that when it was bought up, he retired the
Hornsby shares and immediately declared the overdue dividend. "I
think that was the greatest disappointment of my life," Hornsby
said, "having to sell out a substantial interest in the only business I
ever wanted to be part of. I would have liked to have stayed with
the Cardinals for the rest of my life. But that's how it goes in base-

ball. When you sign a professional baseball contract, you sign your life away."

Not anymore, you don't, and Hornsby may have had as much to do with that as Curt Flood and Catfish Hunter did.

There probably isn't a publisher in the world who wouldn't agree with this, so, although I hate to say it, the truth is that nothing stimulates original thought quite so powerfully as poverty. A painful lack of money in the editorial budget forces an editor to compensate by thinking. *Saga*, put out on a shoestring, was a classic example.

I was riding into Grand Central Terminal on the seven thirty-six from Crestwood when I saw a piece in the *Times* about the death of the Indian who had been one of the Marines who put up the flag on Iwo Jima. A famous drinker, Ira Hayes had been found lying on the ground, frozen to death, after a hard night of boozing. I was glad Ed Linn was willing to fly out to Arizona and talk to the people at the Gila River reservation forty miles from Phoenix.

He came back with a hell of a story not only about Ira but about the flag-raising itself. Both of them: the real one, when a little flag was defiantly stuck up there under fire, and the staged one an hour and a half later, when a big flag borrowed from an LST (landship ship, tank) was pushed into position by six guys who looked heroic because they were trying to plant the flag against the gusts of a vagrant island wind. Because nobody in the months and years after would believe the flag-raising was anything less than one of the most heroic acts of the whole war in the Pacific, Ira freaked out with guilt. He also drank, and drank, and drank. "That's how we Indians are, aren't we?" he said. "We get together and we get drunk."

Eddie wrote it this way:

Ira Hayes came to fame upon the soft, volcanic sands of a mountain crater and died upon the hard, cold sands of an Indian reservation. He died, according to the death certificate, of overexposure to cold weather and alcohol, and yet it would not be inaccurate to add that he died, also, of the accumulated bruises of ten years of hurling himself against a legend. It had taken just 1/400th of a second to bring him his unwelcome—

and, he insisted to the end, undeserved—fame, but Ira Hayes was a long, agonizing time dying.

Ira wasn't the only one of the three survivors among the six flag-raisers who had trouble with his conscience. The others also denied that they had done anything except follow a lieutenant's orders and do a routine job. But the more they said it, the more their listeners nodded and smiled and thought that's how real heroes are, modest. "If there is one thing the human animal can do better than anything else," Eddie wrote, "it is to believe what it wants to believe." Ira learned that once a legend gets rolling, nothing can stop it.

Linn understood the difference between Ira and his companions on the War Bond circuit. John Bradley and Rene Gagnon knew it was all hype, all done to sell bonds and recruit bodies, but they simply surrendered to the inevitable. They never lied about it, but they shrugged and went along with it.

But Ira Hayes was different. Since Ira was first and foremost an Indian, everything that was happening to him was being fitted into an entirely different context. There was, first of all, the matter of the guaranteed equality of all Americans—which, he had always been aware, his country absolutely refused to grant him. At the time, Ira, as an Indian, did not have the right to vote, to drink, or—most ironic of all—to bear firearms. To that was now added the obvious fact that he was no hero for putting up a flag, though everybody insisted on treating him as though he were. The world had quite obviously gone crazy. What he deserved, he could not get; what he did not deserve, they forced upon him. It was something for a man, already depressed, to brood upon.

They buried Ira Hayes on a snowy slope in Arlington National Cemetery, and General Lemuel C. Shepherd, Jr., made the ritual presentation of the flag that had covered his coffin to his stolid-faced mother. One major newspaper's story the next day said, "Hayes, Gagnon and four other Marines, in an inspired gesture, raised an American flag atop Mount Suribachi during the fierce fight for Iwo Jima ten years ago." They didn't come right out and say the flag was raised under fire, but the implication was there. "The legend, you see," Linn wrote, "held to the end."

Helping us make the most we possibly could out of the anemic budget we had to work with, Eddie did colorful, thoughtful pieces on Robert Oppenheimer after the father of the A-Bomb was denied security clearance because of alleged Communist associations, and on Jimmy Hoffa, the tough-guy boss of the Teamsters.

The irony of denying secret information to the man who had invented many of the A-Bomb secrets appealed to the quixotic in Linn's nature. "It was being demonstrated," he said, "when the hearing room was about to be cleared of those underprivileged souls who did not have a high enough clearance to listen to a top-secret report on thermonuclear warheads, meaning the H-Bomb. 'Since this is a report I wrote,' Oppenheimer asked drily, 'is this one I may listen to?' "

There is food for thought, too, in Eddie's opening quote from a Jimmy Hoffa speech before a meeting of Detroit Teamster Local 299 in October 1958. "I've told it to you before," Hoffa said, "and I'll tell it to you again. The strong survive and the weak disappear. We do not propose to disappear."

Roger Kahn did his part for the cause with pieces on a heterogeneous group of subjects including the architect Frank Lloyd Wright, the romantic pirate Jean Laffite, the medical scientist Jonas Salk and world citizen Garry Davis. I suppose the only one of those who was a logical candidate for a story in a men's adventure magazine was Laffite. But I've always believed that running a newspaper, a magazine or a book-publishing company is no different from commanding an army or coaching a football team or being the mayor of New York City. You've got to be bold, you've got to take chances and, above all, you've got to put yourself at risk, you've got to be willing to lose everything. We were always willing and we had a gang of hungry young writers who were willing, too. They had talent to burn and they were in a hurry to burn it.

I even challenged Ed Linn to dig up John Henry, the steel-drivin' man, immortalized in ballad for working himself to death trying to beat the steam drill the captain had brought in to take over the job of laying the iron on the railroad ties:

> John Henry told the Captain
> A man ain't nothin' but a man
> And if I don't beat your steam drill down
> I'll die with a hammer in my hand.

"The first anybody ever really saw of John Henry," according to anthropologist Linn, "was down at the docks of Columbia, Louisiana, where the riverboat *Good Gal Irene* was loading cotton for New Orleans. All them other stories, like how the moon turned blood red and the rivers flooded over when he was born, and how he rassled 300-pound razorback hogs when he was a boy, all them stories, they came afterwards, the way stories are always looking to attach themselves to a man like that."

I never asked Eddie where he got all his material, but he managed to give his piece a beginning, a middle and an end, and even a love story with purty Pollie Ann, who always wanted John Henry to leave the levee and settle down in the back country. Pollie Ann's problem was that when John Henry had a few dollars in his jeans he was more interested in the back o' town, and the only way he knew how to get those few dollars was to swing his hammer, which is why he took on the Captain's steam drill for a $100 purse and killed himself trying to beat it. It was a fight while it lasted, but, like the Captain said:

> There was a day for muscle and sweat,
> And that was the day for you.
> But now is the day for rope and steel,
> And it looks like you is through.

John Henry began the contest against the steam drill swinging the twelve-pound hammer with which he'd won his fame, but he could see that he wasn't going to beat the machine with that, so he switched to a twenty-pounder, and after a while his friend Li'l Alfie sang softly:

De news is gettin' better, Boss,
But, alas, dere's still a lack,
We am movin' fast as it
But it ain't movin' back.

That was the end of John Henry, the steel-drivin' man, but *Saga* was alive and kicking and Ed Linn had probably made another whopping $350 for his research skills and his creativity. Ira Hayes was one thing, but this time we'd made a lead story out of a folk song. You can't get much more resourceful than that.

To tell the truth, I wore out my copy of B. A. Botkin's 1944 edition of *A Treasury of American Folklore* looking for stories for *Saga*. We did Mike Fink, the greatest of the Ohio River flatboat men; Wild Bill Hickok; Billy the Kid; Paul Bunyan; Big Foot Wallace, the Texas Ranger; and Sam Bass, the intrepid bank robber who thought nothing of giving a farm woman one of the Union Pacific's $20 gold pieces for a dozen eggs or a pan of hot biscuits and was admiringly dubbed the American Robin Hood. We even did a piece on Judge Roy Bean, "The Law West of the Pecos," a saloonkeeper who got himself appointed justice of the peace and was judge, jury and executioner all in one. Because Roy Bean went to his own just reward in 1903, the story of his life was in the public domain and didn't cost us anything except whatever modest sum we paid John Groth, the nonpareil illustrator who regularly performed miracles to make our magazine look richer by far than it was.

So we kept learning how to get the job done on Welfare wages and we also learned never to pay any attention to anybody who wanted to tell us that the American people were tired of reading about the heroes of the old frontier. There was a place in the country for Cary Grant, but there would always be a place for John Wayne.

We didn't get everything for nothing, of course, and sometimes we had at least as much luck as brains. *A Stillness at Appomattox* was like that. I read a good report on the book in *Publishers Weekly* and asked the publisher, Doubleday, if I could have a review copy with an eye toward buying second serial rights—the right to publish an excerpt from the book after publication. *Stillness* was the last volume of a trilogy by the distinguished Civil War historian Bruce Catton, who called it *The Army of the Potomac*. The first book of the trilogy was *Mr. Lincoln's Army* and then came *Glory Road*, which included Gettysburg, where the Union broke the Confederacy's back. *Stillness* saw the war through to its end. I wanted it badly and got it for $500. When it won the National Book Award and then the Pulitzer Prize, I felt I was the luckiest editor in the world. Don't let anybody tell you there aren't just as many satisfactions in editing as there are in writing.

Nobody made the war, even the end of the war, as plain and as real as Catton did:

Out from the Rebel lines came a lone rider, a young officer in a gray uniform, galloping madly, a staff in his hand with a white flag fluttering from the end of it. He rode up to Chamberlain's lines and someone there took him off to see Sheridan, and the firing stopped, and the watching Federals saw the Southerners wheeling their guns back and stacking their muskets as if they expected to fight no more.

All up and down the lines the men blinked at one another, unable to realize that the hour they had waited for so long was actually at hand. There was a truce, they could see that, and presently the word was passed that Grant and Lee were going to meet in the little village that lay now between the two lines, and no one could doubt that Lee was going to surrender. It was Palm Sunday, and they would all live to see Easter. . . .

Down by the roadside near Appomattox Court House, Sheridan and Ord and other officers sat and waited while a brown-bearded little man in a mud-spattered uniform rode up. They all saluted him, and there was a quiet interchange of greetings, and then General Grant tilted his head toward the village and asked: "Is General Lee up there?"

Sheridan replied that he was, and Grant said: "Very well. Let's go up."

It gave me a chill then and it gives me a chill now.

Sometimes, of course, ideas can turn on you and bite you in the behind. That happened to me with a lot of things I did at the Literary Guild for Doubleday in the 1960s. When I got to the Book-of-the-Month Club in the '70s, I wished in vain I had saved them. But you can't do that. Anyway, ideas are like streetcars—there's always another one coming along in a minute. The thing is never to run away from the one you've got. Today always has to come before tomorrow.

Thinking about the Literary Guild reminds me of one of my ideas that took a totally unexpected twist. It taught me something about the unpredictability of authors, and maybe even more about the strength of their egos and the length of their memories.

I had wanted for a long time to do a collection of John O'Hara's short stories. Along with a lot of other people, I thought the stories were O'Hara's finest work, better by far than his big novels or even than his short novels. Ironically, although I wasn't asking to include the short novels in the Guild's collection, it was one of them, *Appointment in Samarra*, that provided the last stumbling block to my quest.

Bennett Cerf was buying me lunch to go over his fall list when I hit him with the O'Hara idea. He had just taught me a new Yiddish word when he asked me for a $5,000 advance for one of his admittedly chancy first novels and I had said okay. Bennett was horrified. "Don't do that," he said, "you're taking all the fun out of it. You've got to learn to hondle a little." But, amused as he was by my naïveté in what was my first year as editor-in-chief of the Literary Guild, he wasn't about to talk O'Hara with me. He wouldn't even hondle. "I would if I could," he insisted. "My business is to sell you books, not to tell you you can't have them. But John would kill me if I even so much as encouraged you. He hasn't let any club, not even the BOMC, have one of his books since Clifton Fadiman wrote that review of *Samarra* for the *Times Book Review* and called it 'Disappointment in O'Hara.' Forget it. It will only remind him."

But I was too new to the business to take no for an answer and I kept trying. I asked Bennett for permission to write O'Hara myself, and he finally said, "So go ahead. It won't do you any good, but go ahead and try."

About a month or so later Bennett called me up and said, "I don't believe it myself, but John says all right, if the money is fair, he'll do it."

"Twenty-five thousand dollars advance," I said. "Usual royalties."

I sent a contract off to Bennett in a hurry before the Squire of Gibbsville could change his mind, and I waited nervously for the piece of paper to come back with the great man's signature on it. But what I got instead was another phone call from Bennett. "I'm really sorry to bother you with this," he said, "but you've got to give me two checks for O'Hara. The $25,000 advance is okay, but he wants a separate check for another $25 to pay him back for the $25 Doubleday charged him for the Somerset Maugham quote he used for the *Samarra* title."

"Are you kidding?" I said.

"I'm not kidding at all, and neither is John. He wants his money back."

So I had to have two checks made up, one for $25,000 and one for $25. It was worth it. Almost twenty-five years later the Guild is still selling the book.

This is the piece that cost O'Hara $25:

DEATH SPEAKS: There was a merchant in Bagdad who sent his servant to market to buy provisions and in a little while the servant came back, white and trembling, and said, Master, just now when I was in the market-place I was jostled by a woman in the crowd and when I turned I saw it was Death that jostled me. She looked at me and made a threatening gesture; now, lend me your horse, and I will ride away from this city and avoid my fate. I will go to Samarra and there Death will not find me. The merchant lent him his horse, and the servant mounted it, and he dug his spurs in its flanks and as fast as the horse could gallop he went. Then the merchant went down to the market-place and he saw me standing in the crowd and he came to me and said, Why did you make a threatening gesture to my servant when you saw him this morning? That was not a threatening gesture, I said, it was only a start of surprise. I was astonished to see him in Bagdad, for I had an appointment with him tonight in Samarra.

What mattered, and it's the only thing that ever matters, is that we got the book. In that crucial sense, the book business wasn't any different from the magazine business. But then, I've always argued that the two are the same business. You're creating and selling words and ideas, information and entertainment, in both worlds. My son, Kevin, once asked me why I said so quickly that between the two I preferred the book business. "That's easy," I said. "In the book business you don't have to sell advertising."

I did once catch Irving Manheimer in a weak moment and got him to agree to let me pay Paul Gallico $1,000 over our regular budget for each of two articles Paul was willing to write for us on what you might call a quid-pro-quo basis. Paul had an assignment for a whole lot of money to do a piece for one of the general magazines on the divorce trial of Daddy Browning and Peaches Heenan, one of the more lurid sagas of the 1920s. He wanted desperately to get at the files of the New York *Graphic*, the Macfadden-owned tabloid, long dead, that had latched on to the case with a lip-smacking enthusiasm that didn't even hesitate to invent photographs with posed bodies and superimposed heads of the genuine characters. "Composographs," the *Graphic* editors called them without a touch of embarrassment. One of them showed fifteen-year-old Peaches, who had all the physical attributes of a twenty-one-year-old, and Daddy on their honeymoon. He was wearing a sheik's costume and she wasn't wearing a great deal—a low-cut, sleeveless, bare-backed, short-short apron dress that in the mid-'20s would have got a woman arrested on a public beach and was a circulation-building shocker on the front page of a New York City daily newspaper.

Meyer Dworkin, the company's treasurer and one of the few survivors of the Bernarr Macfadden days, didn't want to let Gallico near the old *Graphic* files. He thought a story like the one Paul wanted to write would reflect badly on the company. "How can we sell Breck on advertising their shampoo in *True Story*," he argued, "if the company's image is going to be so scandalous?" But the prospect of a little scandal didn't bother Manheimer. When he saw how eager I was to have the great Gallico do two boxing pieces for *Sport*, one on Mickey Walker and one on Paul Berlenbach, he gave his gracious approval. So Gallico spent a week in our office poring over the old files.

Paul gave us fair value for this compromising of our corporate virtue. He even threw in a couple of sermons. In the Walker piece, which we ran first, he looked between the lines of Mickey's fight in December 1926 with Tiger Flowers, the middleweight champion:

> Mickey took a beating for ten rounds and at the conclusion was awarded one of those mysterious and wholly unwarranted decisions that happen every so often in the sweet-scented game. It took months for the uproar over that one to die down but Mickey was the champion and that remained on the books. And actually, nobody but Walk Miller, manager of Tiger Flowers, and a few people with a sense of justice and outrage, cared about what had happened to Tiger Flowers. The Tiger was a kindly, good-hearted Negro, a reader of the Bible and a church deacon, who was always being skinned, diddled, crossed, robbed and hornswoggled. In the pre-Joe Louis days of the Golden Decade, it was still the custom to do this, and some time if you really want to be made to feel sick, you can go back in the files and read a famous sportswriter's article praising Flowers for being a Negro "who knew his place." That is to say, he maintained an humble and servile attitude in the presence of the white blackguards who cheated him right and left.

Gallico's other piece for us was just plain wonderful sportswriting, a little old-fashioned maybe, but touching, sympathetic, nostalgic and illuminating. This is how it began:

> Not long ago, at Katonah, New York, there died and was buried one of the handsomest and most glamorous figures of the prize ring of a quarter of a century ago.

When his casket was taken to the grave, of all the men he had enriched—managers, seconds, trainers, hangers-on, and opponents—there was only one who was present on that occasion to pay his last respects. This one was an ex-fighter, a dark, still-slender chap of medium height, piercing brown eyes, coal black hair beginning to thin from his forehead, and a peculiar and characteristic forward carriage of his head on his shoulders. His nose was mashed, the relic of bitter and sensational glove battles, and about his eyes and brows there was scar tissue, the wound stripes of the ring wars. Much of it had been put there by the slashing blows of the man he was following to his last resting place.

His name was Paul Berlenbach and in his day he was known, among other descriptive and affectionate nicknames, as "The Astoria Assassin." Once he had been light-heavyweight champion of the world, a brave and lion-hearted fighter, and in his time one of the most sensational punchers in the history of the ring. The man whom he came to mourn had been his most bitter, persistent, and dangerous foe, the French-Canadian born Ovila Chapdelaine, whose ring name was Jack Delaney.

Four times these two men fought each other in dramatic, pulse-stopping encounters. They battled one another into a fortune for each. Twice the French-Canadian reduced Berlenbach to a reeling mass of blinded, semi-conscious flesh, the wreck of an athlete who had to be rescued by the referee from serious injury. Yet a strong friendship grew up between the two men, and at the end it was only Berlenbach who remembered Jack Delaney and cared enough to attend his funeral.

And this is how it ended, after Gallico told how Berlenbach's dream was to become a referee licensed by the New York State Athletic Commission:

His life has been full and was crowned with achievement in his youth. Today he is content with his family and his job. But he would not be human if, as he approached the ringman's twilight, he did not long once more to feel the scrape of rosined canvas under his elkskin shoes, the thrust of the ropes against his back, the bright glare of the ring lights, and to hear once more from the fighting platform the great roar of the crowd flowing inwards from the darkness.

Unfortunately, Irving's generous moods didn't come along every day and neither did his approval of over-the-budget $1,000 fees for writers. He let me pay $750 to Quentin Reynolds for a *Saga* piece on London during the war, but I suspect that was only because he enjoyed Reynolds' stories at lunch, especially his description of Cardinal Spellman: "He doesn't know his ass from a hole in the ground about ecclesiastical matters, but he's a wizard with a lease." We mostly had to live within our budget of $4,000 for editorial material and that had to pay for fourteen or fifteen articles a month. The only answer, besides working our editors to death, was to find young writers who wanted the experience and the exposure badly enough to work for peanuts. We came up with some big winners in Kahn, Linn, Jimmy Breslin, Josh Greenfeld and Jack Pearl, who wrote for us regularly. One way we managed it was to guarantee them as many assignments as they wanted up to one a month. That way, even though they didn't get a lot of money—unless you considered $250 a month a lot of money—they got it every month and they could count on it to pay the rent. Rosemary Breslin, Jimmy's first wife, said the $250 Jimmy got from us every month in the '50s meant more to them than a lot of the bigger checks he extracted from richer magazines later on. Another twice-told story of the former Rosemary Dattalico's affection for the checks from *Sport* is that she used to salt the money away in a sugar bowl to keep it safe from her too easily tempted husband. Inevitably, one day Jimmy came home from the track with a friend who had lent him enough money to lose the last few races. Jimmy left the friend in the cab while he went upstairs to hit the sugar bowl, which, sadly, was empty. When he confronted Rosemary, she admitted that she had used it to pay the rent. "Jesus," he hollered when he got to the sidewalk, "it's all gone! Every dime. She blew the whole goddam thing on the rent."

Roger Kahn and I stood on the corner of 42nd Street and Third Avenue one afternoon after a pleasant expense-account lunch and shook hands on a bold arrangement. Medium bold for me, nervously bold for him. Roger hated his job writing baseball in the summer and whatever in the winter for the *Herald Tribune* and he wanted to quit and freelance full time. "But I've got to have a nut," he said. "Joan and I don't need a whole lot, but we have to know something is coming in regular." Roger, like most of us, doesn't write like that, but he talks like that. "Can you manage four hundred a month?" he needed to know. I could spend the money in the editorial budget any way I wanted to, so the only risk I was running was that Roger wouldn't deliver. It wasn't much of a risk, I figured, so, standing in the shadow of the Third Avenue El, I shook hands with him. "They made good martinis at Carver's," I tell Roger when we remember that less than historic but, to us, important handshake.

Roger told his own version of our partnership in the introduction to his book *How the Weather Was,* comparing us favorably with the stifling editorial policies of the *Saturday Evening Post.*

Ed Fitzgerald, who edited a small magazine called *Sport,* encouraged a number of writers to publish seriously there and in a companion magazine for men, called *Saga.* Much of *Saga* described ministers playing dry variations on *Rain,* but that still left room for occasional adult articles. Among *Saga*'s adventurers and bawds, I published long and increasingly intense stories about Frank Lloyd Wright, Jean Laffite, Jonas Salk and Garry Davis, the world citizen. Fitzgerald did not demand a pablum overview, nor did he superimpose stylistic oddities. Still, a *Sport-Saga* author faced certain drawbacks. There was no feedback from readers, and Fitzgerald's employers had wedged him between cost accountants. Before me lay a big, two-hearted world: pap, attention and Beef Wellington with the *Saturday Evening Post*; integrity, obscurity and stew meat with Ed Fitzgerald.

Ed Linn began with us as an associate editor and then decided he wanted to try to make it as a freelance. He's been making it ever since. For us, he became the Ted Williams specialist on a magazine that managed to maintain even worse relations with Williams than the Boston newspapermen did. Eddie could get Williams to talk to him even if he couldn't ever get him to stop insulting him—and the magazine. His account of "The Kid's Last Day," Ted's last game for the Red Sox in September 1960, is a classic of informal reporting which achieves its goal of showing the real man by letting the man speak for himself. Eddie, of course, is the unnamed "our man."

Sure enough, when our man started toward Ted's locker in the far corner of the room, Ted pointed a finger at him and shouted, "You're not supposed to be in here, you know!"

"The same warm, glad cry of greeting I always get from you," our man said. "It's your last day. Why don't you live a little?"

Ted started toward the trainer's room but wheeled around and came back. "You've got a nerve coming here to interview me after the last one you wrote about me!"

Our man wanted to know what was the matter with the last one.

"You called me unbearable, that's what's the matter."

The full quote, it was pointed out, was that he was "sometimes unbearable but never dull," which holds a different connotation entirely.

"You've been after me for twelve years, that flogging magazine," he said in his typically well modulated shout. "Twelve years. I missed an appointment for some kind of a luncheon. I forget what happened . . . it doesn't matter anyway . . . but I forgot some appointment twelve years ago and *Sport* Magazine hasn't let up on me since."

Our man, lamentably eager to disassociate himself from this little magazine, made it clear that while he had done most of *Sport*'s Williams articles in the past few years, he was not a member of the staff. "And," our man pointed out, "I have been accused of turning you into a combination of Paul Bunyan and Santa Claus."

"Well, when you get back there, tell them what (he searched for the appropriate word, the *mot juste* as they say in the dugouts) what flog-heads they are. Tell them that for me."

An objective reporter, Eddie wrote:

Although we are reluctant to bring Ted into the context of the story itself, Ted's abiding hatred toward us tells much about him and his even longer feud with the Boston writers. Twelve years ago, just as Ted said, an article appeared on these pages to which he took violent exception. (The fact that he is so well aware it was 12 years ago suggests that he still has the magazine around somewhere so that he can use it to fan the flames whenever he feels them dying.) What Ted objected to in that article was an interview with his mother in San Diego. Ted objects to any peering into his private life. The piece in question said this:

"Ted's mother, Mrs. May Williams, is an ardent Salvation Army worker in San Diego. Up and down the Southern California coast she's known as 'Salvation May,' 'The Sweetheart of San Diego,' and 'The Angel of Tia Juana.' As single-minded about her religious work as her famous son is about his hitting, she is proud of her reputation for being able to force her way into any establishment in behalf of the Salvation Army, and she has laid claim to the world record for selling the Salvation Army newspaper *War Cry*.

"I didn't get a chance to go to San Diego to see her," the author of the piece wrote, "but my friend and colleague Hannibal Coons took care of that detail and came up with some interesting information. He found out that Ted's father, Sam Williams, had left his wife nine years before and they were now divorced. He found out that May had been an Army officer but had been busted to a non-commissioned rank when she didn't marry an Army officer. He found out that Ted had been sending sizeable sums of money to his mother ever since he began making it. He had the old family house on Utah Street in San Diego completely remodeled for her. 'Don't say anything about Teddy,' Mrs. Williams said, 'except the highest and the best. He's a wonderful son.' "

The author of that piece was Ed Fitzgerald, and twelve years later he was still fresh in Ted Williams' mind as Public Enemy No. 1.

If we had a lot of luck with our young writers, we also owed an unpayable debt to the famous guys who wrote for us in the beginning and kept on writing for us even after *Sports Illustrated* came along in 1954. Not only my good friends Red Smith and Frank Graham but John Lardner, who hated the kind of group journalism he thought was personified by the Time Inc. magazines, and Bill Heinz and Dick Young and stars from other cities, Emmett Watson of Seattle and Shirley Povich of Washington, for instance, stayed with us at considerable financial pain to them. "The Bird Watchers' Manual," our gang called *SI*, which used a bird-watchers' cover on its May 16, 1955, issue, showing sixty-six birds ranging all the way from the pileated woodpecker to the yellow-billed cuckoo. When *SI* sent William Faulkner to cover the Kentucky Derby, we fought back with Red Smith.

This is how Faulkner's piece began:

This saw Boone: the bluegrass, the virgin land rolling westward wave by dense wave from the Allegheny gaps, unmarked then, teeming with deer and buffalo about the salt licks and the limestone springs whose water in time would make the fine bourbon whiskey; and the wild men too—the red men and the white ones too who had to be a little wild also to endure and survive and so mark the wilderness with the proofs of their tough survival—Boonesborough, Owenstown, Harrod's and Harbuck's Stations; Kentucky: the dark and bloody ground.

And knew Lincoln too, where the old weathered durable rail fences enclose the green and sacrosanct place of rounded hills long healed now from the plow, and big old trees to shade the site of the ancient one-room cabin in which the babe first saw light; no sound there now but such wind and birds as when the child first faced the road which would lead to fame and martyrdom—unless perhaps you like to think that the man's voice is somewhere there too, speaking into the scene of his own nativity the simple and matchless prose with which he reminded us of our duties and responsibilities if we wished to continue as a nation.

And knew Stephen Foster and the brick mansion of his song; no longer the dark and bloody ground of memory now, but already my old Kentucky home.

This is how Red Smith wrote it:

This was after dinner in Conn McCreary's home on one of those little Miami Beach islands dotting Biscayne Bay. The jockey sat in a big easy chair with his feet tucked under him; if he'd sat up straight, his feet wouldn't have reached the floor. "I try to explain to myself," he said, "what the Derby means to me. I can't find the right words. But one thing I do know. . . ."

Some knowledge of McCreary's professional background is useful here. In 1944, when Conn was turning 23, he went whooping out of the gate at Churchill Downs wearing the devil-red and blue silks of Calumet Farm, steered Pensive through an opening on the rail turning into the home stretch, and won the Kentucky Derby going away. He was still just a kid, not many years along from the day when he had gone hitch-hiking out of St. Louis hunting a job on the Kentucky horse farms. Now he was a Derby winner, a full member of the lodge along with Eddie Arcaro and Johnny Longden and Earl Sande and all the others back to Isaac Murphy.

Red, being Red, even threw in a touch of wry humor that itself said a lot about the Derby:

Mr. Society Kid Hogan, out of Chicago, arrived without a hotel reservation and took a room in the house of a little old doll who could have doubled for Whistler's Mother. When he retired the first evening, he was holding $500. In the morning he was clean. He reported his loss to the landlady, who was properly shocked and sympathetic. She cheered up quickly, though. "You know, this is Derby time," she said brightly, "and at Derby time everybody robs everybody else."

"I'm positive the old doll rolled me," Hogan said later, "but I didn't have the nerve to put the finger on her."

I don't want to imply that everything *SI* did was wrong. In the same issue in which they ran Faulkner on the Derby, Sid James and his merry men ran five color pictures of the matchless Gwen Verdon playing Lola in *Damn Yankees*. No magazine that has that much respect for the way Miss Verdon looks in a Washington Senators shirt and a pair of tight red pants can be all bad.

That, two years after its first issue appeared in August 1954, may have been when Harry Phillips, the publisher, was summoned upstairs to Time Inc.'s executive suite on the thirty-fourth floor to listen to the riot act about all the money his new magazine was losing. "We expected you to lose money," the story goes, "but, my God, not this much. Do something about it." So Harry went downstairs and assembled his senior lieutenants, told them what he had just been told and said, "Whatever you had on for lunch, cancel it. This is an emergency. We're all going over to 'Twenty-one' and talk about cutting costs."

SI still holds the all-time record for money lost by a new American magazine, more than $20 million. But it's been bringing it in for its happy owners for a long time now, another proof of the genius and the tenacity of the Founding Father, Henry Luce. (And, many say, of Clare Boothe Luce, Harry's lady, who simply refused to allow the magazine to go down. When it came to putting money at risk, Mrs. Luce was no Irving Manheimer.)

SI had a lot to do with my trading the magazine business for the book business. First, the competition inspired us to come up with the idea of giving a sports car to the Most Valuable Player in the World Series every year. Phil Hyland, our advertising manager, sold the idea to Chevrolet's ad agency, Campbell-Ewald, and they agreed to sell us a Chevy Corvette, their expensive new sports car, at cost and to support the promotion with six full-color pages. It was the biggest advertising breakthrough we'd had for our struggling magazine and the fact that right from the beginning, in 1955, the award made the sports pages of every newspaper in the country gave us a circulation boost, too.

It was a happy thing for us that 1955 was the first year the Dodgers won the Series. They had lost it in 1916, 1920, 1941, 1949, 1952 and 1953. Every year, after the last game, the Brooklyn *Eagle* ran the same headline in big black letters on the front page: "WAIT TILL NEXT YEAR!" But in '55, after Gil Hodges scooped up Peewee Reese's low throw for the last out in the last of the ninth to save a 2–0 seventh-game victory, the borough of Brooklyn threw an all-night party, and the *Eagle*'s extra had a headline that said: "THIS IS NEXT YEAR!" We couldn't have picked a better time to give away our first car.

We never had a jury or a poll to decide who got the car. From '55 to '60 I made up my mind about it myself. From '61 through '72 Al Silverman did it. It wasn't really so hard. The winner usually picks himself. There was no argument about Johnny Podres in 1955, or Don Larsen of the Yankees in 1956, the year he pitched the only perfect game in World Series history, or Lew Burdette of the Braves in '57, or Bob Turley of the Yankees in '58 or Larry Sherry of the Dodgers in '59—all three-game winners. The only trouble I had was with my last one, in 1960. That was the year the Yankees and the Pirates went down to the seventh game at Forbes Field on October 13 in Pittsburgh. It was some ball game. I was selfishly happy when Yogi hit a three-run homer in the top of the sixth to put the Yankees ahead, 5–4, leaving me with visions of our newly finished book selling off the shelves because the author had won the Series, the car and everything in sight. But the Pirates fought back. It was 9–9 when the Pirates came up for last licks in the ninth and the first hitter, Bill Mazeroski, drove the second pitch over the left-field wall for a home run that won the game, the Series and everything. Except the car. I gave the car to Bobby Richardson, the Yankees' peerless second baseman, who had set a Series record of twelve runs batted in, including the seventh grand-slam homer in Series history. He's still, twenty-four years later, the only member of a losing team to win it.

While the Yankees were finishing their showers, Harold Rosenthal of the *Trib* and I walked up the street past where the press bus was waiting and had a drink at a little neighborhood bar. "If these people knew you were the guy who just gave the car to Richardson," Harold said, "neither of us would get out of here alive." And when we got back to the bus, Bob Fishel, the Yankees' press secretary, said, "Hey, Fitz, Roy Face was out here a few minutes ago with a champagne bottle looking for you, and he didn't want to give you a drink, either. It was disgraceful. No Yankee would ever behave like that."

I was glad to get home. Milton Gross of the *Post* asked me on the airplane why I had bothered to go to Pittsburgh in the first place. "I hear you've got a new job," he said. "What the hell did you need this for?"

"Well," I said, "I hadn't expected to be the target of assault by champagne bottle." Actually, until that seventh game the most exciting thing that had happened was Mickey Mantle refusing to fly to Pittsburgh on a Lockheed Electra, several of which had dropped into the waters of Flushing Bay in recent months.

"You have to, Mick," the traveling secretary told him. "It's all they've got."

"I'll take the train," Mickey said.

They got rid of the Electra, which shows how much influence you have when you've hit 320 home runs.

Luckily uncrowned, I put away my last World Series press button and got ready to do something else for a living.

"I don't have to tell the kids, do I?" my son, Kevin, wanted to know.

Chapter 10

W HAT happened in 1960 proves how little we know about what's going to happen. I got a new job that I would never have dreamed of asking for and my world was changed forever.

Naomi Burton, my sports-fan agent, liked my *Sport* Special on Yogi Berra and thought it was time for a book to be done on Yogi. She made a deal with Yogi's business manager and sold the book to Doubleday. Despite Carmen Berra, we got the book done. But Naomi got to Doubleday before the book did. I hadn't finished it yet when she agreed to go to work for the company as a senior editor.

The first two games of the World Series that year were played in Pittsburgh and the second three in New York. The Pirates were ahead, three games to two, when it was time to go back to Pittsburgh. I was in my office the morning of October 11, getting ready to catch the Yankees' press plane at La Guardia, when the telephone rang. My secretary said Milton Runyon of Doubleday was calling. When I reached for the telephone, I assumed I was going to talk to somebody about publicity for the Berra book. Instead, the man on the line said he was the first vice-president of Doubleday and he had heard about me from Naomi Burton and he wondered if I would have lunch with him.

"Sure," I said. "But not right away. I have to go to Pittsburgh this afternoon for the end of the World Series." We agreed to meet the day after the last game. "The University Club," he said. "That's at the corner of 54th and Fifth." I still didn't have any idea why he wanted to talk to me, but a few minutes later Naomi called. "He wants to talk to you," she said, "about being the editor of the Literary Guild."

That gave me a lot to think about on the plane. I knew what the Literary Guild was. I knew what book clubs were. I'd joined the Book Find Club a month or so after I got home from the Pacific. But that was all I knew. It was a good thing I had a head full of problems about the Series and the car and the magazine's deadlines to worry about or I would have had a heart attack thinking about it. I'd been wanting to do something else for more than a year. I had taken Liby to the Dodger (Los Angeles)–White Sox games in Chicago the year before and had told her, in our bedroom on the Twentieth Century, that I thought I had to get away from *Sport*. "I'm forty years old and it's time for me to do something else. If I don't do it now, I never will. Maybe *Sports Illustrated* will want me. Anyway, I'm going to ask."

I did ask, and I had a couple of interesting luncheons with Andre Laguerre, Sid James' successor as managing editor, but he thought I had too much experience to fit in comfortably with the *SI* staff. "You make more money than anybody besides me," he said, which I thought would have made Irving feel better than he should have felt, "and you're too accustomed to running your own show. That's not how it's done here. I don't think it would work."

So much for *Sports Illustrated*. Maybe they were mad at me, anyway, because Irving and I had taken them to court in 1955 and charged them with unfair competition because the logotype of the new magazine had a great big *Sports* and a tiny *Illustrated* underneath it on the cover. Judge Saul S. Streit, the same judge who had sentenced the 1951 college-basketball fixers, heard the case and ended it by suggesting to Harry Phillips and the Time Inc. lawyers that they ought to change their logotype. The judge even measured the *Sports* and found that it was one and a half inches deep, then measured the bar in which the *Illustrated* was printed and found that it was less than half an inch deep. That was with the bar and all. The word *Illustrated* itself was only an eighth of an inch deep. We had argued that they were stealing our name, and the judge, although he said "Sports" was a generic term and couldn't be copyrighted, agreed with us. After only a few minutes of consultation in front of Judge Streit's bench, the Time Inc. people agreed to make *Sports* and *Illustrated* equal in weight. That's the way it's been ever since.

But I hadn't become an editor of *Sports Illustrated*, so I was warmly interested, and more than a little nervous, when I met Milton Runyon at the University Club. He explained that the man he was looking for would be the editor-in-chief of the Literary Guild and all of its affiliated book clubs, more than twenty of them. There was the Dollar Book Club, which was much bigger than the Guild, the Mystery Guild, the Cook Book Guild, the Fireside Theatre, the American Garden Guild, the Science Fiction Book Club and God knows how many other guilds and clubs. "I like the cut of your jib," he said over his coffee and my iced tea. "Let's go back to the office and meet Douglas Black. He's the president of the company. The job is mine to fill, but he ought to meet you and say what he thinks."

We went to the office at 575 Madison Avenue and Mr. Black shook hands with me and wanted to know what I had done in the war. I told him I had been in the Infantry and he said, "So was I, in the first war. That's great." I was hired.

That was the easier of my first two meetings with Mr. Black. The second one was at lunch, at Café Argenteuil, and we had three martinis before lunch, a bottle of wine with lunch and two brandies after lunch. I think I did some reading that afternoon before I walked down the street to Grand Central, but I've never been sure. I do remember that it was Friday and he had called ahead to make sure a specific wine would be ready for us, and I ruined everything by ordering fish, which would hardly go with his red wine. I compounded the problem by saying that it didn't matter, but he brushed me off and had the captain bring him a white wine which he said was stout enough to stand up to my fish and his steak. I wished I could sink under the table, which probably would have been easy anyway. But when I got to work the next morning, I was still the editor-in-chief of the Literary Guild.

It was no big deal, I soon found out. The Guild's membership was at the vanishing point. The first meeting I went to was called to discuss the wisdom of killing the Guild and folding its membership, most of which was in the department-store units, into the Dollar Book Club. I protested. "I don't know anything about it," I said. "Let me have a chance to look at it." So they set another meeting for the next week and by then I had a plan. It was outrageous, but it was a plan.

"I think what we ought to do," I said, "is take on the Book-of-the-Month Club head to head. Let's just say we're going to be the same kind of book club they are and do a better job of it than they do. They take some terrible books and they pass up a lot of good books. There's plenty of room for two clubs in there."

The Guild—which had been chartered in 1925, a year before BOMC, but had actually begun operating in 1927, a year after Harry Scherman did—had always been known as the low-neckline club. Historical romances were its chief stock in trade and the jackets of the books uniformly featured the kind of women in the kind of clothes you see today on the covers of the Gothics. The Guild was an early and a cleaner source of the "sweet remembered passion" school of fiction. I couldn't wait to get at it.

I had got the chance, Milton Runyon told me as we walked out of Mr. Black's office, because an ancient publishing maxim had worked for me: "Once an agent, always an agent." Naomi Burton had been at a meeting of senior editorial people and the Doubleday brass, including Mr. Black, Milton, John Sargent, who was Neltje Doubleday's husband and a vice-president of the company, and young Nelson Doubleday, who owned it. Nelson's father and grandfather had believed in the Commodore Vanderbilt philosophy of management of family-owned businesses, which is that one heir has to be in charge or they will all fight and the company will fall apart or have to be sold. So, although Nelson's mother and sister owned much of the stock, he had all of the votes—or would have in a few years. So even then, when he was only twenty-eight years old, what he said mattered.

"Milton," he asked when all the editors except Naomi, who was picking up some papers, had left, "what the hell are you doing about the Guild job?" Nelson and Sargent, I found out later, had been after Milton for months to retire John Beecroft, the curmudgeon who had been running the Guild for decades, and replace him with somebody younger. The Guild, unlike the Book-of-the-Month Club, didn't have an editorial board; there was no panel of distinguished judges—it is mandatory to say "distinguished" before "judges"—with the sole power to select the book of the month. Beecroft did it himself and so would his successor, who, the Doubleday brass hoped, would pick books that the members would buy more enthusiastically and that might even be appealing enough to attract new members.

"Well," Milton is said to have said, "I haven't had any luck at all. I've been all through the book business, I've talked to everybody I know and I haven't found anybody."

"Milton," John Sargent said, "we've simply got to do something. We're even worse off now since Jerry Hardy went over to *Time*. Now we not only need somebody for Beecroft, but we need somebody to be behind you, too."

"I know," Milton said. "I've been thinking, since I haven't had any luck in the book business, maybe I ought to try the magazine business. There might be somebody there who would be right for us."

That was when my agent stepped in. Heading for the door with her papers clutched under her arm, Naomi stopped by the group and said, "I couldn't help hearing what you were saying. Forgive me, but if you're going to look in the magazine business for somebody to run the Guild, I know somebody you ought to talk to." Which is how Milton Runyon happened to call me and make a lunch date.

Milton gave me $5,000 more than Irving was paying me in base salary, taking me from $22,500 a year to $27,500, which sounded wonderful until we began living off my paycheck and found out

how much of the money we had been spending to keep up the house
and buy clothes for ourselves and Eileen and Kevin and pay all the
other bills that make life challenging for suburban families had come
from magazine articles and books that didn't seem likely to be a part
of the Doubleday picture. I liked the work a lot, but we were always
broke.

But that was something to worry about later. Right now the
problem was finding my way around in my new job. Peter Schwed
of Simon & Schuster, who had been my editor on the Bobby Riggs
book, was the first of scores of editors and publishers who wanted
to take me to lunch and tell me about their books. "I find this an
astonishing appointment," Peter said encouragingly when we met.
Going to lunch was the main thing I did for the first three months.
I had lunch at restaurants still alive and restaurants long dead, at
Lutèce and Café Chauveron and Chateaubriand and the Laurent
and La Côte Basque and L'Aiglon and the Lafayette and the Peacock
Lounge at the Waldorf and even, God forbid, at the Century Club,
which—no matter how much I liked Evan Thomas, who took me
there—struck me as a mausoleum then and strikes me as a mausoleum
now. I went all the way uptown to the Lotos Club on 66th Street,
where they at least had paintings of naked women on the walls, to
have lunch with one of our advertising-agency heads, Frank Vos,
and all the way downtown to 12th Street to eat with Roger Straus
at Charles French. I had lunch at the Rainbow Room with Leon
Shimkin and lunch at the Brussels with Blanche Knopf and lunch
with Harry Abrams at the Italian Pavilion. I had chicken hash at
"21" with Nat Wartels. Every time he came to New York from
his splendid townhouse office on Beacon Hill in Boston, I had lunch
at the Plaza's Oak Room with Arthur Thornhill, Sr., the best book
salesman I ever met. Once I went to the Plaza by mistake when I
was supposed to be having lunch with Evelyn Shrifte at the Oak
Room at the St. Regis. I had lunch at Giovanni's and at Le Bistro
and at Monsignore and at the Voisin and at Quo Vadis and Sardi's
and the Russian Tea Room. I ate at Christ Cella's and La Caravelle
and The Pen and Pencil and Reuben's. I even ate at Reuben's, on
58th Street between Madison and Fifth, by myself because you

could sit at the big round bar and have a drink, a bowl of soup and a sandwich and be out in twenty minutes. I could and did do the same thing at P. J. Moriarty's on Third Avenue, where a set of railroad trains ran on a rickety track just under the ceiling over the bar. I ate at Tony's Wife and at Charles à la Pomme Souffle. For somebody who is famous for not eating much, I ate a lot of fancy lunches.

The good news was that the book business didn't seem all that arcane. I'd been reading books all of my life and it wasn't hard for me to talk about them, even with people who edited them and published them. It made it easier that I was the customer and if I said something stupid nobody was likely to expose my inexperience too cruelly. The purpose of the occasion was for the publisher to sell me books; no luncheons were ever more legitimate expense-account deductions. Arthur Thornhill told me what Edwin O'Connor was working on, Blanche Knopf told me what Jorge Amado was doing, Roger Straus told me that Bernard Malamud's next book was going to be even better than *The Magic Barrel* or *The Assistant*. Marshall Best told me what John Steinbeck was writing. Larry Hughes told me that Morris West was doing a book I would love.

The people who worked with me were harder to deal with, mostly because they were used to doing what they were told. I didn't know what to tell them yet, so they were confused and withdrawn and I was just confused. One thing that didn't confuse me, though, was the bell. John Beecroft had left it up to his assistant and office manager, Alice Ford, to summon the troops to the weekly editorial meeting. Alice, an incredibly efficient woman, did all by herself work that at the Book-of-the-Month Club, I found out later, was done by at least four people. Alice had been a WAVE officer during the war and, having a lot of Navy in her, had decided that the easiest way to tell everybody to come to the meeting was to ring a bell. So she took an old-fashioned brass bell, the kind schoolteachers used in the early days of the Republic, walked out of her office into the hall that connected all the offices and rang the hell out of it. This was no friendly call for a get-together. This was a summons to await the captain's pleasure. Frances Bolton, Marie

Reno, Clint Simpson, Wailes Gray, and Maggie Bowes dropped whatever they were doing and shaped up.

That was too much for me. I told Alice the bell had to go. "Actually," I said, "I not only want you to stop ringing it. I wish you would take the damn thing home." The bell was never seen or heard again, and the staff began to talk to me as though I was a person and not just the new boss. Marie Reno even asked me how old I was.

I won over the receptionist, who was a baseball buff, the day Yogi Berra walked in and asked if I had a few minutes to talk with him.

But nothing was going to do me any good if I couldn't back up my ambitious plan to take on the Book-of-the-Month Club in a literary *mano-a-mano* with some good books as weapons. Important books. The first painful indication I got of how hard it was going to be came when I discovered that the Doubleday editors were worse than the people at the other publishing houses. They looked down on the Guild and didn't care who knew it, especially me. They sent all of their most promising new fiction to BOM, as they called it, and they were surprised that I thought the least they could do was let the Guild see the book at the same time. Lee Barker, the number-two editor, who had been number one while Ken McCormick was away during the war and who was more or less co-equal with Ken, handled book-club subsidiary rights himself—and he was brutally candid in telling me that it was the Book-of-the-Month Club he wanted for his authors, who included the likes of Leon Uris and Irving Stone and Arthur Hailey. "I wouldn't be doing my job for them," he said, "if I didn't try to get them the BOM. We have enough trouble as it is convincing the agents and the writers that we do our business with the Guild at arm's length."

I had no complaints with the management. All of my bosses—John Sargent, who had been elected president when Douglas Black retired, Nelson and Milton Runyon—had given me a license to go after the Book-of-the-Month Club even though I had said carefully, and they knew themselves, that it was going to be expensive. They never complained about my spending money and they never blamed me for the losses the Guild was running up. I was lucky, anyway, that the Guild wasn't losing as much money as the Dollar Book Club was making. But I knew I couldn't count on their support forever if I didn't at least show that I was making a beginning. With the Guild's mail-order membership under 200,000 by the time my first selection was shipped, I knew I'd better make some progress or I would have been hired just in time to preside over the death of my first book club.

One of the reasons the membership had fallen so drastically was that the Guild was no longer being supported by print advertising— not even in the New York *Times* Book Review, where Doubleday still maintained a host of prime franchise positions like back covers and center spreads, the two pages that open so readily in the dead center of the magazine. With no books worth advertising, they had reasoned, why waste the money? They spent it on their other clubs and on Doubleday trade books. I remember how chagrined I was to see on the back cover of the *Book Review* for Sunday, February 5, 1961, an ad for the Fireside Theatre. *24 Favorite One-Act Plays*, edited by Bennett Cerf and Van H. Cartmell, was offered for ten cents as a premium to new members promising to buy at least four regular selections at the standard member's price. The plays the ad showed as examples of what you could expect to be offered as a member included three musical comedies, *The Sound of Music*, *The Unsinkable Molly Brown* and *Fiorello*. The whole thing offended me, not only the lack of a Guild ad but even the content of the Fireside Theatre ad. But I disagreed with many things Doubleday did, and it is to their credit that they gave me a lot of chances to prove that I was right.

Wallace Stegner, a good writer who had had a major success with *The Big Rock Candy Mountain*, had a new book I liked coming from Viking. It was called *A Shooting Star*, it was laid in the West, Stegner's part of the country, and it had an exceptionally appealing heroine. I bought it from Marshall Best at lunch for what was then the regular Guild guarantee of $25,000 against royalties of 7½ percent of the club price. That 7½ percent was one of my crosses as long as I worked for Doubleday because the Book-of-the-Month

Club paid 10 percent and wasn't shy about reminding publishers about it. (The Guild did and does pay the full club royalty on books used as premium and dividend books and BOMC pays 5 percent, half the regular royalty on copies actually sold.) I wrote Stegner a letter telling him how happy I was about my first selection and thanked him for his confidence in the Guild. He wrote back, "When you have written as long and as hard for a living as I have, getting a book club selection feels like an old man being smiled on by a very young and very pretty girl."

Milton Runyon wasn't quite so happy about *A Shooting Star*. He thought a novel about a rich woman involved in an adulterous love affair was a dangerous experiment for the Guild. I thought if the handful of members we had left had been able to survive the blood-less and deliberately titillating sex of a lot of books the club had been using, they ought to be able to handle the more literate and seriously undertaken sex of Wallace Stegner. "Adultery," Sabrina Castro, his heroine, thought in her pain.

What a ridiculous Old Testament notion, and how vile that after resenting her mother's New England–Victorian notions all her life, she should find herself netted in a New England conscience of her own. When practically every woman she knew had had, or now had, or would have, a lover or many lovers; when adolescents were as promiscuous as street dogs, and every movie you went to, every play you saw, every novel you read, was sex-obsessed; when the accepted way to recover from guilt feelings, if you were unfortunate enough to have them, was to repeat the offense that caused them, until you could accept it as natural; then, then, right at that moment of history, she would have to be torturing herself with notions like adultery. In Arabia, she thought, they would stone me to death.

I was convinced, and I've never let go of my conviction, that you can interest enough serious book readers to make all the money anybody needs by publishing good books. "We'll give them the best

books," Irv Goodman used to say, "that they are willing to take."
We did a better job of doing what we wanted to do after Irv came
to work for us, and an even better job after his friend Charlie Sopkin followed him. Our team stayed together for about seven years
and we did what we had set out to do: we made the Guild a believable competitor to the big club.

It always helps to be lucky, and we had a lot of luck. But our first
big break wasn't luck, it was more support from upstairs. My impatience with the publishing division's scorn of the Guild boiled
over when I tried to buy the Bruce Catton *Army of the Potomac*
trilogy both to sell and to use as a premium offer and got a curt no
for an answer. "What the hell is this?" I demanded, charging into
John Sargent's office. "Are we working for the same company or
aren't we? I've got to put together a list of books that can carry an
ad in the *Times*. The Catton set will help. The company isn't doing
anything with it to speak of. It's just sitting there on the backlist. I
wish you would change this no into a yes." Sargent, Nelson and
John O'Donnell, a cheerfully pragmatic Irishman who was the third
member of the Holy Trinity, did exactly that. I put up a piece of
paper on my bulletin board and began to list the books I thought
had a chance of winning the argument for the new Guild in our
first comeback ads in the *Times*. To *A Shooting Star* and *The Army
of the Potomac* we added *Rembrandt* by Gladys Schmitt, *The Winter of Our Discontent* by John Steinbeck and *Wilderness* by Robert
Penn Warren. More good ones followed quickly: Morris West's
Daughter of Silence; Harrison E. Salisbury's *The Northern Palmyra
Affair*, Hiram Haydn's *The Hands of Esau, Portrait in Brown-
stone* by Louis Auchincloss and a string of ten-strikes that owned
the number-one fiction place on the *Times* best-seller list for months:
*The Shoes of the Fisherman, The Spy Who Came in from the Cold,
Herzog* and *Catch-22*. We were on a roll. John Sargent talked his
friend Charlie Scribner into letting me have *The Stories of F. Scott
Fitzgerald* and that gave us the idea to put together three-volume
sets of the best novels of Fitzgerald, Ernest Hemingway and William Faulkner.

"Have You Looked at the Literary Guild Lately?" was the headline I wrote for our first centerspread ad in the *Times*. Lester Wunderman, whose personal as well as agency contributions supplied a lot of the muscle for our drive for new members, gave us superlative advertising—eye-catching advertising that not only made you look at it but made you feel good about what you were looking at. "These are good books," Lester and I agreed. "The ads have got to have substance. We're not selling cheap bars of soap here. And with the substance, we've got to have style." I never did understand exactly what Marshall McLuhan meant by "the medium is the message," although I could see what he was getting at when he wrote that mesh stockings were sexier than nylons because the eye had to act as a hand in filling in the image, but I knew in my bones that we had to wear the right kind of graphics and speak in the right tone of voice if we were going to attract the kind of people we were after.

We never would have got so far so fast if the Book-of-the-Month Club hadn't behaved like a hibernating bear. It had never occurred to them that the day might come when they wouldn't be able to have any book they wanted, any time they wanted it, just for the asking. If the judges didn't anoint a book as the main selection, they would just wait and see, or, as the phrase was generally used around their august halls, watch and wait—follow the book's progress on the best-seller list before condescending to make a modest offer for it as an alternate. In the better restaurants on the streets and avenues of the East Side, we fought them tooth and nail by persuading publisher after publisher in case after case not to let BOMC get away with their lord-of-the-manor attitude but to sell the book to us and let us give it a chance right now. "Who's looking out for the author?" I would ask over and over again.

That's how we got *The Shoes of the Fisherman*. John T. Lawrence (Sam to his friends), who along with Larry Hughes and Jim Finkenstaedt had bought William Morrow from Thayer Hobson for cash and a promissory note, thought Morris West's new novel had a chance to go all the way. The idea of a dead Pope being replaced by a Russian was intriguing. "Well," I told Sam, "it ain't literature,

but it's a good story and I'll make it a selection. Okay for $35,000?"
I had talked Sargent, Nelson and O'Donnell into letting me raise
the guarantee.

Sam was interested but cautious. "They've made it an A book,"
he said. "If they take it, I've got to sell it to them."

"Sure you do," I agreed, "but they won't take it. So what I want
is your agreement now that if they say no, we get it for the thirty-
five unless they top that right away."

"They won't do that," Sam said. "They never have."

"I know they won't," I said, "so do we have a deal?"

We had a deal, the same one I had struck with Marshall Best on
the Steinbeck novel. The BOMC judges had turned down *The
Winter of Our Discontent*, and they turned down *The Shoes of
the Fisherman*, too. We put both books in the first ads we were allowed to use them in, meaning the weekend following their official
publication date—a date nobody pays any attention to except the
book clubs.

It sounds dreadful, but there is no way to say it except truthfully.
If I was happy about *The Shoes* when we had it safely tucked into
an ad, I was dizzy with good fortune by the time the ad appeared. I
felt like a horseplayer who had just hit the Daily Double. Every day
we reached eagerly for the reports from Garden City on the thousands of orders that *The Shoes* was bringing in because Pope John
XXIII had died the week before the book was published. I'm afraid
that when Sam took Joyce and Morris West and Liby and me to
lunch to celebrate publication day, we spent more time talking about
the incredible sales the book was achieving than we did about the
death of the most popular Pope of our lifetime.

When he thanked Sam for being such a generous host, Morris
told us one of my all-time favorite publishing stories. Remembering it always makes me laugh even though I'm sure it's apocryphal.
"You know," he said, "an English publisher would never dream of
standing his author to a lunch like this just because he was lucky
enough to have his book published. They're not like you, they don't
think much of writers over there. I remember I dropped in at

Charles Pick's offices one day a year or so ago and asked the receptionist if I might see him for a moment. 'May I ask what is your business?' she wanted to know—quite properly, I thought. 'I'm one of his authors,' I said, having already given her my name with no noticeable reaction on her part. 'Oh,' she said, 'I'm sorry, but Mr. Pick never sees authors.' "

The Shoes of the Fisherman was such a hit that the *BOMC News* carried a shameless fib a couple of months after we offered it. "This was one of the rare titles to slip through the Book-of-the-Month Club's elaborate editorial net," it explained righteously to readers who wanted to know why they weren't getting it. "It simply was never offered to our judges." It probably wasn't, but it was not for lack of trying by the publisher. Somebody lower in the club's hierarchy turned it down. I let them use it as an alternate a year later in exchange for our using Truman Capote's *In Cold Blood*, which had been a Main Selection of theirs. It was a straight player trade, no cash involved.

Jack Geoghegan, who like most of the other people in the business had got his start working for Doubleday, took me to lunch and pitched a novel he had picked up cheap in England—*The Spy Who Came In from the Cold*, by John le Carré. "That's not his real name," Jack told me. "His real name is David Cornwell. He has to use a pseudonym because he used to be in British Intelligence. But this is a hell of a book by any name." He gave me a copy of the English edition to take home. I read it that night and called him the next morning. "You've got a deal," I said. "I'll give you $1,500 for it and start it out in the Dollar Book Club. After all, it's a suspense story and it's more Dollar's kind of thing than the new Guild's, but I like it and I'm game to give it a try." I wanted to cut my throat over that one for years because by the time it had taken off like a skyrocket, two years before the Richard Burton movie, we had already used it as a Dollar selection and had to settle for making it an alternate and a premium book in the Guild. But it was one of the books that helped us steadily push the Guild's membership back up over 200,000 in 1963, over 300,000 in 1965 and over 400,000 in 1966.

Another surprise winner, and the one that came to me under the most memorable circumstances, was the novel Joseph Heller delivered to Simon & Schuster for publication in the fall of 1961. Bob Gottlieb, who hadn't yet left S&S (along with Tony Schulte and subsidiary-rights wizard Mildred Marmur) for the quieter precincts of Random House and Knopf, called and asked if he could personally deliver a manuscript for me to read. "I can't send this one by messenger," Bobby said, "it's too hot." Then, when he sat down in front of my desk, he said, in his characteristically restrained style, "This is, quite simply, the greatest piece of fiction I have ever had in my hands. This book is going to make history." He pushed the bulky manuscript across the desk to me and I looked at the title page: "Catch-18," it said, "by Joseph Heller."

"Hey," I said, "do you know Doubleday is publishing a new Leon Uris novel called Mila 18? That's an interesting coincidence."

"No kidding?" Bobby said. He reached for the telephone, got Joe Heller, told him about the Uris book and asked if maybe they shouldn't think about changing the title. "Can it be changed?" he wanted to know and, as he explained it to me later, he found out that not only could it be changed but the change didn't make any difference at all. There was no such thing in Army Regulations, only in Heller's head. "It just has to sound right," Joe told Bobby. So they went over all the possibilities—"It's got to be two numbers," Joe said—and they settled on Catch-22. When S&S sent us more copies of the book for our other readers, that's what the title page said: "Catch-22 by Joseph Heller." A piece of American language, used somewhere every minute of every hour of every day, just missed being Catch-18.

We worked hard to get our hands on good books to throw into the fight against the Book-of-the-Month Club, but we worked just as hard to stay away from bad books. I've often heard people say there's no way to guess the best-seller list, but that's nonsense. Anybody in the business can guess two thirds of the best-seller list months before the books are published. You don't have to have any brains to know that books by the likes of Jacqueline Susann, Harold

Robbins, Jackie Collins, Irving Wallace, Judith Krantz and Robin Cook are going to sell; what you have to do, if you're trying to run a good publishing house or a good book club, is stay away from them.

I've never understood why it should be necessary for a serious publishing enterprise to increase its sales and profits by 10 or 15 percent a year. Harvard MBAs don't know everything; I'm not sure they know anything. But I am sure that if you make money every year selling good books to people who care about them, you shouldn't be held accountable for becoming bigger every year, you should be held accountable for becoming better. Doubleday gave me a chance to do that in the beginning, but, except for Sargent, the top men lost enthusiasm for it. Nelson wanted to be the biggest and, except for the beginning of our war against the BOMC, his idea of what constituted the best hardly ever agreed with mine. O'Donnell's job was to feed the presses and, being an amiable Irishman, which is probably redundant, he was reasonably tolerant of most editorial foolishness except where it threatened to hurt the profits of the manufacturing division. After all, they were a sure thing. Profits from the books were risky at best. But we always got along well—he even held still for my insistence on changing the bindings of the Guild books from plastic to cloth—so it was surprising even to me when I finally had a crunching battle with Nelson and him over the physical appearance of Doubleday trade books.

It was a weekend that is easy to remember because it was the weekend Bobby Kennedy was shot. We had flown to San Francisco to open a new Doubleday bookstore. It was the first stop before Los Angeles on our way to El Paso to visit KROD-TV, which Doubleday had just bought along with half a dozen other radio and television stations. Because the weekend would end on June 6, our twenty-sixth wedding anniversary, I talked Sargent into letting Liby come with us on condition that she would fly home the day before we left San Francisco for El Paso. It would have been a memorable weekend anyway, because Liby was late for lunch after watching Bobby's motorcade through Chinatown and picking up a Bobby campaign flier done in Chinese calligraphy. "I was scared to death," she told us and our host, Herb Caen. "There was a loud sound like a shot and Rosie Grier dived at Bobby from one side and Ethel dived at him from the other side and we all thought it was a shot. I'm sure Bobby did, too. But it was only a firecracker."

Gene McCarthy, whose victory over Lyndon Johnson in the New Hampshire primary had encouraged Bobby to get into the race, was to debate him on national television that night. We saw Jimmy Breslin at the bar in the Fairmont and asked him if he wanted to come upstairs with us and watch the debate on the tube. "Nah," Jimmy said, "I've heard everything they've got to say." We went up and watched the debate and rooted for Gene, who had made our kids as well as a lot of other people's kids Clean for Gene, and decided regretfully that Bobby had won. In the morning, before Liby left for the airport, we watched Bobby and Ethel show the bellhops how they wanted their station wagon loaded for the drive to Los Angeles. Then I got a cab to take Liby and me to her plane, and a few hours later the Doubleday gang got into a limo for the airport and into a plane for L.A. "I hope you've got a radio," Sargent said to me on the plane. "We ought to listen to the primary tonight."

We did listen, in the Polo Lounge at the Beverly Hills Hotel, and we turned up the volume a little when Eunice Shriver, who was sitting a few tables away from us, asked us to. She asked us just before the announcer's voice changed from a happy recital of Bobby's victory margin to the hysterical report of his shooting. Eunice was gone out the door before we could say anything. Anyway, there wasn't anything to say except what Sargent said. "Let's go somewhere and have a drink."

We went to Chasen's and had more than one drink. The radio told us Bobby was still alive and that was about all it told us. So we began to talk about books and I said I thought it was time we began to spend some money to make Doubleday books look a little better. Nelson didn't say anything, but O'Donnell did. "Wait a minute," he stopped me. "I don't mind spending money on books, but you're always saying we ought to spend it on what goes into the books. I don't get this about making them look better. I think they look pretty good now."

"They look terrible," I said with the evangelistic fervor of the dedicated. "The bindings are terrible, the dust jackets are terrible, the paper is sawdust and the rubber-plate printing is like what comes out of the boxes kids get for Christmas."

O'Donnell opened round two. "Okay," he said, "if our books are so terrible, whose are the best? I mean, give me a comparison."

I was patronizing to the unlettered. "That's easy," I said. "Everybody knows the best are Knopf's. There are other publishers who make good-looking books and use good materials, but Knopf consistently makes the best. They care more about how their books look than anybody else does. Even if Alfred Knopf thinks the book won't sell more than a couple of thousand copies, he still makes it look like a million dollars."

"Well," O'Donnell said, waving to the waiter for another drink, "that does it. I think Doubleday's books are the best-looking and Knopf's are the worst."

I didn't even say good night. I got up and left. I could hardly go off in the limo that had brought us, so I walked three or four blocks until I found a cab and went back to the Beverly Hills. Back, in fact, to the Polo Lounge, where the half a dozen people still up were talking about the shooting of Bobby Kennedy. I sat alone at the bar and had two brandies and wondered how much longer I could stand this.

Not much longer, it turned out. When I walked out of Chasen's that night, I was a senior vice-president of Doubleday in charge of the book clubs, the trade publishing division, and the bookshops. In the eight years I'd been there, I'd had little to complain about. Nobody had ever told me I had to use a bad book, even a Doubleday bad book, and nobody had complained about my using a book that was so good that everybody, including me, knew it wouldn't sell. I was allowed to take chances, from *Malcolm X* to Dag Hammar-

skjold's *Markings* to Ralph Nader's *Unsafe at Any Speed* to Chaim
Potok's *The Chosen* to Tom Wolfe's *The Electric Kool-Aid Acid
Test*.

It was Irv Goodman's father who put the seal on our buying *The
Chosen*. Irv, Charlie and I all loved it, but were in varying degrees
worried about how it would sell. I was the most nervous. "You've
got to be very literary and very Jewish to want to read it," I said.
Irv's father heard us arguing about it at a dinner party, and he heard
me say for the nineteenth time that nobody would buy it except
Jews who cared about serious books. "There are," he said gently,
"a lot of them."

I was also allowed to spend serious money for books I thought
we had to have. We broke the almost-half-century-old book-club
peace by bidding out of sight for Theodore H. White's *The Making
of the President 1964*. I'd bitten my nails over the success of Teddy's
first *Making of the President* book, the account of the Kennedy–
Nixon campaign, and I wanted this one badly. At first Harry Scherman fought back, topping each of our bids almost contemptuously,
as though everybody knew how it would all turn out, so why was
everybody making such a fuss about it? But I wanted the book, I
thought the Guild had to have it and I got it when Mr. Scherman
abruptly stopped bidding. There has never been any question in my
mind that Teddy would rather have had the Book-of-the-Month
Club, but he wanted the money more, so we got it. Harry Scherman
thought the numbers had become ridiculous and he wouldn't go any
higher. I think that was the first of the now commonplace telephone
auctions between the two book clubs; we had joined the paperback
houses in turning money into confetti. But it was the only way I
knew to break BOMC's stranglehold on the best books, and Sargent,
Nelson and O'Donnell went along. In 1960 and 1961 we had said we
were going to become an equal competitor of the Book-of-the-
Month Club; now we were asserting that in fact we were.

There had been other steps. Wolfgang Foges, who ran Aldus
Books for Doubleday in London, arranged a meeting for me with
C. P. Snow in 1961. I wanted a Snow book on our list and I had an
idea I thought he might respond to, especially because he was now

a Minister of Technology in Her Majesty's government and presumably wasn't making much money. I was interested in a book on men whose lives and ideas had made a profound impact on the world, whether for better or worse. Even Hitler, I thought, could be considered. The man's influence didn't have to be benign. Hitler didn't make it because Snow hadn't known him, but nine interesting men did, including Robert Frost and Joseph Stalin, Winston Churchill and Albert Einstein.

Wolf Foges had left my name with Snow's secretary, so when I called his office in the English Electric Company, of which he was a director, she was ready to make an appointment and I saw him that afternoon. I should say we saw him because Liby went with me and her presence made it easier for us to have the kind of informal conversation I had hoped for. It became clear right away that Wolf had briefed Sir Charles—he hadn't become Lord Snow yet—as well as his secretary, and that Snow had had enough time to think over the idea and was generally in favor of it. "I'm not earning much these days, you know," he said in what I always thought, over the years I knew him, was a curiously un-British speech. There was an occasional "you see?" in his speech, but that's more French than English, and I never heard him commit a "don't you know?" He did break us up twice at that first meeting. The first time was early on when I said he might like us to pay the money we would advance against royalties—$50,000 U.S., I suggested—to his son, Philip, rather than to him. "No, no," he said cheerfully. "I did that with my last book with Scribner's. I rather think I'll keep this one for myself." Except to agree to the whole of my proposal, he never discussed the terms. The second surprise came at the end of our stay when he was helping Liby on with her coat. "He's quite an operator, your husband," Snow said to her. We had a happy cab ride back to the Connaught, which had been commended to us by Naomi Burton and praised lavishly by John Sargent. "It's a very chic hotel," Mr. Sargent said, "and when you leave, they will give you a very chic bill."

Snow's book was delivered on time and did everything we had hoped it would. It was, most of all, one more solid stone in the foundation of respectability we were building underneath our club. It looked good in the ads and it helped make our claims believable. It also gave me a particular friendship I treasured. So did Liby, who wasn't always crazy about book people. She said they intimidated her. Snow, who was made a life peer by Queen Elizabeth soon after we published his book, and who by any standard was one of the massive intellects of the Western world, didn't intimidate her. Whenever we had a meal with him alone, or with him and his Lady, Pamela Hansford Johnson, Liby took an easy and animated part in the table conversation.

We had a steady stream of letters from him over the years and they were always a joy to read. They were worth a great deal more than a nickel an inch. "Please don't worry about the major magazines," he wrote when I told him I wasn't having any luck trying to sell pieces of his book, which he called *Variety of Men*, to the likes of the *Saturday Evening Post, Life, Look* or the *Reader's Digest*. "Do they expect me to write about the Beatles? In fact, the sales to *Atlantic* and *Commentary* are being settled, and John Cushman is screwing rather more money out of them than he usually does."

Another time he offered the conviction that his readership, "contrary to all impressions, is based on intelligent wives in various parts of America."

"When are you two coming to London?" he wanted to know in one letter. "I want to give you a meal in the House of Lords—dim food, excellent wine." With our friends Dorothy and Donald Nyland we got not only the meal and the wine but even a visit to the House galleries with a few graceful speeches thrown in. Then, when I had caused the Book-of-the-Month Club to reprint in three hefty volumes his eleven-novel masterwork, *Strangers and Brothers*, he wrote a touching thank-you letter. "I heard the news from Charlie Scribner yesterday," he wrote. "I know that this is entirely due to you, and I want to say that I'm deeply grateful. To have a definitive edition in print on this kind of scale is a piece of fortune which doesn't happen to many writers. This is all your doing. After I have given the Einstein lecture in Washington on 8th December [1978], I propose to come to New York to spend a few days seeing the people I want to see and no one else. I do hope you will be free. Much love to you and Liby."

My favorite was the letter he wrote me soon after he had become Lord Snow. "My friends," he said, "call me Charles. I hope you will."

Another landmark book for us, not a total surprise but more successful than we had hoped, was *We Seven*, the book put together by editor John Dille from the *Life* articles on the seven original astronauts. We got it from Simon & Schuster for a modest price and got a lot of mileage out of it.

The year Goodman, Sopkin and I knew for sure we had made it was 1966 when our thirteen selections included books by John Fowles, Graham Greene, Dan Jacobson, John Hersey, Gwyn Griffin, Roderick Thorp, Zoe Oldenbourg, Edward Crankshaw, John Knowles, Bernard Malamud, Edwin O'Connor and the first of four projected volumes of *Winston Churchill* by the great man's son, Randolph.

I also knew we had made it when Orville Prescott, the erudite and, I thought, somewhat pompous book critic of the *Times*, asked me at a cocktail party if it was true that the Guild was going to use Oldenbourg's *The Crusades*. When I said it was indeed true, the little sparrow of a man with so much power over the fate of a book shook his head. "I was surprised," he said, "that's a *good* book."

The Churchill book was introduced at a splendid party thrown by its publisher, Houghton Mifflin. The Goodmans and the Fitzgeralds were invited and, in fact, were invited not only to the cocktail party for 150 or so of the press and assorted literati but even to a small dinner party afterward for the author and a handful of his and the publisher's friends. Bobby Kennedy was there with Arthur Schlesinger, Jr., and John Kenneth Galbraith; everybody who was anybody was there. Toward the last minutes of the cocktail party we were tipped off that soon it would be time to go in to dinner and were shown the door through which we should go. Liby and Roz Goodman decided they would go to the ladies' room first and disappeared. Just as they did, Jackie Kennedy came in, electrifying the room. Irv and I hoped our women would come back before

Jackie left; people were leaving quickly now. Bobby shook hands with Randolph Churchill and said to Schlesinger, "We'd better go, Arthur." Jackie, who had been sitting next to Randolph, got up, too, and my heart skipped a couple of beats. I wanted Liby to see her, and now she was leaving and Liby and Roz were still nowhere in sight. But just as they reappeared, Jackie took the arm of Houghton Mifflin's Harold Miller and walked gracefully into the small dining room where we were to eat dinner. The four of us walked in happily behind them.

The luck of the draw put both Liby and Roz at Churchill's end of the table. Jackie was at his right. Nobody could have asked for more and I'm sure the four peasants from the Literary Guild, startled to find themselves in such exalted company, didn't even notice what they were eating. I know that when we had made our good nights to the guest of honor, our host and our fellow diners, including Mrs. Kennedy, and found ourselves on the sidewalk outside the hotel, Roz Goodman said to Liby, "Don't call me tomorrow, I'll be on the phone all day."

Chapter 11

L IFE at Doubleday in the 1960s was made exciting and often downright hair-raising by the pursuit or at least investigation of four bold possibilities to add important new businesses to the company's profitable book operations in the United States and Canada. Three of them failed to come off; the fourth made it.

The three acquisitions that didn't happen were the Curtis Publishing Company, a deal which we rejected; the Dell Publishing Company, which I was interested in but nobody else was and so was never seriously pursued by us; and *Newsweek*, which we wanted very much and went after fiercely. The one that did happen was the launching of an American-style simultaneous book club on the green but hostile islands of Great Britain. That one is alive and flourishing today.

The *Newsweek* opportunity hit us first. Nelson was friendly with Malcolm Muir, Jr., who with his father ran the editorial side of the magazine. Gibson McCabe ran the business side. The magazine's principal owners were Vincent Astor, of the Astor Foundation, and Averell Harriman, who owned about a third of it. After Captain Astor died in 1959, rumors about the Foundation wanting to sell the magazine hit the street every week. Osborn Elliott, the managing editor, and Gib McCabe knew it was going to be sold eventually

and wanted to see it go where they wanted it to go. Their choice
was the Washington *Post*. Ozzie Elliott liked Phil Graham, president of the *Post*, a power in Washington and the son-in-law of
Eugene Meyer, who loved Phil almost as much as he did his daughter, Katharine, and who had already paid some $9 million to buy
the Washington *Times-Herald* so Phil could kill it and take on the
Washington *Star* in a knockdown fight for the championship of the
city. Why wouldn't Meyer buy *Newsweek* for Phil?

He would, and he did. But Nelson and his company were the
choice of the Muirs, who wanted to pick the new owner just as badly
as Ozzie and McCabe did. Each contender was given a chance to
make a final bid. We had a meeting and decided the magazine was
worth $14.5 million and Nelson sent in the bid. Some publishing
historians insist that the Doubleday bid and the *Post* bid were pretty
much the same and that the Astor Foundation felt it simply had to
pick the best home for the magazine and the people who worked on
it. Nelson was so sure we had it that he invited Douglas Black, Sargent, O'Donnell and me to a celebration lunch. But at something
like half past eleven in the morning he got us together and said Mac
Muir had just called to tell him *Newsweek* had been sold to Phil
Graham and the Washington *Post*. I remember him telling us, "It
was Joe Kennedy who did it. He called up Eugene Meyer and reminded him that if *Newsweek* went to Doubleday, both of the
country's news magazines would be owned by Republicans and that
would be terrible. He said if money was a problem, he would help.
'But you've got to get it,' he told Meyer. 'You can't let it get away.' "

Coming from the father of the newly elected President, that was
powerful stuff. Phil Graham had already charmed Brooke Astor,
Vincent's widow, and had persuaded friends to work on Averell
Harriman, and when he sent in his bid he was sure of two things—
that the money he was offering on behalf of his father-in-law was
an acceptable figure, and that if it came down to simply choosing
the more desirable buyer, the *Post* would beat out Doubleday. He
was right. We went out to lunch that day anyway and we drank
some martinis, but not to celebrate. We had really wanted it and we
had lost it.

166

I had been invited to join the inner circle in the *Newsweek* discussions because I was the only one who knew anything about the magazine business and there were all kinds of details about circulation, particularly subscription liability, and about such arcane advertising matters as cost per thousand and the desirable balance between editorial and advertising content, that they needed help on. I hadn't gone to the Harvard Business School, but I had gone to the Irving Manheimer College of Publishing Knowledge. I was able to help out.

I was called in again when Doug Black's friend Admiral Lewis Strauss, the former chairman of the Atomic Energy Commission and a big man on Wall Street, told Doug he ought to look into the Curtis Publishing Company. Everybody who read the newspapers knew that Curtis was in bad trouble, mostly because its flagship publication, the *Saturday Evening Post*, was losing readers and advertisers faster than the accountants could keep track.

"How can a magazine that still has a circulation of over five million a week lose money?" Nelson wanted to know, reasonably.

"Because it costs more money to put it out than they sell it for," I said, "and they have to sell a lot of advertising to make up the difference. Once the advertising begins to fall off, the way it has on the *Post*, the more copies you print, the more money you lose."

"Why don't they print fewer, then?"

"Because they've already got all those subscriptions signed up," I said. "They've probably spent the money already, but they still have to fulfill the subscriptions. Their newsstand sales, which mean fresh money and cost a lot less than the subs, are way down, just like almost everybody else's since television. What they ought to do is begin to cut down on new subscriptions, save that money, let the magazine drop to its natural level, to the size the people who really want it make it, and then sell the circulation for what it's worth. A lot more pages at less money per page, with a big reduction in manufacturing costs, might turn it around."

"Should we look at it?" Nelson wanted to know.

We all thought we should look at it, provided Admiral Strauss and his friend Milton Gould, a member of the Curtis board of directors, would guarantee that we could look at everything. Gould told Black that could be arranged, which was why we all met for lunch at the St. Regis on a Saturday afternoon early in 1962 on our way to La Guardia to fly to Philadelphia in the Doubleday plane. No fancy airplane for Doubleday in those days; it was a twin-engine Beechcraft Bonanza. But their own. "What it is," Sargent explained, "is that the airplane takes off when you get there."

I was impressed. But I was less impressed when our pleasant lunch at the St. Regis was over and the captain presented the bill. "Does anybody have a charge account here?" Doug Black asked. Nobody had.

"Well," Sargent said in his amiably authoritative voice, "then we'll just give you a credit card. American Express?" He reached into his pocket.

"No credit cards," the captain said. "I'm sorry, sir. We do not accept credit cards."

"Oh," the unflappable Sargent said. "Why don't I just sign the bill and you can send it to the office?"

"I'm sorry, sir," the captain said. "We require payment in cash. A personal check would do." He looked happy, as though he had solved the whole problem. But nobody had a personal check with him.

It was my first lesson in life with the really rich. They don't carry money and they don't carry checks and they don't worry. I was a poor boy and I worried. "Let me see the check," I said to Sargent. (I hadn't learned yet that in Anglophile publishing circles it is never a check, it is always a bill.) I looked at the numbers, calculated the tip at 20 percent and saw that I could handle it. I gave four $20 bills to the captain—don't forget, this was 1962—and we all got up and left.

When we got to Philadelphia, we set out for the marble palace that was the Curtis Publishing Company. We were ushered promptly to the office of the president, Robert MacNeal—the successor, Admiral Strauss had explained to Doug, to George Horace Lorimer and Walter Deane Fuller. "It's no wonder," I said irreverently to Sargent, "that he's having trouble. He hasn't got three names." We dutifully walked around the offices and adjourned to the Downtown Club next door for lunch, another palace in which generations of *Post* executives and editors had eaten and drunk at the company's expense. MacNeal made it clear right away that he was interested in our interest. "I think Curtis and Doubleday would make a great combination," he said. "Just tell me what I can do to help."

Douglas Black took over. "What we'd like," he said, "is two things. If you will put John O'Donnell here together with your financial man and let John take home the numbers he's interested in, what we would like is to leave Ed here for most or all of next week."

That was interesting; nobody had told me, and I hadn't told Liby, and the only clothes I had with me were changes of underwear and shirts. No matter, I decided. First things first. I could call Liby and tell her, and I could buy some clothes. Wasn't there a place in Philadelphia called Strawbridge & Clothier?

My week was both exciting and frustrating. The more I saw—and nobody stopped me from going wherever I wanted to go—the less I thought of what I was seeing. Not only Irving Manheimer, who hated to spend a dollar, but *Time*'s Jim Linen, who didn't mind spending money but wanted to know what the company was going to get for it, would have sent for the cops. I was shocked at the kind of money the *Post* editors spent for ideas that never came off, for finished pieces that were never published and for pieces that were published that never should have been.

Even before I went back to New York, I found myself befriended by the contenders for editorial power. Bob Fuoss, who had succeeded Ben Hibbs, had been succeeded by Bob Sherrod, a Time-Life graduate, and now Sherrod was under frontal and flank assault by Clay Blair, who couldn't wait to take me in as part of taking over. He gave me a copy of a long memorandum he had written for Joe Culligan, who according to Barney Gallagher, the newsletter rascal, was the most likely candidate to succeed MacNeal. The memo was Clay's battle plan for a new Curtis Publishing Company. He wanted to get rid of the Sharon Hill printing plant of which MacNeal was so proud and in which the company had in-vested more than $30 million; he wanted to kill the *Ladies' Home Journal* and *American Home*, both of which had been losing money for years; he wanted to sell the Curtis Circulation Company. He would rather have become the president, but he would settle for becoming the editorial director or general manager or both. He also gave copies of his memorandum to Douglas Black, Admiral Strauss and Milton Gould. There was nothing halfway about Clay Blair.

My major contribution was to tell MacNeal that the editorial offices of the *Post* ought to be moved to New York. "It's not only a real problem having them here," I said, "it's also an advertisement for what's wrong. The editors sit here and work Philadelphia hours and go home at four thirty to their fancy houses on the Main Line and expect that everybody in the world will come to them. That's the way it used to be, but that isn't the way it is now. There's too much competition. They should be in New York riding the subway and fighting for taxis and taking out authors and agents and digging up stories with their bare hands."

MacNeal picked up the telephone and told his secretary to ask Bob Sherrod to come up. "Ed thinks we should move the editorial offices to New York," MacNeal said. "What do you think?"

"I think he's right," Sherrod said. "No question about it. People won't come here anymore the way they used to. We'd better go where they are."

"How soon can you move?" MacNeal asked him.

It seemed to me clear that Sherrod had been thinking about this on his own. He didn't hesitate. "A few months," he said. "Maybe July, maybe August. It will cost some money, but it will be worth it." He turned away from MacNeal and looked at me. "Thanks," he said.

"I just moved the *Saturday Evening Post*," I told Liby when I called her up before dinner that night.

But that was our biggest impact on the *Post*. When we all got together back at 575 Madison Avenue and O'Donnell gave me the money I had spent on our lunch at the St. Regis, we agreed it was not for us.

I was a lot more interested in Dell because I thought the company ought to own a paperback house. "Why?" Sargent wanted to know when we talked about it one weekend at the country house he and Neltje had in Tannersville, New York, in the shadow of Hunter Mountain. "We already have the book clubs as a hedge against the trade publishing business."

"We need it," I said, "because the trade business depends on the fifty-fifty split of sub rights, and the split isn't going to last. It's being broken down already, book by book, house by house."

"Not by us," John said emphatically.

"I know," I agreed, "but it will be. It's inevitable. Right now we buy off the Wouks and the Urises and the Haileys and the Stones by giving them secretaries and paying for their offices and their airplane tickets and their hotels and God knows what. But sooner or later they're going to insist on getting more than half the sub rights. What makes us think, anyway, that we're entitled to fifty cents of every dollar they make from somebody else?"

"Because that's the way it is," John said. "It can't be any other way. If we let go of the fifty-fifty split, we'd go broke. How else would we make up for all the books that don't make a dime? We'd go to the poorhouse."

My daughter, Eileen, saved the day. "Mr. Sargent," she said with the innocent candor of a thirteen-year-old, "I don't understand that. How could you go to the poorhouse? Daddy says he's never met a poor publisher."

But we didn't buy Dell, which we could have had for a lot less money than Doubleday paid for it ten years later. George Delacorte and Helen Meyer were ready and willing to talk about it, but we never asked them.

The English book-club effort went better, outside the company if not inside it. Enthusiasm for it was, in the beginning, somewhat muted, probably because it was Milton Runyon's idea and Nelson thought any idea Milton advanced had to be bad. Nelson thought Milton was too old-fashioned, too conservative, and wished he would retire. But I was all for it and Sargent diplomatically allowed the project to get off the ground. John was at heart an international-

ist and could see important benefits in a major Doubleday presence
in the U.K. Milton had already exported minor book-club activity
to Australia, with mixed results, and had a going business, although
a small one, in France—a partnership with one M. Maurice Dumon-
cel. Now he wanted to go for the big one. I think that Sargent, a
world-class manipulator of events, managed to persuade Nelson that
among the benefits of a successful Literary Guild launch in England
would be the need for Milton to run it.

Milton and I made the first invasion of England in 1964. We saw
twenty-three British publishers in three days and got twenty-one
Savile Row cold shoulders. Most of them were polite, and some
were even friendly. Only a handful, like Sir Stanley Unwin, were
forthrightly hostile. "But we don't do things like that here, you
know," he told us as he walked us out to our car.

Even the fierce Captain Robert Maxwell, the baron of the Perga-
mon Press, who introduced Milton to his lieutenants as "the doyen
of the book-club business," predicted that his near neighbor Ronald
Barker, secretary of the Publishers Association, would throw us out
the door. "You don't understand the depth of antagonism these
people feel about anything foreign," he said. "I do. And you will
find out."

But we did pick up two allies, both of them powerful and respected. They were Charles Pick, co-managing director with Dwye
Evans of William Heinemann & Co., perhaps the closest thing to
Doubleday among the major English houses (and not surprisingly,
because in the 1920s Frank Nelson Doubleday, Nelson's grandfather, had bought a controlling interest in the company and later
sold it), and Ian Chapman, managing director of William Collins
and Billy Collins' trusted right-hand man. Both of them were in the
mainstream of British publishing activity but far out of the mainstream of British publishing thinking. They thought like Americans.
They didn't think everything had to be done the way it had been
done a hundred years ago, and they thought the times were right
for the establishment in the U.K. of a simultaneous book club—
meaning a club that would issue books to its members at the same
time they were published and sold in the stores.

That was a revolutionary concept for England. There were several book clubs there, the largest of them being World Books, which was somewhat analogous to the Dollar Book Club in that it offered books about a year after publication. It was owned, in an inimitably English fashion, by five trade publishers, including Heinemann and Collins, each of which had the right to pre-empt two selections a year. The other two could, if the board chose, go to other publishers. Cozy, we thought; in the United States of America, you could go to jail for that. But in England, we learned quickly, such joint endeavors are not only legal, they are the order of the day. Fostering these activities, we came to feel, was the real reason the English gentlemen's club was invented.

We made another trip the next year, but got no further except for one significant development. Charles Pick, who had begun by favoring a strictly fifty-fifty partnership between Heinemann and Doubleday and had then progressed to the point of looking favorably upon a three-way partnership including Collins, showed the entrepreneurial spirit that had earned him the nickname "Pick the Pincher" because of his cheerful willingness to take an author away from another publisher. "I think what you need," he said, "is a British partner who can tell the Publishers Association where to get off. I think you ought to talk to Peter Bennett of Smith's."

It turned out to be an inspired suggestion. To a man, the other English publishers had argued that what we wanted to do—establish a book club that would operate the way the Book-of-the-Month Club and the Literary Guild did in the U.S., offering new books the same month they were published—would enrage the bookstore people on whom the trade depended for its sales. No matter how forcefully we argued that experience had proved exactly the opposite back home, where book-club use had increased bookstore sales, we got nowhere. "The bookstores will never stand for it," we were told. Ronald Barker, who had great influence in the PA, of which he was the principal paid employee, was especially vehement on the subject. Pick and Chapman were important figures in the business, but it was as if everybody expected *them* to behave unconventionally, so what else was new? Captain Maxwell thought all the English publishers were Colonel Blimps, but his real interest in the book-club possibility was in owning it himself. The captain did not take either prisoners or partners. When he did take a partner years later, he regretted it bitterly.

Pick—with some help from Wolf Foges, who knew everybody—arranged a meeting with Bennett. Peter had been the youngest brigadier general in the Canadian Army during the war, had met a beautiful war widow, Ann Smith, in London and married her. Ann's father, David Smith, belonged to the Smith family that controlled W. H. Smith & Sons Ltd., distributors of national newspapers and owners of bookstores. In fact, some hundreds of bookstores. Peter liked our idea and sold it to his father-in-law and we were in business. It was going to be hard for Ronald Barker to argue that the British bookstores would never put up with us when half of us was a company that owned half the bookstores in the country, most of them on the High Streets of the United Kingdom's cities, towns and villages.

If you ever wonder how the British have managed to survive so long, consider their skill at politics, which I think may not be so much the art of the possible, as American politicians are always saying, as the art of persuading other people to do what you want them to do, which is what the English are surpassingly good at.

The first action of the partnership, which took the name Book Club Associates, was to buy World Books and the Reprint Society from Heinemann, Collins, Jonathan Cape, Michael Joseph and Macmillan. Charles Pick and Ian Chapman still hoped to become advantageously involved in our schemes, so they helped persuade the others to throw in their shares and take the excellent price we offered. With the clubs we bought a small warehouse and fulfillment operation in Aldershot, the home of England's biggest military-training base.

Milton took a flat on Park Lane and set about multiplying the clubs' membership and sales. In five months, although by English standards he had spent a fortune in advertising and a lot more giving away expensive premiums to new members, he had kept his losses to an insignificant £2,500. He got little credit for this back home, where they were more likely to grumble that he had spent £100 for an original print for the living room of his flat, but a lot of credit in London where they were astounded by his energy, his determination and his willingness to do the work of copywriters, layout men and whole advertising agencies. His lively ads brought in the members he wanted and his determined efforts to improve the quality of the books they were offered kept them happy and made them profitable.

Everybody was ready to move on to the main event. We left the talking to Peter and the other Smith's people, who pressed Book Club Associates's ambitions by dressing them casually in the language of what would be best for the English book business as a whole. Every now and then, in somebody's office, at lunch in the Smith's board room, in the lobby of a West End theater over drinks between the acts or during a late-night supper at the Savoy, they would make a convert. Finally, enough people were at least nominally on our side to press the PA executive board to put on the agenda our request for a change in the rules to allow the operation of a simultaneous book club. We felt we had much to celebrate when it was agreed that the motion would be heard at the meeting of September 21, 1967.

Our only disappointment was that Milton had been suffering from a variety of ailments—a residue of phlebitis and now a gallbladder infection—and probably wouldn't be able to make the meeting. But the script was played out faithfully. When Milton knew for sure he couldn't be at the meeting, he had time to tell me to fly over on the twentieth. "At least," he said, "it will give you an excuse to leave the meeting at the Brook Club early on the evening of the nineteenth." What he meant was that I had told him there was going to be a meeting of Doubleday's executive committee at the discreet club on East 54th Street, which, unfortunately for some of us non-family members, tended at a Doubleday meeting to become anything but discreet after midnight. That's when everybody was in peril of being fired by Nelson for insubordination or even just plain disagreement, and Milton knew I would be happy to leave. Pan Am flew me to London in the morning and the historic change we wanted was put into effect.

John Attenborough of Hodder & Stoughton was the chairman of the PA and he spoke mildly in behalf of the motion, pointing out that the simultaneous clubs had helped sell more books in the United States and that the desire of Book Club Associates, the Smith-Doubleday partnership company, to launch such a club in the U.K. deserved a chance. Representatives of Michael Joseph, Hamish Hamilton, Jonathan Cape and Macmillan also spoke for the measure. There was no outright opposition, only some sniping in the form of several amendments aimed at requiring the clubs to manufacture editions markedly different in appearance from the publishers' editions. "So people will know they're not getting the real thing," was the general theme. In the end we settled for a BCA colophon to be printed on the spine of every jacket and every binding. The vote was taken and the motion was passed. Peter didn't say anything. He just sat there with his several hundred bookshops in his High Street pockets.

Peter took me to lunch at one of the West End hotels where they know how to make a proper martini and we celebrated a major milestone for both our companies.

It has always pleased Sargent and me that, although Smith's appeared to American eyes to be almost a para-military organization, with uniformed doormen and guards saluting the senior officers every time they walked in or out the door, the men who ran the company liked to eat and drink well. That's as British as saluting. But it was always a welcome sight to see the side table in their board room, which, with its slanted, lead-lined windows and heavy wooden beams, looked much as an American might imagine Lord Nelson's cabin on HMS *Victory*. It was generously lined with bottles of gin and vodka as well as whiskey. And always in the center of the dining room there was a gleaming crystal decanter decorated with strips of silver and filled with the richly dark port that is so dear to the Englishman's heart. It might, depending on the season of the year, be a trifle chilly for an American's taste, but there was no lack of warming stimulants.

I had a direct lesson in the similarities between our side and theirs when the Hon. David Smith himself paid us the honor of a visit in the spring of 1968, a few months before the official launch date for the Literary Guild in London. I was elected to give him the grand tour of Doubleday's Garden City fulfillment operation. Whether he really wanted to see it or Milton had suggested it and he had agreed out of politeness, I had no idea. At least, I thought, even though nobody would salute us as we walked in, the building itself did look suitably collegiate in its brick-and-ivy handsomeness, and the beautifully paneled office of Nelson's grandfather was at least the equal of David's office in Strand House. (The chairman was the only one of the officers who had a private office in Smith's executive suite; the three other managing directors, Peter, Dick Troughton, and Bill Rowe, all made do with desks in a common room outside David's sanctum.)

We managed the tour in about an hour. When I noticed David looking swiftly at his watch as we rounded a corner in the hall, I suggested that, unless there was something more he particularly wanted to see, we might head back to the city. He agreed instantly, and at a few minutes after noon we were settled comfortably in the Brussels restaurant just a few doors east of the Brook Club. Unsure what was the right thing to do, I asked if he would like a drink. I hardly had got the words out before he said cheerfully, "Yes, I would indeed. A dry martini, I think, straight up." I relaxed, and I was even more relaxed an hour and a half later when we were on our third martini. David graciously accepted my invitation to choose a wine from the Brussels' extensive cellar and altogether it was a pleasant lunch. The Hon. David was positively American in his willingness to discuss candidly the problems as well as the opportunities that confronted us in our brave new venture. "It won't be easy," he said thoughtfully, "Englishmen don't like change."

First Douglas Black, then John Sargent and now David Smith. John was right when he ignored my complaint about being dragged off to a luncheon at McGraw-Hill the first day we were back in the office after two weeks in London and Paris. "Not me," I told him. "You go. I'm having a Coke and a tunafish on rye right here. I don't even want to look at another drink." But John was firm. "Come on," he said, "you've got to go. Curtis Benjamin is leaving for London tonight and he wants to talk to us first about what we're doing over there." That's when he strengthened my resolve with his matchless directive. "Fitz," he said, "let's face it. It's a drinking business. Drink or get out." I went to lunch.

The only time I can ever remember the drinking habits of either company becoming a problem in our Anglo-American partnership was when Simon Hornby, then a young man being groomed for big things and now the chairman of Smith's, visited Garden City. Not only because he was tall, but because of his haughty outlook on the world and especially the colonies, Simon was to us the personification of the British Raj and we were the Indians. When you were with Simon, there was never any question about who belonged to which class. The worst moment of his inspection—calling it a visit would be a misnomer—of the Garden City plant came when he told Ed Stoddard, our advertising manager, who had been unlucky enough to draw him as a partner on the walk to lunch, that he was unalterably opposed to drinking at lunch and was sure that "eventually the Smith-Doubleday company will enforce a no-drinking rule."

When Simon disappeared into the facilities at the restaurant, Ed, shocked, reported the exchange to me. "My God," he said, "what are you going to do?" Ed was wetting his lips nervously the way somebody does when a drink that was there a moment ago is snatched away without warning.

"It was," I told Sargent solemnly, "clearly a crisis. It would be either my finest hour or my most disastrous. But I decided I really had no choice, and, in the best Sargent tradition, I instructed the waiter to take drink orders from everyone and I told him, in a clear voice, that I would have a Beefeater Gibson on the rocks, very dry. There was, after all, nothing else I could do. Doubleday's honor was at stake. I did what I had to do."

John approved. "Anyway," he consoled me, "that ain't no ginger ale they give you before lunch in that fancy board room of theirs."

Whenever I think of the Doubleday years, I think of John. He never fired anybody after midnight and, indeed, could conduct a dinner meeting with all of its before and after drinks as imperturbably and as profitably as he could one at nine o'clock in the morning when only the supply of ice water was being depleted. Nobody could have asked for a more sharing friend in or out of business, and to work with him in the pursuit of the company's profit and our own publishing ideals was a joy. It didn't hurt any that Liby thought so, too. Being with him made a lot of business trips and elegant dinners much more enjoyable for both of us than they would have been without him.

John is so much bigger than I am that he could outdrink me any time he felt like it, and eating was no contest at all. He had been born with the kind of confidence that made him certain no airplane would think of leaving without him or club refuse him membership or attractive woman deny him her company—a confidence that was foreign to me. But we got along together so well that we didn't have to think about each other's reactions, we could anticipate them. I learned a lot from John, including a few modest lessons in assertion. When he saw a stewardess hurrying into the galley with half a box of caviar in her hot little hands, he moved out a foot and slowed her down. "Before you take that home, love," he said, "we'll each have a few more spoonfuls. And some more vodka, please." We rented black ties at Moss Bros. in London so we could accept an invitation to the Cirque de Paris and watch the best entertainers in Paris risk their necks trying to perform circus stunts for the benefit of some lucky orphanage. We ended that night drinking brandy at a sidewalk cafe in Les Halles. Once while we were having lunch at Lasserre's we discovered that it was March 16 and he suggested that we fly to Dublin for St. Patrick's Day. It would be hard not to like a man like that. I liked him so much and spent so much time with him that it ended with my working somewhere else.

It was a case of creeping inevitability that Nelson would shake things up. He began to show signs of restlessness early in 1967 soon after he put the company into the broadcasting business by engineering the acquisition of half a dozen radio and television stations from a Texas combine run by one Cecil Trigg, who had carefully explained to Nelson that what broadcasting was all about was investment and depreciation and taxes and operating losses and taxes and taxes and taxes. Meaning taxes you don't pay. Now, it seemed, it was time for red-faced Cecil to cash in his chips, give the government a few dollars and ride off into the sunset with his capital gains. Some of us thought he meant Doubleday gains, but no matter. We were now in the broadcasting business and could make practically free trips to such oases as El Paso and Odessa, Texas. I thought it might be an omen of some kind that the first time we went to El Paso to look at the property we had bought, the Rio Grande was dry right through the middle of town.

Another omen of sorts was dropped in our laps when the Texans made their first invasion of New York. This is how I reported the highlight of their visit to Milton:

The funniest event of the day by all odds must have been what happened at lunchtime. It was snowing like hell and the snow was being thrown in your face by a gale-force wind. A bunch of the Texans left our office on their way to lunch at, of all places, the University Club, which may never be the same again. When they walked out the front door and began shouting imperiously for a taxi, a chauffeur popped out of a huge black Cadillac and asked respectfully, "You gentlemen from the Doubleday party?" Mr. Trigg allowed that they were, the chauffeur opened the door for them, and off they went to the corner of Fifth Avenue and 54th Street. About ten minutes later big John, who had been holding a high-level meeting in his office with Frank Stanton of CBS, hurried out to the sidewalk with Dr. Stanton on the way to a lunch date they had downtown. No Cadillac. Not even a lousy VIP taxicab. No taxicab of any kind. You can bet that by the time John got his distinguished companion out of the snow and into some warmth on wheels, there was very little left of the Uppmann he was chewing.

Nelson had laid on a dinner in a room at "21" that night and John got there late enough to make an entrance. "I'll thank you sons-of-bitches," he said grimly as he took his seat at one end of the table, "not to steal my transportation in the future." The Depreciation Dandies didn't say a word.

The shoe I had been afraid for a long time was going to drop hit the floor with a dull clunk in the fall of '67. Liby and I were traveling in Europe. John had left word for me in London that Nelson's long-awaited reorganization plan would be announced within the week, so I was braced for it.

We met Sargent in beautiful, decadent Paris and got the official word that we would now have two executive vice-presidents, Nelson and O'Donnell, with the company split into two reporting halves. Everything connected with business—manufacturing, accounting, financial—would report to O'Donnell. Everything connected with books—the club, trade publishing and the bookshops— would report to Nelson, who would also continue to oversee the broadcasting group. I was to become a senior vice-president in charge of the clubs, trade publishing and the bookshops. "Maybe it will work," I said. "It depends on how much Nelson leaves me alone."

But before I had to worry about that, I enjoyed the artistic dinner John gave us and a few other Doubleday people at L'Escargot in Les Halles, where the sommelier carries the frighteningly expensive bottles of wine up a periously circular flight of stairs from the cellar below. Liby and I restricted ourselves to one martini each before dinner, saving enough strength to deal with John's relentless assaults on the wine list. We finished with framboises buried under buckets of thick yellow cream. Life, we agreed as we went to bed at the Hotel de Crillon on the Place de la Concorde, wasn't so bad. The hell with Nelson.

Chapter 12

NELSON, of course, wasn't so easily dismissed. It's hard to ignore the man who is not only your boss but owns the company. Sargent had an easier time with his former brother-in-law's increasing appetite for command because Nelson would take more needling from John than he would from me, and, after all, John was the president and you don't fire presidents as readily as you do senior vice-presidents. Anyway, even though John and Neltje were in the process of being divorced, Ellen Doubleday, the grande dame of the family, still thought John was exactly what the company needed.

I would never have got away with Sargent's handling of the wine issue at a dinner Nelson threw at the Racquet Club for a few of our directors, Elbridge T. Gerry, John Sengstack and Douglas Black. With a *filet mignon* dinner, and with the eminent Chevalier du Tastevin Black at the table, Nelson brashly served a white wine. He explained interestingly that he had been quietly keeping score at all of our lunches and dinners and had discovered that when we had both red and white wines with the meal, we tended to use four bottles of white to one bottle of red. So he had decided to go with the white. "Cut it out, Nelson," Sargent said majestically, "why don't you just say you like white wine?"

John wasn't above making light of his own tastes and, for that

matter, idiosyncrasies. We all had, for business reasons, pet subscriptions to use for entertaining our best customers or suppliers.
"Nelson," John said, "has a box at the Jets, Fitz has a box at the
Mets and I have a box at the Met." I used to try to get Nelson to go
to a ball game with me once in a while—our box was right behind
Joan Payson's, the wonderful old lady who owned the ball club, and
Nelson knew her and her whole family—but he would have none
of it. No baseball for him. Too dull. Football was where the action was.

Sargent's love of the opera gave him three more points on Liby's
1–10 scale, especially because he frequently invited us to help fill
the eight seats in his box in dead center of the parterre level. The
first time we were invited, Liby whispered to me, as John led her
to a front seat in the three-three-two arrangement, "I feel like the
Queen of France." Liby didn't know then that the middle three
seats were kept for those, mostly men, who might rather be somewhere else, and the back two for those who wanted to, and most
probably would, sleep through the whole thing.

We turned the tables on John one night when he had given me
the whole box and I had invited Sol and Pat Stein, the husband-
and-wife team of Stein & Day, and their celebrated author, Elia
Kazan, and his lady. She was Barbara Loden, who played the Marilyn Monroe part in Arthur's Miller's *After the Fall* and was well
equipped for it. "Help me out, John," I pleaded. "I can't ask just
any slob to help me get through an evening with Kazan. Come on."
John came and was gracious about it, even when Barbara, who
turned out to have been anointed the new Mrs. Kazan, spent most
of the evening—in sight of the whole world, at least as the world is
constituted by the Metropolitan Opera House—curled up in Kazan's
lap. Actually, we had a good if uneven time. Kazan was an entertaining talker, especially on the subject of the imposing sets of the
Carmen we were watching and hearing. He was more interested in
talking about books than the theater, which wasn't so surprising,
not only because Sargent was there but because Stein & Day had
sold some 200,000 copies of his novel *The Arrangement* and we
were probably going to sell another 700,000 copies between the

Guild and the Dollar Book Club. Gadge, as the Steins pointedly called him, gave up on the opera at the end of the third act. He leaned over to John and said, "Hey, why don't we just go over to '21' now?" So we went over to "21." That was about eleven fifteen and Liby and I fell into bed at half past two. They'd had to unlock the front door of the restaurant to let us out.

There was always something out of the ordinary going on at Doubleday in those years, or maybe it's more accurate to say there was hardly ever anything ordinary going on. *Book Publishing in America*, a massive work detailing the histories of all the U.S. houses, said in its long study of Doubleday that Nelson was "Sargent's young brother-in-law." He was, but, with his reorganization an accomplished fact, the Falcon, as he was sometimes called by a less than gruntled employee, was out from under John's shadow for good and things would never be the same again.

I made the mistake of thinking Nelson would be amused, as I was, by another *Book Publishing in America* observation, this one that the main reason Doug Black had been able to take over the company with a minimum of disruption after Nelson's father died was because Black's publishing philosophy coincided with that of the Double-days. He believed, as they had, that "publishing is a commerce first and a noble calling second." Nelson agreed. "That's right," he said, "that's the way it ought to be." This was at lunch, a novelty for Nelson and me. But I soon found out why I had been invited to break bread with the young master. "We've got to do this regularly," he told me. "I don't want you having lunch with Sargent so much."

Nelson didn't interfere with the picking of books for the clubs. I was free to do my own wrestling between the claims of art and commerce—never an easy matter. I refused, for example, to use Jacqueline Susann's *The Valley of the Dolls* as a Guild selection, but was willing enough to use it as a selection in Dollar, where it made truckloads of money. "We've sold 90,000 copies so far," I reported to Milton, and it's an overwhelming number one on Dollar's list of the most popular premium books. "My conscience gives me a twinge every now and then, but I'm sure O'Donnell won't

feel any pain when he puts the money in the bank." It wasn't generous of me to blame it even indirectly on O'Donnell. He didn't
have anything to do with it except to see that his printing presses
made us the books we needed.

Looking back, I can see that all I needed to give in to the temptation to use an explicitly sexual book was the support of an accepted
literary name. I tried hard for John Updike's *Couples*, more popu-
larly known around the office as "Coupling," and was disappointed
when the Book-of-the-Month Club took it away from us for
$50,000. The BOMC paid all that money for a book Knopf's Bill
Koshland, who told me he was sure neither club would touch it, had
asked me hesitantly to take "even if for only a few thousand dollars,
just so it can have a book-club imprimatur." As we used to say
whenever an old Brooklyn Dodger mainstay like Dixie Walker
moved on, "It's the end of an area." For the staid BOMC to take a
novel that by any standard was a poem in praise of oral sex was
certainly a departure.

On a BOMC cable television program, "First Edition," in 1984,
Nancy Evans asked Updike if his concentration on the joys of oral
sex came somehow out of his religious upbringing, and Updike said
he thought it might. "You know," he said, "the chalice and all that."

Mostly, Goodman, Sopkin and I fought to carry out our self-
imposed charge to trade up the Guild. In a twelve-page supplement
all our own in the January 7, 1968, issue of the *Times* we risked a
few hundred thousand dollars' worth of Nelson's money on a classy
Wunderman presentation of a proud list of books. In fiction we had
Angus Wilson's *No Laughing Matter*, Chaim Potok's *The Chosen*,
Thomas Berger's *Killing Time*, Ira Levin's *Rosemary's Baby*, Isaac
Bashevis Singer's *The Manor* and Gore Vidal's *Washington, D.C.*
And in nonfiction we had John Kenneth Galbraith's *The New
Industrial State*, *The Autobiography of Bertrand Russell*, Susan
Sontag's *Death Kit*, Stephen Birmingham's *Our Crowd*, W. A.
Swanberg's *Pulitzer*, Henri Troyat's *Tolstoy*, Willie Morris' *North
Toward Home* and Justin Kaplan's Pulitzer Prize-winning *Mr.
Clemens and Mark Twain*. As throw-ins we had the stunning Oscar
Lewis study of life in the slums of Puerto Rico, *La Vida*, Catherine

Marshall's *Christy*, *The Complete Poems of Marianne Moore* and my personal trademark or, by now, good-luck charm, Bruce Catton's *The Army of the Potomac*.

If you sent in the coupon on the back of that supplement, you could also order the three-volume *U.S.A.* by John Dos Passos, *Under the Volcano* by Malcolm Lowry, *The Fannie Farmer Cookbook*, *The Boston Strangler* by Gerold Frank, *Renoir, My Father* by Jean Renoir, *Giles Goat-Boy* by John Barth or collections of the works of Irwin Shaw, Shirley Jackson, Edgar Allan Poe, Mark Twain, Nathanael West and Ernest Hemingway.

"Any 4," the advertisement said, "all for only $1." The Book-of-the-Month Club had been going with "Any 3 for $1 each," but our ads did so well they had to change first to the four-book offer and then, reluctantly, to "Any 4, all for $1." I have to take as much blame as anybody else for the fact that the book clubs are their own worst enemies when it comes to giving away the store. Instead of doing as the English do, or tacitly acknowledging that each club has its own clearly defined turf and can operate on it as it sees fit, we ripped into each other with the ferocity of a tiger pouncing on a wild pig. The next great challenge for the clubs is to figure out how to stop outdoing each other giving away more to new members and instead spend more money giving greater rewards—lower prices and more gift books—to the members who stay with them for a long time.

Quality Paperback Book Club has at least made a start in that direction. The rationale is simple enough: the rewards ought to go to the people who have earned them.

Irv, Charlie and I would not have been happy with a lot of the books the Guild offered in the *Times* on a Sunday almost seventeen years after our shoot-the-works supplement. In the January 20, 1985, issue of the *Book Review*, a new member filling out the Guild coupon could write in the numbers for *Love and War* by John Jakes, *Dream of Orchids* by Phillis A. Whitney, *Love* by Danielle Steel, *Past Imperfect* by Joan Collins, *Pleasures: Women Write Erotica* by Lonnie Barbach, *The Miracle* by Irving Wallace, *Making Love Better* by Patricia E. Raley and *Strong Medicine* by Arthur

Hailey. We wouldn't have minded Norman Mailer's *Tough Guys Don't Dance*, which ain't literature but is Mailer, *Ride a Pale Horse* by Helen MacInnes or *Blue Highways* by William Least Heat Moon. I think we would have worried a lot about Bob Woodward's *Wired*, the John Belushi story, and John Cooney's *The American Pope*, the biography of Francis Cardinal Spellman that discussed allegations of homosexuality, and which I rejected for BOMC.

Well, as somebody said once, you pays your money and you takes your choice. That's what happens when you choose commerce over art. I know Sam Goldwyn said about the movies that if you want to deliver a message, go to Western Union. But there is a middle ground.

If I had been filling out one of the competing book-club coupons on that Sunday, I would rather have picked from the Book-of-the-Month Club's list. On the nonfiction side there were *Iacocca: An Autobiography* by Lee Iacocca, *The March of Folly* by Barbara Tuchman, *The Living Planet* by David Attenborough, *Heritage* by Abba Eban, *Remembering Kennedy* by William Manchester, *Fatal Vision* by Joe McGinniss and even *Mayor*, the immodest account of the life and times of Edward I. Koch. On the fiction side there were *Lincoln* by Gore Vidal, *The Little Drummer Girl* by John le Carré, *. . . And Ladies of the Club* by Helen Hooven Santmyer, *The Fourth Protocol* by Frederick Forsyth and even *God Knows* by Joseph Heller, a raunchy, often profane and always shocking retelling of the King David story.

God Knows is a textbook case of the kind of book that club editors and managers have to be wary about using as a main selection. The way the clubs work, the selection is shipped automatically if you don't send in the reply card after checking one of the boxes to indicate that you don't want the selection, that you want another book instead or that you don't want any book at all. You can even say you want the selection and another book. But if you forget to send in the card, or you're away on a vacation, or for any reason don't put that card in the mail, you're going to get the book. It doesn't seem reasonable to run the risk of sending you by accident a book in which David talks like this about Bathsheba:

I wanted to be with her more often than either of us would have imagined. Occasionally, she chided me for barging in without notice and interfering with her work. I think it's true—I liked my women very much more than they liked me, and I enjoyed lying with them more than they enjoyed having me with them, until Bathsheba. She was a hot one. She wanted it at least as much as I did, and I soon discovered something else eccentric about her: if I didn't come as swiftly as I hoped I would, she herself would eventually go off like a string of firecrackers hung from the tail of a vixen, exploding in a climax of her own with those marvelous and shocking tumults that are incomparably titillating and began causing talk through the whole neighborhood. Who'd ever heard of a thing like that? She called it her orgasm. She awarded me points for giving her multiples.

My uncertain relationship with Nelson became even more strained, on my part anyway, when he shot down a tentative plan to make shares of Doubleday stock available to members of the executive committee. He regretted that some shares had been distributed by his father during the rocky years of the 1930s and that some of those shares had found their way onto the open market when their holders needed money. Nelson had a horror of outsiders knowing anything about the business and, worse, thinking they had the right to ask questions about it. He seemed amenable to the stock plan when we had assembled at a little inn in Amagansett for an "away from it all" session, which meant that we could drink more than usual because all we had to do was walk up a flight of stairs to bed. But a month later he laid down his ruling, which was simple enough: No. We would continue to be paid salaries and profit-sharing payments that Nelson considered generous, and that was that.

I was amused that Jack Laidlaw, one of the two brothers who had sold their River Forest, Illinois, textbook business to us for a considerable amount of money, was so angry that Nelson wouldn't sell

him any stock that he raged at Nelson at a Brook Club party until
we literally carried him off to bed. He was already rich; he just
wanted the stock as a club tie of sorts. I wanted it because I needed
the money it would be worth someday.

What made me angriest was that other people had been able to
make a lot of money selling their businesses to Doubleday. Unhappily for me, I didn't have anything to sell them. All I had done was
build them a business.

Nelson or no Nelson, I invited Sargent to lunch one day and put
my case to him. He was sympathetic but non-committal. He did
think he could get me a long-term contract and more money. He
thought the stock matter was dead. He thought I ought to look at
the long term and see that I would have a pretty good life with
Doubleday. "With the company, you mean," I said with a certain
wistfulness. "I don't think you mean with Nelson." John signed
the check.

A couple of days later I found myself with no lunch date and
decided to stay in and read. I asked Penny Williams, my secretary—
we had secretaries in those days, they weren't all assistants—to order
me a sandwich and Coke. A little after noon Penny came in with
my sandwich and said, "There's a man outside who wants to see
you. He says he hasn't got an appointment, but if you can do it,
he'd like to talk to you for just a minute. His name is Al Casey." She
waited. "Do you know anybody named Al Casey? He says he's
from California."

"No," I said. "The only Casey I know is, if you can believe it,
named Irving, and he doesn't live in California. What does he want?"

"I don't know," she said. "Want me to ask him?"

"No, it doesn't matter. Bring him in."

So I met Albert V. Casey, president of the Times-Mirror Company, who said he was in New York looking for a man to succeed
Kurt Enoch as the head of New American Library, the paperback
house Enoch had started with Victor Weybright and then sold to
Times-Mirror. "Kurt is retiring," my visitor told me, "and I came
here to look for a replacement for him. I've talked to four publishers

this morning and three of them told me I ought to talk to you." He looked at the unwrapped sandwich and the unopened Coke on my desk. "You're not going out to lunch?"

"No," I said.

"Why don't you come across the street and have a sandwich with me in my office—well, it's really Kurt's office—and talk a little? Would you do that?"

I did it, and I was suitably impressed by the beautiful office high up in 280 Park Avenue with a glorious view of the East River. We talked for more than an hour, and when I left he said he was interested in me and he hoped I was interested in him. "I'm not sure," I said, "but it's true that I'm thinking about doing something different." We got all the way out to the elevator before he dropped on me the thought that the job he was talking about would be worth a lot of money. "We could," he said, "begin talking at $75,000."

That gave me something to think about when Sargent handed me a piece of paper that was, he said, intended to make me secure forever. Or practically forever. In addition to increasing my salary by $5,000 to $52,500 and guaranteeing me not less than $10,000 a year in profit-sharing even if the plan didn't earn that much, it said this:

> The Company hereby agrees and guarantees that in the event of 1) termination of your employment ten years from this date, or sooner if by mutual agreement, 2) normal retirement unless extended by mutual agreement, 3) death, or 4) total disability, the total amount of deferred compensation credited to your account at that time will be paid to you or to your beneficiary in ten equal annual installments.
>
> Your salary and corresponding pension and deferred compensation benefits may be increased in the discretion of the Company but there is no commitment to make any increase.
>
> We both contemplate the continuance of your employment as specified herein. In the light of circumstances as they arise from time to time this agreement may be modified by future agreement between us.

When Casey called me a couple of weeks later he said he had talked to the Chandlers, who owned Times-Mirror, about me and everybody was interested. He asked if I would be willing to make a trip out there. "Out there," I thought. "That's pretty funny. That's the ultimate insult New Yorkers lay on California." But I said, "Okay. Let me know when."

He let me know right away. "Can you come either of the next two weekends?" I said sure, even this weekend. "Wonderful," he said, "I'll make airplane and hotel reservations for you and your wife. You can fly on Friday? Is the Beverly Hilton okay?"

"Wait a minute," I said, looking quickly at my pocket calendar. "I can do it this weekend, but Liby can't. She has a date she's been committed to for weeks. Just make a reservation for me."

"Oh," he said. There was a pause. "Well, we can't do that. You see, this is a sensitive job. The Chandlers will want to interview both of you."

"Interview my wife?"

"Yes, they'll want to see her as well as you."

"No kidding?" I said. "You know, Liby is a very nice woman, she looks good, she has good taste, she's a hell of a cook and I think she's wonderful, but she's really a lousy editor. Why do they want to see her?"

"Well," Al said, "as I said, it's a sensitive job. They want to be sure they're going to be comfortable with both of you. Let's just make another date when you can both come, all right?"

"No," I said. "I'm afraid it isn't all right. If they have to interview my wife for the job, it's not for us. She wouldn't like it and I wouldn't like it. Let's just forget it, and maybe we'll talk again someday. Thanks anyway."

Al didn't argue. Clearly, he knew the Chandlers. And when I told Liby about it, it was just as clear that I knew her.

So things were quiet for a while. Until I got a telephone call one morning from a man who said he was Alexander Black and he worked for an executive recruiting firm and would like to make a lunch date with me. "I'm sorry," I said, "but this is a bad time for me. If you want to talk about somebody I can help you with, why don't we just talk about it over the phone right now?"

"Well," he said, "actually, I want to talk about *you*. Can you block out a lunch date for me some time this week or next?" Never having been approached by a head-hunter before, I said yes, made a date and had lunch with Sandy Black at the Union League Club. I'd never been in the Union League Club. I looked quickly at the menu and ordered a hot turkey sandwich with gravy and mashed potatoes. I figured I'd show them how Democrats eat.

Sandy said he had been asked by a client of considerable importance to talk to me. "The job he wants to fill," he said, "is a big one."

"In publishing?" I asked.

"In publishing, yes. But not the kind of publishing you're in now. In fact, I would say you're a very long shot for this job. The only thing is he's a man who likes long shots, which is why we're here. He has a hunch you might be just what he wants."

The next voice I heard was Jack Clumeck's. I'd never heard of him either, but after he had explained that he was a close assistant to the man Sandy Black had talked to me about, I agreed to have lunch with him. As soon as he had hung up, I looked him up in *Who's Who*. Jack Clumeck, it said, was vice-chairman of the finance committee of Norton Simon Inc. I knew that Norton Simon Inc., was the conglomerate that had been put together by Norton Simon, the man, out of Hunt-Wesson, Canada Dry, something called the Glass Container Corporation and the McCall Corporation. So it had to be *McCall's* he wanted to talk to me about.

I had lunch with Clumeck and said yes when he asked me to fly to Los Angeles and meet Simon. They had too much class to ask me to take Liby with me.

Actually, I have always regretted that Liby wasn't invited. Norton gave me lunch at his home, and walking through the house from the front door to the living room and on to the dining room was like walking through the Jeu de Paume. Manets and Monets and Renoirs were on one side and Henry Moores and Modiglianis were outside the glass wall in the garden, and even I knew that the

picture across the dining-room table was a Van Gogh. I told Norton
it was too bad Liby wasn't there and he said she'd have to come the
next time, but there never was a next time. Norton's son Robert, a
young man married to a beautiful young woman who was seven or
eight months pregnant, killed himself, and Norton was never the
same again. He and his wife agreed to divorce, he sold the house and
his controlling shares in the company that carried his name, and
changed his life. Liby never got to see all those beautiful paintings.

At lunch Norton offered me $100,000 a year for five years to be-
come the president of McCall's. Well, half of McCall's. He wanted
to split the printing company and the publishing company into two
separate companies, and he wanted me to run the magazines—
McCall's, *Redbook* and the *Saturday Review*. In addition to the
$100,000 a year, he would give me 20,000 stock options in Norton
Simon Inc. at the market price on the day I signed the contract.
Norton is a man with a narrow, lined, craggy face and a manner
curiously shy, I thought, for somebody so rich. I liked him. I
thought I would like working for him. But I didn't say yes, I said I
would think about it. It was a hell of a long way from a nickel an
inch.

The next time I went out there, I spent an hour with each of the
three men he had picked to run the company, Dave Mahoney,
Harold Williams and Bill McKenna. Then we went to lunch. Norton didn't feel good; he hadn't gone to the office that morning. "I
think I'll go home," he said about one o'clock. "I feel rotten. Anyway, everything's all settled, isn't it?" I didn't know if I should say
anything or not. I looked around the table and nobody else was
saying anything either. "Well," I said as Norton was getting up,
"don't we have to give these gentlemen a little time to decide if they
want me? They haven't even had a chance to caucus."

That was when I met the real Norton Simon. "They've caucused,"
he said.

But I still had to talk it over with John Sargent. We thought hard
about it together. On the one side there was a lot of money; on the
other side there was the kind of work I loved to do.

"You just don't want to leave the high-class world and go back

to the world of the peasants," Norton had said to me in California.
"You like it here," Sargent said.

Well, sure I did. Anyway I wasn't sure I wanted to fight with
the magazine business again. So I said no to Norton in one of the
most extraordinary telephone calls I've ever made. He had asked
me to call him at noon, and when I did, his assistant said he was in a
board meeting but that he had said he should be interrupted if I
called. I was in a phone booth at the Tavern on the Green and I
waited patiently until Norton came out of his meeting. "Well?" he
said. "No," I said. "Too bad," he said. "I think we'll change your
mind. The reason I went after you was because Al Casey told me
he couldn't get you but maybe I could. Maybe I can. Let's keep in
touch."

Keeping in touch wasn't easy because working for Nelson wasn't
easy. Nelson had never been to Europe and he decided he wanted to
go that fall, first to London and then to Frankfurt and then to Paris.
He wanted to show the Europeans that he was taking charge of the
company.

We stayed at the Berkeley, a pleasant hotel on Piccadilly. Nelson
liked it and particularly liked the fact that it was a place Sargent
wouldn't have stayed at. "Not fancy enough," one of the world's
richest young men said. He didn't mind staying at the Frankfurter
Hof in Frankfurt and seemed happy with the Crillon in Paris. We
never had a fight while we were traveling, but we never had a lot of
fun, either. Nelson didn't think much of the Doubleday people we
had to deal with and I liked almost all of them, so there wasn't much
for us to agree on.

My not infrequent characterization of Nelson as "the last of the
plantation owners" was not just irony. I always felt he treated his
employees like serfs, which is defined by Webster as "a slave" or
"someone who is oppressed or without freedom." Because all of
them were my friends, I took it personally.

Wolf Foges is an Austrian and my favorite memory of him is the
morning he appeared in the doorway of my office in New York
blowing clouds of smoke from his ever present cigar. I'd had no
idea he was coming. "Surprise," he said in his enigmatic European

way. "But it's more than surprising," I said, "it's a hell of a coincidence. Here I am reading a novel by Sara Gainford called *Night Falls on the City* and it's about how anti-Semitic Vienna was before the war." Wolf took out his cigar and shook his jowls and said, "Yah, especially the Jews."

Beverley Gordey, born in Minneapolis, had married a Frenchman, Michel Gordey, a foreign correspondent for *France Soir*, and was Doubleday's scout not only for Paris but for Europe. She worked out of her apartment in Saint-Germain rather than in the office, and Nelson didn't like that. He also didn't like the fact that when Danny the Red disrupted the Book Fair at Frankfurt one night when we were all there, I took Beverley back to the hotel where we were all staying. When we met Nelson in the bar, he acted as though we had abandoned him to the Red Brigade. He went on about it for so long that I went quietly to bed.

Nelson had bought Paul Feffer's book distribution business and it seemed to me that in his eyes that meant he had bought Paul, too. It was probably Nelson's proprietary behavior toward Paul that made me dispute Harry Abrams' wife, Nina, when we were having a pleasant lunch with friends in St. Thomas a few months after Harry had sold his company to the Times-Mirror. "We haven't really sold it, you know," Nina said. "They're just providing the capital to expand it. Harry will still be in complete control of it." I thought about one of my Irving Manheimer legacies. "Nina," I said, "don't kid yourself. When you sell it, you sell it." That's how it was between Nelson and Paul. Paul had sold it and Nelson had bought it. There wasn't any doubt about who owned it now.

But my unenthusiastic participation in Nelson's responses to the genuine efforts these three, and lesser employees, made to please him was mild compared to my reaction when he began to treat me the same way. If you sell it, you sell it, I reminded myself, and if you work for him, you work for him, but there is a difference. Once you've sold it, it's done; but there's no law that says you have to keep on working for him. That's up to you.

What it came down to was that I would never get along with Nelson the way I did with John. But Nelson, not John, owned the company and he was going to have his way whether I liked it or not. When we got off the airplane in New York, I walked across the parking lot with Liby and said, "Liby, I don't know what I'm going to do for a living next year, but I'm not going to work here. I've got to get out. I can't live with him and I'm afraid he won't let me live with John."

"That's interesting," Liby said. "Norton Simon called last night and said somebody had told him you were coming home tonight and he wanted you to call him."

When I called Norton, I said, "If you want to ask me what I think you want to ask me, the answer is yes." I did tell him that the only money problem I had was that I would lose $55,000 in profit-sharing money that I had accumulated at Doubleday; the rules said it would be forfeited if I quit. Norton said, "Okay, we'll change the $100,000 for five years to $110,000. Fair enough?" I thought it was fair enough, and I bit the bullet and called Sargent at home on Saturday night and asked if I could come to his house at nine o'clock in the morning to talk. "You're quitting," he said, and I said yes, I was. I didn't get to talk to John about it until Monday morning in the office because it snowed all day on Sunday, maybe a foot's worth, and I couldn't drive in.

"I suppose," John said when we met, "Goodman and Sopkin will follow you right out the door."

"Not if Nelson gives them a little tender loving care," I said. "They like their jobs."

But a couple of months later Vilma Bergane, Stan Donaldson, Irv Goodman, Charlie Sopkin and I were all together again at 230 Park Avenue, home of The McCall Publishing Company.

Nelson was generous to Irv and Charlie. He let them go off with the profit-sharing money they had earned, which was good of him because he knew they couldn't afford to lose it. And I got the message.

Leaving Doubleday wasn't easy. I hadn't known what I was getting into when I went there and I didn't know what I was getting into when I left, but it had provided me a Master's degree in Education, if not in Business Administration. There were, and are, lasting benefits, lasting memories and lasting friends.

Among the things I learned there were two invaluable lessons about the unique—not arcane, but unique—business of mail-order selling. The first one, which I laughed at in the beginning, but learned to take seriously, was that "Ten Cents is Better than Free." This was before the Federal Trade Commission cracked down on "Free" offers by forcing the advertiser to make so many disclosures about the customer's obligations that even the gullible could see through the "Free" subterfuge. But Milton proved to me with test after test that an ad asking the customer to send ten cents with the coupon would out-pull a straight Free offer every time. "Ten cents is better than free," Milton explained patiently, "because the crooks, or even the reasonably honest customer who just isn't sure he's going to want to fulfill his whole commitment, figures that if he's sent you the dime he's paid you. He hasn't cheated you because he's done what you asked him to do. That makes him more willing to send in the coupon.

"And that," Milton said, "ties into the other old mail-order rule. The activity element is very important. Make them fold a corner over the dime, or fit it into a slot, or Scotch-tape it over a printed circle, and they love it. It's something to do, an activity element."

It's a truth that fits a lot of things in life. If you have to do a little something, perform some small task, to get what you want, you enjoy it more. That's why some people like to squeeze their own oranges or wash their own cars. It's the activity element they like. That's why an offer of a specific group of four books will never do as well as one inviting the reader to pick his own four out of thirty-six. It's the activity element.

I learned, very early on, that one of the things you have to fight in the book business in general, and the book-club business in particular, is the avid desire some people have to test. "Let's test three different offers," they say, and a couple of months after you go away and leave them alone, you discover that they've tested eight different possibilities. Sometimes although not always, it is important to test a major change in an offer, but, no matter how important the change is, there are times when you have to lead, not follow. You have to rely on your own instinct to push you into offering something new the public doesn't know it wants. MBAs think that when they have all of the company's experience in the computer's memory, they can just push a few buttons on the magic machine and be told what to do. I don't think so. The fanciest, most expensive computers can only add and subtract. They can't think. You still need people to do that. People who aren't afraid to be fired when they're proved wrong. Computers don't worry about being fired. "Go with IBM," a Doubleday family director told me after we had sat through interminable presentations by IBM, RCA Spectra and Minneapolis Honeywell. "Nobody will ever blame you if something goes wrong if you go with IBM." I wasn't so sure when the RCA salesman finished his pitch by claiming, "Our equipment beats IBM's in its capacity for graceful deterioration." How could you beat that?

My Doubleday experience reinforced my conviction, learned at Macfadden, that a publishing business ought to be run by people who are essentially editors or, at least, people who are in love with the newspapers or magazines or books the company is publishing. Nelson thinks people like that ought to be allowed to work for a living but not to decide anything.

Just the same, Doubleday and Nelson made it possible for me to talk with Duke Ellington about his autobiography over breakfast—for him—at one o'clock in the morning in his Manhattan apartment. That was a date Nelson made through Stanley Dance, who had done a biography of the Duke in 1970 and who took it upon himself to respond to my request that Ellington think about doing an honest-to-God autobiography for us. Dance thought it was a good idea as long as he wrote it, but Nelson, bless him, agreed with me that what we had to do was talk to Ellington alone and find out if he was willing to write—with the help of whomever—the kind of soul-searching book we had in mind. Proposing soul-searching to the man who wrote "Sophisticated Lady," Mood Indigo" and "Solitude" was probably unmitigated chutzpah on my part, but Nelson got Duke to make the appointment and there we were at one o'clock in the morning, sitting in his living room, being served gins-and-tonics by two beautiful white women whose average age might have been twenty-two and who came back in fifteen minutes or so with the great Edward Kennedy Ellington on their arms. He looked like an Arabian king.

"There are two things in particular I'd like to talk about," he said. "The first is how hard it was to get people to let me play the serious music I wrote, like *Black, Brown and Beige, Harlem* and *Liberian Suite*. Everybody wanted to hear "Take the 'A' Train," which I always had to remind them I didn't write, anyway, Billy Strayhorn did. And they wanted me to play other people's music which they identified with my band and my arrangements, but never anything I wrote that was serious. Sure, they wanted to hear "Lady" and "Indigo" and "Solitude," and they wanted to hear "I'm Beginning to See the Light" and "Do Nothing Till You Hear from Me," but I always wanted to play the other music and it was years before they would let me.

"The other thing is how hard a life we had then. We rode the buses and we played wherever the money was, but we never knew where we were going to spend the night. Sometimes we had to get back on the bus and just drive on through the night until we got somewhere where they would take us in. I used to love the train trips, when we could afford them, because you knew you were going to eat and sleep on the train. The black musicians today don't know anything about that and somebody ought to tell them."

Duke never did the book, but that one time with him is a memory to cherish. He looked old, but he talked young.

Nelson also went along with our offering Eugene McCarthy, after he lost to Hubert Humphrey in the 1968 Democratic primary, $100,000 for a book to be called *The Year of the People*. He even held up well when McCarthy asked us what the initials of the Three-Eye League stood for and I knew they meant Iowa, Illinois and Indiana because I had worked in the business. Nelson still signed the check—or let me sign it.

Watching the CBS film *Robert Kennedy: His Life and Times*

reminded me, when one of the newsreel clips showed him standing with James Meredith at the door of the administration offices at the University of Mississippi on October 1, 1962, that I had tried hard and failed to get the story of James J. P. McShane, Chief of U.S. Marshals under President Kennedy. Jim McShane was a friend of mine through the ubiquitous Red Smith–Frank Graham axis, of which he was a card-carrying member. Liby and I had first met him and his wife at a Sunday-afternoon gin-and-tonic time at the Graham house in New Rochelle. Jim was a former New York City detective with a chestful of decorations, not an especially tall man but burly and fearsomely intimidating when he wasn't laughing. He was a fight buff who had been banished from Manhattan to the Ryer Avenue station in the Bronx because the *Daily News* had run a front-page picture of him holding an umbrella over Rocky Marciano's head as the heavyweight champion walked out of Madison Square Garden in the rain after a weigh-in. His banishment to the boondocks had disenchanted him with the New York City Police Department and he accepted in a hurry when he was offered a job as head bodyguard for Jack Kennedy during the 1960 campaign. When Kennedy won, he rewarded pugnacious, good-hearted Jim with the prestigious job of Chief of United States Marshals. Jim was involved in a lot of black-white confrontations during the Thousand Days of Kennedy's administration, but his grimmest hours were the ones he spent in Oxford, Mississippi, a town he had never expected to see.

The day of the great admissions showdown, October 1, 1962, Jim was on the Old Miss campus commanding a force of three hundred Federal Marshals. His boss on the scene was Deputy Attorney General Nick Katzenbach, a close and trusted friend of both Kennedys. Katzenbach and Jim had two jobs to do, and they knew, as did the Kennedys, that the two weren't going to be easy to do at the same time. They had to see that Governor Ross Barnett's reluctant agreement with the President to admit Meredith to the university was carried out without personal harm to Meredith. They also had to do everything they could to keep more than a thousand rioting students from forcing a pitched battle between the people and the militia of Mississippi and the government of the United States. It was a heavy responsibility. The rioting students, led by segregationist retired Major General Edwin A. Walker, forced Katzenbach to call in Regular Army troops that the President had sent to Memphis, Tennessee, to stand by in case the trouble got out of hand. Two men, a French reporter and a Mississippi television repairman, were killed in the ugly fighting that seized the attention of the whole country, but Meredith, with James J. P. McShane standing tough next to him like Gary Cooper in *High Noon*, be-came an enrolled student at the University of Mississippi and another milestone had been erected to stand with Little Rock, Birmingham and Selma in the history of the Civil Rights movement.

I thought Jim had a story to tell and I thought it ought to be told. So I had lunch with him in the Oak Room of the Plaza Hotel. We sat looking out of the windows at the hansom cab on 59th Street and the green trees of Central Park and talked for three hours. He had a lot to talk about. He had spent a lot of time with Jack Ken-nedy. His Irishness and his New York street smarts had made it easy for the Irish Mafia around the President—Dave Powers, Kenny O'Donnell and Larry O'Brien—to kid around with him and to trust him. His book, I was sure, could open a brand-new window into the whole Camelot story. Jim was interested, and because of my rela-tionship with Smith and Graham, whom he revered, he knew he could trust me.

The trouble was he had dozens of freelance advisers, most of them former cops who tend to trust nobody except their own. They all thought that if he stayed away from the big publishing companies and did it by himself—"the way Evelyn Lincoln did," he said a couple of times, "when she wrote the book about being Kennedy's secretary"—he could keep all the money for himself. I explained to him patiently that a big publishing house like Doubleday, with its huge sales force, would do a better job for him than some little pub-lisher or, God forbid, vanity publisher could ever do unless lightning struck all over the place. I argued that he would be better off with a tough agent like Sterling Lord to look after his interests. "Sure, he'll get ten percent," I said, "but you know the old saying that ninety percent of something is better than a hundred percent of nothing." I explained to him that a good agent would almost certainly get a better price for the paperback rights and the best possible prices for other subsidiary rights. I told him that if he didn't want to involve a stranger, Doubleday would do all that for him for the same ten percent. He worried about taxes and about money for his wife if anything happened to him. I told him he could choose the amount he wanted paid to him every year, I explained how that would work to hold down his taxes the way it did for all the big-name writers and I said we would make an advance payment against royalties of $50,000, half of that when he signed the contract and the other half when he delivered the manuscript. "If something happens to you," I said, "your wife will get all the money you would have got."

I got in touch with him a couple of times after our lunch, but both times he said only that he was still thinking it over, that he wasn't sure what he ought to do. Then one morning, riding from Crestwood to Grand Central on the train, I read in the *Times* that James J. P. McShane, former hero cop and Chief of U.S. Marshals under President Kennedy, had died of a heart attack.

If you're going to work in publishing, you have to get used to the fact that you're going to win some and lose some.

Life wasn't, I knew, going to be any easier in the magazine business, even with Norton Simon's money and his willingness to spend it, but now that I had made up my mind to do it, it was easy to get excited about it. It didn't hurt that the day the story about my appointment came out in the *Times* and the *Wall Street Journal*, I had lunch at "21" and met Irving Manheimer there. "You'll do fine," he said. "But you won't get any kosher hot dogs in places like this." Mostly, Irving couldn't get over the fact that Phil Dougherty of the *Times* had called our house to ask some questions about me and had got Kevin, who did his best to answer the questions, but, in owning up to the truth about my educational background, gave Dougherty an opening for one of his funny last lines. "If you want to grow up to be the president of the McCall Publishing Company," Phil wrote, "don't go to college."

"I've decided to follow the ancient injunction about rape," I wrote Milton when all the handshakes were shaken. "You know, the one that says if it's inevitable you might as well relax and enjoy it. I can't say I'm terribly relaxed. I've been wrestling with it for weeks. But I finally decided that if Norton Simon was so determined to make me rich, I would stop fighting and let him do it. I also want to prove that I can do what he wants me to do."

At Norton's request, I had lunch with David J. Mahoney at "21" and agreed on everything. The troika was on its way toward being dissolved and Mahoney was obviously running the NSI show all by himself, with Norton looking interestedly over his shoulder. I met all the McCall Publishing Company people at a meeting at 230 Park one morning before Christmas and went home to wait for the new year and my new job to begin.

I wouldn't have any more Doubleday escapades like the executive committee's visit to Jack Laidlaw's place outside Chicago. We showed up more or less on time for that seminar at Jack's baronial castle, ate and drank when we were invited to and tried to make do on two or three hours of sleep a night. It was hard to describe Jack to Liby, who had never met him. "Well," I said, "he must be one of the most likable unregenerated right-wingers in the United States."

Jack offered us the use of his heated swimming pool, his Mercedes and an engaging Chinaman named Patrick to drive it. He filled us full of Beefeater gin, made hamburgers for us by folding grilled squares of filet mignon between soft rolls and handed them to us with the injunction that "I'll kill the first son-of-a-bitch who asks for ketchup."

Actually, the highlight of the trip was not Laidlaw's hospitality but an athletic event. Two of the Chicago crew challenged Sargent and Nelson to a tennis match the next day. The New Yorkers accepted with enthusiasm and bets began to pile up on the table by the swimming pool. All this was over after-dinner stingers and each stinger was probably worth another $20 a man. The match finally was set for $250 a side, winners take all.

The next day, before lunch, the contestants were back at the pool, taking nourishment from Patrick's exceedingly dry martinis.

203

Sargent and Nelson kept looking wistfully at the cloudy sky, wishing it would rain. But it didn't, and they had to face up to the fact that they had to have some tennis equipment if they were going to meet their doom properly dressed. Patrick drove them to the nearest shopping mall, where there was, he said, a Sears Roebuck store with a sporting-goods department. It was probably the first time in their lives either John or Nelson had ever been in a Sears Roebuck store. But they manfully struggled through the ordeal of buying the necessaries, and when they walked hesitantly out onto the field of honor they looked ready for the center court at Wimbledon. The Chicagoans casually wore the kind of bleached old clothes that only real tennis players wear. Jack was holding the $500 and I could tell that he was ready to hand it to the Champions of the West right now and spare the Effete Easterners the agony of losing it on the rack.

So, after a few erratic rallies, big John and Nelson won the first set, 6–1, and the second set, 6–2, taking home not only the $500 but the $2.95 Jack Laidlaw Challenge Trophy. They also left behind with their employees the message that the Chicagoans might be able to play tennis better, but the New Yorkers could drink better. So much for publishing priorities.

I was afraid I would miss all that nonsense, but I felt better about it after my first trip to an NSI board meeting in Fullerton, California. After the meeting, and over so-so martinis before lunch, I saw Norton, a passionate corporate-brand defender, and I decided to complain to him. "Look," I said, "I work for the company, so Liby uses Hunt's tomato sauce, which she always used anyway, and Wesson Oil instead of Mazola, and even Hunt's ketchup instead of Heinz's. But this booze is something else. Johnnie Walker is great for the Scotch drinkers, but Canada Dry for gin drinkers? That ain't fair." Norton looked at me with a quizzical expression that said eloquently he knew he was talking to the new kid on the block. "See that cut-glass decanter down at the end of the table?" he said. "That's the Beefeater."

Right away I knew it wasn't going to be so bad.

Chapter 13

WHENEVER I think of my time at *McCall's*, all two years and eight months of it, I think about Shana Alexander. She was the worst great idea I ever had.

She happened to me, as a lot of things have, on the train. I was reading *Life* and stopped at her column, "The Feminine Eye." It was about Dwight Eisenhower's funeral, and one short sentence convinced me that she was the editor I needed to make a new *McCall's*. I already knew I wanted a woman for the job. She would be the first woman editor *McCall's* had had in forty-eight years.

"Hearse, caisson, riderless horse—they were all so familiar," Shana wrote.

TV has shown us four state funerals in five years, four deaths in living color. . . . The honor guard is getting better at it, I reflected idly as the young men moved in punctilious slow-motion military choreography. . . . Or it may be that I am getting used to it. Either way, the sole astonishment for me this time was the sheet of plastic over the flag. Plastic is a fit cover for a grapefruit half, perhaps even for a general's hat. But not a general's casket. Rain may spoil a parade but it decorates a cortege, and if there ever is a time when the flag should be wet, surely it is at the funeral of a great general. . . . When his body is returning at last to the earth, and the coffin that contains it, by his own request, is the standard military box, what is being protected from the rain?

Shana finished her piece with the sentence that did me in—in more ways than one. "I made my mourning from that," she wrote.

The only person I knew at *Life* was Jack Newcombe, so as soon as I got home I called him. "I need a favor, Jack," I said. "Can you get me Shana Alexander's home phone number?"

"Oh, Jesus," he said. "They'll kill me if they ever find out I helped you steal her."

"I haven't stolen her yet," I said. "First I have to talk to her."

I held on while Jack got the number and then I called her. She was home, and when I introduced myself and told her what I wanted, she said, "Well, it must be some kind of an omen, but I'm going to be in New York next week."

"Will you have lunch with me, or dinner?"

I should have learned something from the unhesitating way she chose dinner. Shana always goes first class. She told me she would be staying at the Regency and we agreed that I would pick her up there at seven o'clock on the evening she named. The next morning I told David Mahoney about my idea and my date and he was impressed. "I'll join you," he said. "It will be easy anyway, I'm staying at the Regency, too." David's main office was still in Fullerton, California.

On the fateful evening I went to the apartment the company had leased for me in the Beaux Arts on 44th Street, east of Second Avenue, put on a clean shirt, watched the six-o'clock news and left for the Regency in plenty of time to have a six-forty-five drink in Mahoney's suite, as he had suggested. When my cab pulled up in front of the hotel and I climbed out, Mahoney got out of a cab that had parked right behind mine. It was, we agreed, good timing, but it got even better because we got on the elevator behind a short, expensively dressed woman with streaky blond hair who, in the proper New York fashion, turned around to face the door once we were all on. "May I push a button for you?" David asked politely. "We're going to five," he said, pushing the button.

"Then you've already done it," she said. "I'm on five, too."

"No kidding," David said. We had already found out that Mrs. Alexander was staying in 510. "You aren't by any chance Shana Alexander?"

"I sure am," she said, giving him back smile for smile. "So you must be Ed Fitzgerald."

"He is," David said, pointing to me. "I'm Dave Mahoney."

We had drinks in David's suite and rode in David's limo to the Chateaubriand and told her how much we needed her. She said she was interested but she had a lot of things to think about. "Not to be funny about it," she said, "but *Life* is my life. I'm not sure how I'd feel about leaving it."

"Can we have lunch tomorrow?" I asked her. I didn't throw in the possibility of dinner. I've never been much on business breakfasts or dinners; lunches are for business. Shana agreed to have lunch at the Regency and I had bought my ticket on the Shana Alexander roller-coaster.

"You've got the right one," David told me the next morning.

"I haven't got her yet," I said. "But I want her. The big women's magazines have always been edited by men. *McCall's* ought to have a woman. A special woman."

"You'll get her," he said. "She's ready to be taken."

"Well, before I have lunch with her, I'd better warn you that I'm going to offer her a three-year contract for sixty, sixty-five and seventy. Okay?"

"Cheap. Good luck."

On April 8 the lady said yes. "But you'll have to make the contract deal with Swifty Lazar," she said. "He does all my business for me."

I didn't care who I had to make the contract with. She was saying yes, and that was all that mattered. I had wanted to solve the *McCall's* editor problem by a knockout in the first round, a 102–yard kickoff return, a grand-slam home run, and I had done it. *McCall's*, I was sure, would never be the same again. I had reason to be euphoric. The seduction of this glamorous publishing talent had been easy. I had no idea how hard the consummation was going to be.

"You've got to understand," the worldly-wise Mahoney counseled me, "that she's extremely vulnerable. You're going to have to treat her gently."

After her first overnight at our house, Liby, remembering the Mahoney injunction I had reported to her, said, "She's as vulnerable as a butcher knife."

Mahoney was wrong; Liby was right.

Another authority, Sheilah Graham, Scott Fitzgerald's last lover, said in her candid memoir *A State of Heat* that men are less inclined to send presents to efficient women. She spoke openly about her own experience. "The men preferred to subsidize the helpless-looking girls. I was too intelligent ever to be really helpless, and more organized than people would give me credit for. But I would always give the impression that I needed help. This has stood me in good stead over the years. Whenever I am in a jam I become bewildered and helpless, and men or efficient women take over the problem."

My daughter, Eileen, says it differently, but says the same thing. "How are you going to carry two bags and a tape recorder from the airplane to the cab?" I asked her once. "I'll cry a little," she said. "Somebody will help me."

At the beginning of my time at *McCall's*—which I always think of that way, although when I moved into 230 Park Avenue my empire also included *Redbook* and the *Saturday Review*—I had lots of problems without Shana. Because *McCall's* (the magazine) was losing money, Norton had made two moves, both of them wrong. First, he asked Norman Cousins, whom he respected enormously, to divide his time between the *Review* and *McCall's*. He made Norman editor-in-chief of all the McCall (the company) publications. Second, he asked Herb Mayes, the accepted maven of women's magazines, to sidestep out of retirement and temporarily take over from Bob Stein the editorship of *McCall's* (the magazine). Stein, whose contract hadn't run out yet, was left sitting in a big office with nothing to do. He also had a handsome wooden refrigerator that he later gave to me and I later gave to Al Silverman.

Herb was endlessly helpful to me when I showed up for work. He took me all over the place, introduced me to everybody and said he would make sure that everything was running like clockwork by the time I actually took over. He had an extra reason to be friendly to me because his daughter Vickie had worked for me at Doubleday and had married Charlie Sopkin. But as he gave me the five-dollar tour I worried more and more that this was going to be like having two cooks in the same kitchen. He kept telling me how much he could do to help me learn the ropes, but I wondered where the ropes would be when I had learned about them.

Herb's deal with Norton and Mahoney was that he would run the magazine with its regular budget, plus $400,000 of his own to spend any way he wanted, for the issues dated March through July 1969. No salary, just an expense account. With that kind of expense account, you don't need a salary. Anyway, Herb had total power, and power was Herb's drive. Not glory, not money. Power.

I've always said that all art directors should be strangled at birth, because I'm convinced they couldn't care less about how hard it may be for the reader to make out what the hell is going on. I don't really think that art directors as beautiful as Jessica Weber, Janet Doyle and Alma Phipps of the Book-of-the-Month Club should have been strangled, but even those three have a fondness for reverse type—light type printed on a dark background—and anybody who likes reverse type cares only about art awards and not about whether or not the subscribers can read it. Some editors also like unreadable but pretty layouts, but because they are editors I consider that a weakness rather than a crime. Anyway, despite my feelings about art directors, I gave up on Herb the second or third time I watched and listened while he beat up on the *McCall's* art department. I decided I was going to have to live or die doing it my way. Alone. I told him so bluntly.

"All right," he said. "I can finish the issues I have in the works in about three months, and I'll leave then."

"No," I said. "I think it's important for you to leave now."

"You mean at the end of this month?"

"No," I said, "I mean now. Today."

So Herb left, after a farewell lunch with me at his favorite restaurant, "21," and warm good wishes on both sides. Mahoney was worried because he knew how much Simon liked Mayes. "Be nice to him," he said. And when I was back in my office after lunch, the first person I saw was David. "How did it go?" he wanted to know.

"Fine," I said. "We're still friends. Look." I showed him the St. Christopher's medal Herb had given me in a tiny blue box. "I'm a Jew," he had said, "and I don't know anything about what Catholics do, but I wanted to give you something for good luck, and this is what my friends told me I ought to give you. So I went to Tiffany's and bought you this solid gold St. Christopher's medal. Enjoy."

"See?" I said to Mahoney. "We're still friends."

Mahoney looked hard at the medal. "It should have been St. Jude," he said.

St. Jude is the patron saint for hopeless cases.

Anyway, with Herb appropriately subtracted from the crowded group of deposed generals surrounding me, I was able to turn my attention to Norman Cousins, the editor-in-chief of the whole publishing company. I knew my first big job was to find an editor-in-chief for *McCall's* itself and I had been around too long not to know that you can't have two editors-in-chief on the same magazine. I told Norman I would appreciate his forgetting any responsibility for *McCall's* and returning to full-time supervision of the *Review*. He protested with a vehemence that I found surprising. I had expected he wouldn't be wild about giving up his illustrious title, but I hadn't thought he would care that much. But he did. The day after I had talked with him, he met me in my office and said my request was unacceptable to him and that if I insisted he give up the company title, he would have to resign.

"Resign from the *Review*?" I asked.

"Exactly," he said. "I can't stay in the company if I'm going to be humiliated like this."

I used every argument I could think of. I flattered him outrageously, I told him the *Review* would be lost without him and the whole company would desperately miss his experience and his wisdom. "But," I said, "the decision is entirely up to you. I can't have two editors-in-chief, so I have no decision to make." He left grimly. And the next morning he called and said he would resign the company title and stay on. I thanked him warmly and we both went back to work. I've always been sure he carried his protest to Norton and got nowhere, and when he was confronted with the stark choice of giving in or leaving, he decided he would rather stay. We never had an angry word from that day on.

A couple of days later I came home from the office visibly tired and Liby made me a drink and handed it to me with the question, "What dragon did you slay today?"

Other people had to be fired, and it's never easy to fire anybody, but there were no duels with dragons that came even close to matching the confrontations with Mayes and Cousins. Well, not until the emotionally stormy one that I've always thought of as the Showdown with Shana.

Herb didn't go away as quietly as Norman did. As he was preparing to leave, still with charitable good wishes for my success, he described *McCall's* as a "dreadful editorial product . . . the worst I have ever seen . . . a magazine that has been in the hands of amateurs, unbelievable, utterly inept amateurs. If somebody had been hired to sabotage *McCall's*, no more effective job of sabotage could have been done." He pointed out that his first Christmas issue of the magazine, in 1959, had sold almost two million copies on the newsstands and that the Christmas 1968 issue had fallen below 900,000 copies.

Well, I figured, if there hadn't been a problem, I wouldn't be there. So I was philosophical about it. I decided I would have to find out for myself who were the amateurs Herb spoke of so scathingly. I sent Horace Sutton, who had been running the magazine with his longtime boss, Cousins, looking over his shoulder, back to the *Review*. I didn't know anything about Jim Fixx, who had briefly preceded Horace as editor and gone on to *Life* and later to fame and considerable fortune as the man who turned the whole country on to running. That left Bob Stein, the man chosen to succeed John Mack Carter, who had got the job over Stein when Mayes retired in 1962. Carter had left to take over the *Ladies' Home Journal.* Stein had lasted through 1967 and was still there because his contract had a year to run. He had been isolated, with nothing to do, in the best office in Siberia. It turned out to be next to the one I chose for myself, so I had seen enough of him to have my own opinion when Mahoney told me that he was willing to pick up the tab for the rest of Bob's contract and it would probably be better all around if I got rid of him now.

"Why?" I said. "We're paying him anyway and he knows a hell of a lot about the magazine business. I'd rather pay him for hanging around. I can always ask him some questions."

When the problems I had with Shana became so painful I could barely get through the day, Bob was my main support. He got the magazine out while Shana single-handedly kept Le Pavillon and the Four Seasons in business. But except for her crunching demands about personal accommodations and comfort, Shana wasn't the witch she was sometimes pictured. Pieces were printed that said I had paid $100,000 for her office. Ridiculous. It only cost $45,000, including the shower. Other pieces, written by people who knew something about the magazine business, said she was my second choice—that Gloria Steinem had said no and Shana had said yes because she knew *Life* was going to die. I did say once at an editorial meeting that Shana was "my shiksa Gloria Steinem" and was promptly corrected by Helen Markel, who said, "Gloria is the shiksa. Shana is the Jew."

Norton thought she was a great idea, David thought she was a great idea and I thought she was a great idea. The whole world thought she was a great idea. Well, except for the backbiting publishing newsletter *The Gallagher Report*, which said she was only a token I was using to head off the kind of confrontation John Mack Carter had had with a hundred feminists who barricaded him in his office, taunted him, smoked his cigars and, according to *Newsweek*, "demanded everything from publication of a column on how to have an orgasm to the removal of editor and publisher John Mack Carter." Mr. Gallagher, who awarded gold medals to Mahoney as Marketing Man of the Year as regularly as he speared me with his harpoons, suggested that I was an amateur. That may have been because I refused to give him a preferential rate for selling our subscriptions, as Mahoney had always done. Anyway, Gallagher's blast got me one of my best Shana notes: "Dear Amateur," she wrote. "Love, Token."

The announcement of Shana's appointment won us an outpouring of admiring publicity, although one of the recurring headlines—"MCCALL'S APPOINTS GIRL EDITOR"—made me wince. But one thing was for sure: there was nobody even remotely connected with the publishing or advertising worlds who did not know that *McCall's* had a new editor, that she was the magazine's first woman editor in forty-eight years and that her name was Shana Alexander.

Shana hated to make speeches, but she made a brave effort to help us out. Us was Ray Eyes, whom I had promoted from publisher of money-making *Redbook* (replacing him with advertising director Carlo Vittorini) to publisher of money-losing *McCall's*, and me. Ray was in trouble with the Armstrong Cork account, which was putting all of its 1970 advertising budget into television, and I persuaded Shana to fly to Lancaster, Pennsylvania, with us and meet them. I thought it might help if they not only saw that our celebrity editor was willing to make such a major effort in their direction but also had a chance to get to know her. It would, I hoped, give them a clearer sense of what her magazine might be like.

"We've got to show you off," I told her.

"Then you're in trouble," she said.

But she showed up at the Marine Terminal at La Guardia at nine o'clock in the morning and climbed onto the twin-engine Cessna I had chartered for the mission. The co-pilot offered coffee from a quart-sized thermos and Shana was impressed. "Where did you get this airplane, Fitz?" she asked when we were up in the air over the Statue of Liberty. "Out of the Yellow Pages," I confessed. "I didn't have time to go through company channels, so I just looked in the phone book and picked the ad that sounded best. The one that seemed most reassuring, you might say. So even if the airplane isn't the greatest or the pilot the best in the world, at least we know they've got a hell of a good copywriter."

We didn't get the Armstrong business, but we scored heavily when we took our traveling road show to Fullerton, California, for our first presentation to the Norton Simon Inc. board. Shana's nervousness and beseeching uncertainty over how you were supposed to go about this kind of thing won over the formidable board members as quickly as she had carried the day with Mahoney back in the beginning.

Shana also was the star of the first out-of-town sales meeting we'd had since she took the job. It was held at Dorado Beach in Puerto Rico because, I suppose, it's centrally located. Shana overcame a lot of the early suspicion about her on the part of the troops and she did it without showing her trademark vulnerability. I thought it proved she was smart enough to know she had to stand up on her feet before our own people and prove to them that she could run the magazine.

"Here I am. Hello. This is me," she had said near the beginning of the first signed piece of hers the magazine ran—in the November 1969 issue.

Some of you already know me. For nearly five years I have been standing on another stage, over at *Life* magazine, writing a column called "The Feminine Eye." ... In many ways, say a thousand or so, I'd rather not appear onstage at all. ... Now that I am in the editing business, running a magazine instead of buzzing around the world like a female Green Hornet, I can think of a thousand more reasons to remain backstage, as an editor should. Then, in a year or so, if you like what we're doing—because it will take a year at least to do it; magazines are big, slow-moving beasts like whales and elephants, but beautiful and wise and responsive like whales and elephants, too—then, in a year, if you like the show, I might be persuaded to step out for a modest bow. ...

214

Shana also said in a couple of her early interviews—and God knows she was subjected to enough of them in those first months—that because she had written a piece about them once, she knew it took an elephant almost two years to be born, but she was sure an adult elephant like *McCall's* could be steered in a different direction in a lot less time than that.

She left everybody at the Dorado meeting in a good mood when she promised one thing for sure: that, as good as the *McCall's* Food Department had been in the past under Mary Eckley, it would be even better now because we had a company president who was so interested in food that he even cooked his own gourmet dinners. "Fitz," she said, "takes a can of Franco-American spaghetti and mixes in a can of Campbell's beans and eats the whole thing out of the pot. With a president like that, we ought to do beautifully with the Campbell Soup Company."

Shana did a lot of good things for us that had nothing to do with making speeches or giving interviews or generally being shown off. She talked Garson Kanin into doing a long, touching piece on the love affair of Katharine Hepburn and Spencer Tracy and even talked Miss Hepburn into letting us use a dozen of her own watercolors, including one of Tracy reading a newspaper. "Tracy used to call her Grandma Moses," Kanin wrote.

She got the magazine rights to a new novel, *The Marriage of a Young Stockbroker*, by Charles Webb, author of *The Graduate*. It cost us a lot of money and it was *New Yorker* fiction which probably would have been rejected by the *New Yorker*, but that wasn't Shana's fault. She didn't write it and she was pressured hard by Webb's agent, Robby Lantz, to take it or forget it because he had other places to go with it. Like me, Shana would much rather have had Webb do her first idea, which was "A Letter to Mrs. Robinson," telling what had happened to Mrs. Robinson and her son's friend since they had been lovers. I liked that idea so much I even wrote Shana some thoughts about it:

> I would like to see the letter open like this: "Dear Mrs. Robinson, We've been out of touch for a long time. How's the family?"

The idea of the Graduate writing to say that he and his wife can't go to her Christmas party is a good one. But he shouldn't say he doesn't want to go because he doesn't like Mrs. Robinson's social attitudes, her wearing coats made out of the skins of animals that shouldn't have been killed for her pleasure, her giving Christmas tips to the people who do her dirty work, or her happy participation in a society that pollutes its air and organizes wars and doesn't bother to cure emphysema. It ought to be that he doesn't want to go because he feels guilty about her. This is a personal letter he's writing, and God knows he had a relationship with her which entitles him to feel guilty.

I would have him explain, in his awkwardly intense, Dustin Hoffman way, that he knows he would feel bad being at her party because he even felt bad on his honeymoon when Elaine was proud of him because he knew how to get through all the mechanics of checking into their hotel room. Elaine might have been proud that he knew how to do it, but he wasn't.

Maybe he could say he had seen her on the street recently and thought she looked great, implying that he was tempted all over again. I think the reader would like it if he didn't just beat her over the head, but made it plain that the good-looking woman who made him say "Jesus Christ, Mrs. Robinson" when she took off her clothes for him is still a good-looking woman. That would make his attack of conscience more believable.

Shana had a lot of good ideas. One that I thought was worth going after, even though it was obvious it would cost us a lot of money, was "Four Revolutionary Women." Shana wanted to do a separate *McCall's* piece on each of the four famous women radicals of the time: Bernadette Devlin, the Irish rebel-politician; Leila Khaled, the Palestinian bomb-thrower; Bernadine Dohrn, the American Weatherwoman; and Angela Davis, the black militant from California. Once all the pieces had run in the magazine, we could make a book out of them for the book-publishing division we were getting ready to launch. But that good idea never happened. What did happen was that I signed checks for it as though the magazine was making money instead of losing it. Still, it was a good idea.

Shana's *McCall's* attracted an above-average amount of fan mail. So much publicity had been generated by her coming that it was inevitable a lot of people would have something to say about what they thought of the magazine. Not all of the comments were as bitterly scornful as Herb Mayes' lengthy critique, which I asked for, of her first Christmas issue. "Terrible" was the kindest word he used. He picked up the elephant metaphor. "It may take a year to turn an elephant around," he said, "but it doesn't take a year for a good editor to turn a magazine around."

Lots of old-time readers of the magazine hated the cover on that Christmas 1969 issue. Maybe there was a Reverend Jerry Falwell out there somewhere leading a chorus of protest against anything untraditional. I didn't know what they were so mad about. The cover was simply a little four-year-old girl, shown from the waist up, wearing nothing but a garland of orange blossoms in her curly blond hair. "You call that a Christmas cover?" Marge Waslenko, the wife of my boyhood friend Mike, wrote in mock alarm from Sun City Center, California. "I want to tell you, Edward, a lot of people out here are pretty upset about it." Well, I was willing to admit there was no Christmas tree on the cover, and no colorfully wrapped presents, but that little child was made in the image of God if one ever was; she had the face of a Botticelli angel. It was probably a good thing people were only upset about the lack of conventional Christmas touches on the cover. Today they would probably be accusing us of child pornography.

There were lots of letters of praise, too. Helen Gurley Brown loved the changes Shana had made. So did Harriet Van Horne, who said, "*McCall's* used to look like a suburban matron wearing too much makeup and at least three mink stoles. The sudden transformation is dazzling beyond words. The clutter is gone, the good bones are showing. The piece on Hepburn had some passages that made me cry. . . . It is lovely to see *McCall's* blossoming in your hands." Helena Rubinstein's senior vice-president, Mala Rubinstein, said, "To my joy, February *McCall's* was beautiful to the eye, interest-packed from start to finish, and thoroughly entertaining. Congratulations on your magic formula. . . ." "The difference is fantastic," Shirley Polykoff, the senior vice-president of Foote, Cone & Belding, said. The creator of the "Does She or Doesn't She?" advertising for Clairol, Shirley qualified as a professional critic.

One night in August of Shana's first year Mahoney had dinner in California with Bill Safire, Bob Finch and Daniel Patrick Moynihan. David told me he spent a lot of time listening to Moynihan telling him how smart he was to have Shana Alexander running *McCall's* because the next big revolution in the country was going to be the revolt of the women. "They don't get a fair shake," Daniel Patrick said, "and they are going to insist on it."

The American Newspaper Women's Club gave Shana one of their four 1969 awards for "outstanding personal achievement in professional journalism." The other three women honored were Katharine Graham, president of the Washington Post Company; Charlotte Curtis, women's-news editor of the New York *Times*; and Helen Thomas, White House correspondent for United Press International. At the award dinner Rita Hauser, a President Nixon appointee to the United Nations Commission on Human Rights, offered a Moynihan-like glimpse of the future when she needled Attorney General John Mitchell for saying that "women are a grumbling and malcontent lot." Mrs. Hauser said, "I can hardly wait to see what he does when women really get militant."

So Shana was there, she was attracting a lot of attention and I felt I had every right to hope that what Herb Mayes called my "impossible dream" might not be all that impossible. Shana was, as I had known from the beginning, without experience as the editor of a major magazine. She had never managed anything. But she had worked for *PM*, a liberal New York City tabloid for which her mother, Cecilia Ager, was the film critic. She had worked for Fleur Cowles' *Flair*, the magazine with a hole in the middle of the front cover—"through which," Shana said wryly, "everything inside fell out." She had been first a journeyman and then a star at *Life*. She knew the difference between good writing and bad writing.

She was also a personality, and *McCall's*, I knew, needed that to help it get off the dime or out from behind the eight ball or just plain to keep from drowning in its own dullness. And she was a woman who had taken over *McCall's*, long billed as "The Magazine for Women," at a time when women's consciousness was being raised in a tearing hurry. Shana, whose name means "Little Pony" in Cherokee and "Pretty" in Yiddish, and whose songwriter father, Milton Ager ("Happy Days Are Here Again," "Hard-Hearted Hannah," "I'm Nobody's Baby"), had written "Ain't She Sweet" to celebrate the day of her birth, was going to attract attention whatever she did, and that was all right with me. I was ready to pay the price to get what I wanted, a *McCall's* that, in Shana's words, would be "for the whole woman, not just her glands."

There was never a dull moment with Shana. At least once a month, and usually more often than that, she conducted a salon in our dining room, with a celebrity guest invited to lunch. Billy Graham told us about how he had to have two attack dogs guard his house, Julia Child terrorized our cook by standing over her shoulder in the kitchen while she simmered and stirred and sauteed, and Alan Jay Lerner told us what it was like to be married so many times that you lose count. Ed Bronfman, head of the House of Seagram, thanked us for giving a job and a new life to his wife, Ann, who had gone to work as a Shana assistant for $140 a week. "You've given me back my wife," Ed said seriously.

Shana had a fight with Ray Eyes once when he wanted her to give a lunch in our dining room for some Bristol-Myers people. She said she would do it, or ones like it, only if I was part of it. "So what we've agreed, Fitz," she wrote me, "is that all the whoring around here will be done at the highest level, Ray, me, and you."

Another time she showed me a piece about her in which one of her friends was quoted as saying, "Shana goes out of the house every morning with an empty leash looking for an underdog." She liked that.

This was no ordinary woman. But I hadn't wanted an ordinary woman. Mahoney hadn't. Norton Simon hadn't. And all three of us believed in taking chances the way we believed in breathing.

My first shock of panic, of "what have I done?" hit me when

I carefully went through my first-off-the-press copy of the March 1970 issue, the one that carried the Charles Webb novel and had a cover line proclaiming "The Occult Explosion." There wasn't much occult about Webb's novel, which seemed to be mostly about a strange young man who liked to drop a mirror out of his window to hang outside the window of the apartment below so he could watch the pretty secretary who lived there take a shower. But I didn't need the ladies of Sun City Center to tell me that this was a far-out *McCall's*.

To begin with, there was a lot of occult, which the dictionary defines as "secret, esoteric, beyond human understanding." I'm afraid the main thing that was beyond our readers' understanding was why we laid so much of it on them all at once.

Susanna McBee, our Washington correspondent, went to the University of Virginia and interviewed J. Gaither Pratt, head of the Division of Parapsychology, about extra-sensory perception.

Nicholas Pileggi did a general piece on the flash fire of interest in the occult. "Until five years ago," he said, "the only contact most Americans had with the occult was through Chinese fortune cookies and penny weighing machines. Then, suddenly, the Age of Aquarius was upon us. . . . More than two million ouija boards were sold last year, and the dignified New York *Times* even interviewed a witch."

Kurt Vonnegut, Jr., the Pied Piper of the young, wrote about "The Mysterious Madame Blavatsky," the occult priestess of the mid-1800s.

At least Kenneth L. Woodward's "Seances in Suburbia" was closer to home. "What happens when respectable matrons start dabbling in the spirit world?" the blurb asked. Well, the women in one community imported a "sensitive" from the big city to help them with their first seance, and he gave them the real word. "Thoughts can boomerang," he said. "Bad thoughts we direct toward other people can circle 'round and come back at us. That's because we are all magnets in a psychic field. So it's important to have good thoughts, as Doctor Norman Vincent Peale wrote in his book *The Power of Positive Thinking*." That, I thought, would have made *McCall's* worth fifty cents of anybody's money. After all, Peale's book cost more than that even in paperback. The best part of the piece was this homey touch: "Because she is the only woman in the group who owns a round table, Marge McKinley was chosen as hostess for the first seance."

Priscilla Friedrich did a piece on "Tarot." That seemed an improvement to me. A lot of us had daughters who fooled around with Tarot cards. Shana wrote about them herself in her "Feminine Eye" piece in that issue. "What was it I asked the cards all that winter," she wondered, "laying out the beautiful, strange, heavy pasteboards day after day in precious privacy behind my locked bedroom door?" Shana always wrote better than the people who wrote for her.

"San Francisco's Church of Satan" was Judith Rascoe's responsibility, and she carried it out faithfully by going there and participating in one of the Black Masses. "The Victorian front parlor and dining room now form a single room, the Ritual Chamber," she reported somberly. Then the piece grew livelier. "Suddenly the door opens and a priestess carrying a candle beckons us to follow her to the Ritual chamber, where we grope our way onto folding chairs and are plunged into impenetrable darkness. . . . The organ booms on and on. . . . Finally the lights flicker a little in the other end of the room, flare up, and reveal half a dozen ministers of Satan, some with their heads covered with pointed black hoods, gathered before the fireplace-altar. On the altar a buxom red-haired girl lies nude and artfully disposed on a fur rug, so that her nudity is more suggested than explicit." That at least made you want to tune in next month and find out what happened.

Selma Robinson wrote about Maurice Woodruff, "Astrology's Brightest Star." Tame stuff.

Jean Stafford, searching for some sociological significance in the sordid Sharon Tate murders, wrote about Charlie Manson's dutiful girls who were "at once his daughters, his sisters, and his concubines."

There were features for straight women on fashion and beauty, needlework and patterns, decorating and household equipment.

There was, of course, even one on food—this one on the glories of Irish cooking, the likes of Irish lamb stew, poached salmon, Irish soda bread and steamed raisin pudding. My problem was that by the time I got that far I wasn't hungry.

The occult explosion wasn't the first time I'd been made uneasy by a concentration of coverage on a single controversial subject. The January 1970 issue, the one that promised a look at "The Good Life on Earth," struck out against the Vietnam war with three separate pieces. David Halberstam's essay on the '60s said:

> The old America revered its war heroes, did not question their military judgment; the old America had earned its right to the riches of this land by fighting the nation's wars; the newer an immigrant you were, the more readily you assumed the burden of a war, and then gladly joined the American Legion or the Veterans of Foreign Wars. But now the definition of patriotism was changing. . . . Now the patriot was the long-haired, bespectacled young man who announced, with NBC and CBS in full view, that it was against his own conscience and his own personal definition of the worth of man . . . to fight a war he considered unjust and immoral. He was a man valued by his contemporaries, *he* was the patriot.

A pregnant Joan Baez, whose husband, David, was in a United States government prison for protesting against the war, wrote about what was happening to her husband and her, and what life might be like for their unborn child:

> I cannot tell if it is a sin of some kind to subject a yet unborn soul to the disease which we call society, or if it is a sin of another kind, equal in wickedness, to deny any potential being the magnificence of one orange sunset. The world, after what we've done to it, is barely fit for a cockroach to live in. It gasps for air and is dying. . . . The truth is simply that we are living in the most violent, reckless, and deadly era the world has ever known. And we, the human race, have chosen to be as blind as snakes, as stubborn as asses, and dumber than cows.

Shana had given former Senator Eugene McCarthy, the man who had led the crusade against the war, a monthly column and a free hand, and this month the eloquent poet-politician-essayist wrote about what the war was doing to the country:

> There is unhappiness over the substance of government policy, and particularly over the war in Vietnam. . . . A single act of injustice, if given public approval, is sufficient to tear the whole fabric of society. The Dreyfus case did tear the fabric of France. The war in Vietnam has come very close to doing the same thing in the United States. For the first time in our history we are involved in a war of questionable legality, in a war the purposes of which we do not fully understand, in a war which we have been unable to win and which we cannot justify on moral grounds either to ourselves or to other people of the world. . . . There have been draft-card burnings, raids on Selective-Service headquarters and recruiting offices, suicides in protest against the war.

The three anti-war articles in that issue provoked a disturbing quandary for me. On the one hand, I both greatly admired Halberstam, Baez, and McCarthy and passionately opposed the war myself. So did Liby and our children. On the other hand, I was pouring all of my energy and enthusiasm and more than a little of my blood into the effort to make this magazine work and I knew in my bones this wasn't the way to go about it. Every once in a while I wished I had been given the charge of making *Harper's* or the *Atlantic* work.

Gene McCarthy was a special problem. I had said yes when Shana asked me if I thought it would be all right for her to take him on. It was a sensitive problem because during the campaign, which Shana had covered from New Hampshire to the convention, she and McCarthy had been written about extensively as what the gossip columnists call "an item." Even after she had become the editor of *McCall's*, especially bold interviewers would ask her if she expected to marry McCarthy after he left his wife Abigail. And soon after she had agreed to take the job, she sent me a note saying she had forgotten to tell me that the Los Angeles *Times* had chosen her "Woman of the Year" in journalism. "That," she said, "was shortly before Maxine Cheshire labeled me '*Other* Woman of the Year.'" But that had never bothered me. What did bother me was that I had hoped Gene would write philosophical, even witty pieces for us that would come out of the title he had picked for his column, "One Man's America," and what we were getting was a series of well-written but heavy-handed musings on the most searing problems of our time, war and politics—subjects I had grown up understanding were as difficult to handle in a general magazine as they were at dinner parties.

The only problem about the whispered relationship between Shana and the Senator was that it made people in the business think that the only reason we kept publishing his square-peg-in-a-round-hole column in *McCall's* was because Shana wouldn't let him go. Shana didn't help any by indirectly writing about it in her own column. "Since I had written about other people for years," she said, "I suppose it was inevitable that sooner or later people would begin to write about me. Still the change from author into character is an awful shock. I was not in the least prepared a year or so ago when my own name began to turn up in the gossip columns. To find oneself lied about in public for the first time is surprisingly nasty."

Shana and I never had an argument about it, not even when I told her we couldn't afford him anymore. He didn't complain, either. As problems went at *McCall's* in those days, Gene McCarthy was a non-problem.

An early minor problem was Shana's casual attitude toward her first Christmas issue. I had lectured her endlessly about how important each Christmas issue is to every women's magazine, and I had especially hammered the point that her first Christmas issue would be of crucial importance, but she kept wriggling away from me. "I'm really incompetent to discuss Christmas," she told me, "because my own attitude pretty much goes along with Scrooge's. All I ever want to do at Christmas is run away and hide, and I usually do. But I haven't given any thought on how to handle Christmas in the magazine. Perhaps when I am as incompetent, and as personally

uninterested in an area as I am in this one, I should have as little to
do with it as possible."

Another headache was her scornful attitude toward anything so
shamefully money-grubbing as the publisher asking her help to
squeeze a late ad into the magazine even though it would displace
a column or a page of editorial copy. Considering that our magazine
was trying to come from far back to break even, much less make a
profit, Ray Eyes and I thought it was reasonable to lean on her to
help out. Shana thought it was reprehensible. I tried getting tough
with her. "Our editorial expenses are running so far above budget,"
I wrote her, "it seems to me only fair to ask for editorial help when
it can contribute to lessening our budget aches and pains." Shana
responded that she didn't know what the hell the editorial budget
was and why didn't somebody tell her? "For the twentieth time?"
Ray asked me despairingly. I tried once again with Shana. "Don't
labor under the misapprehension that this only happens here," I told
her. "Believe me, it happens everywhere, even at *Life*. A full-page
ad is awfully hard to turn down." In the end I simply took the
decision responsibility away from her. That was the beginning of
the end.

She didn't want to write "The Feminine Eye" either. She was
too busy. How could she do all the work of running the staff, deciding on assignments, meeting authors and agents, reading manuscripts, approving art layouts and write a column, too? The answer
clearly was that she couldn't do all of those things, but the one that
she *could* do and do best was write a column. "I don't think anything is so important as maintaining the continuity of 'The Feminine
Eye,' " I told her in one of my million memos. "Nothing that has
been or will be said about our recent troubles will be as harmful as
our giving up the commitment to have you talk to the readers every
month. Stay home tomorrow. Stay home Thursday, too, if you
have to. But we can't go without the column."

We got that one, in the April 1970 issue. In it she made interesting
use of letters from readers. One of the readers said, "Your most
recent issue of *McCall's* depressed me. The comforting thing about
your type of magazine is that it has for the most part ignored the

problems that this issue deals with. I have always read *McCall's* with an eye toward being relieved for an hour of the responsibilities of being a woman (a person) in this spiraling world. Now this is gone forever. Oh, I suppose I could subscribe to the *Ladies' Home Journal* and find food charts that do not include yogurt, and the last articles on the social and economic value of virginity to the modern coed, but I know that this is only a muscle twitch after the body has died. When a bright chick like you agrees to edit a women's magazine, one has to expect this. . . . I suppose now, Mrs. Alexander, I'll just have to grow up."

Shana's answer to the critical points the readers made was: "I passionately hope that before long *McCall's* will have evolved into the magazine you long for—literate, beautiful, entertaining, various, helpful, and compelling."

Maybe, I thought, I ought to put her in charge of the promotion department.

But mostly I wished I could keep her writing that column. It never just lay there; it always drew responses. She wrote a few more. After that the "Eye" was closed.

The staff, which had been unsettled since she arrived, was now always in a state of uneasy tension. Nobody knew who was supposed to be doing what, and everybody knew that if you crossed Shana, deliberately or accidentally, the guillotine was going to get you.

Don McKinney, an experienced, unflappable editor, was willing to leave the dying *Saturday Evening Post* and join us. Shana wanted him and I was glad.

Editors came and went. She fired the beauty editor, the fashion editor and the home-decorating editor. Sitting five floors above Shana, torn between wanting to stand behind her and wanting to give her a chance to do it herself, I watched the magazine go to hell. Shana began to refer to the magazine not as an elephant but as a dinosaur, and then, more affectionately, as "Moby McCall's," so I assumed she had moved on to the friendlier whale. She soon formed a dislike for the new managing editor, McKinney, and an attachment for an English refugee, Clive Irving. I let her have Irving, but

I said no to firing McKinney. I began to be afraid that making this monster of a locomotive run at all, much less run on time, was more than she could handle. She had alternate fits of confidence and despair. Her memos to me went up and down:

> I trust me now in ways I sure didn't a year ago, or even six months ago. . . . You know to what extent I am flying blind, going on instinct, but that instinct tells me over and over to try to make a magazine that I, I, I would like to read. . . . It's almost a year to the day that you made that famous trans-continental phone call "You don't know me, but . . ." I think this is a good point to pause and take stock. . . . We don't have to enumerate the stumbling blocks and the hidden icebergs which have loomed in the seven months since you took the crazy step of putting an inexperienced editor in command of a sinking ship. . . . But now I feel a strong sense of confidence that I know what *McCall's* should be like, and a new sense of sureness that I know how to make it that way.

"My own effectiveness," she wrote later, "is rapidly approaching zilch. Personally and professionally, I'm in poor shape, and I don't want to hang on by my fingertips much longer."

God knows she was right. I couldn't beat up her or the magazine any more. Her "fingertips" memo went on to say, ironically, "I'll be away on vacation June 15 to July 1. Love, Token." She did say that the house in which she would be vacationing came complete with a staff of servants and a swimming pool, "in which," she said, "I intend to spend the next week lying face down."

Not even good news could induce me to put on my rose-colored glasses again. Mahoney told me that David Susskind had said to him, "I've fallen in love with Shana Alexander," and I said I thought that was nice. Jack Benny raved about her on the David Frost show: "You know who I'd like to have write my book?" he asked Frost. "Because she's a marvelous woman? Shana Alexander. She followed me on a concert tour once and wrote the most beautiful article I've ever read. Funny, clever, very witty, and she wrote it so beautifully. Sometime, maybe I'd better do it pretty soon, I'm going to say to her, how would you like to write my autobiography?"

Could *McCall's* have first serial rights? I wondered.

There was nothing to do now, late in 1970, except begin to pick up the pieces and make a new start. The first thing I did—and it was Shana's idea, in the depths of our mutual despair—was to hire Patricia Carbine from *Look*. Pat Carbine, as Irish as John Jameson's, was considered in the business to be the consummate magazine professional. She wasn't forty years old yet and she had been with *Look* since 1953. She had been made managing editor in 1966 and executive editor in 1969. She was a pretty, black-haired, slightly plumpish woman with a peaches-and-cream complexion, laughing Irish eyes, the most wonderful smile you were ever charmed by, and a will of iron. She believed that deadlines were made to be met and budgets made to be lived within and, above all, that the magazine came first. She achieved her goals mostly by persuasion and example, but everybody who worked with her knew that, one way or another, she was going to achieve them and you had better not get in her way. She knew Shana and knew what she was getting into, but I promised her I would get Shana out of the way. "The ideal situation," I said, "would be for Shana to write as often as we can get her to write, and to talk to other writers and bring them in. If we can get her to do that, and have you run the magazine, we'll be in good shape."

"Expensive," Pat observed. "You're going to pay me to edit the magazine and Shana not to edit it."

"It happens in baseball all the time," I said. "Anyway, it will be cheaper than what we've been doing. Believe me, you never thought of as many ways to spend money as she has. Let me worry about the money. You put out the magazine."

Ray, who was ecstatic about the change, added, in his conservatively optimistic way, "It's always possible, you know, that a *McCall's* doing what we've been wanting it to do, and looking the way we've been wanting it to look, will bring in some money."

Pat left the starting blocks like a world-class sprinter. She made friends with our newest art director, Alvin Grossman, and told him they would stay friends as long as he got things done, looking as good as he could make them look, in the time she would give him.

"Late," she told him, "is out. Give me the best you can give me in the time you have. If it isn't good enough," she said disarmingly, "we'll get somebody else." It was as though somebody had opened all the windows on the floor. People came to work earlier and stayed later. There were fewer staff meetings and more of the kind of meetings between two or three people that happen in the halls or the open offices or even the bathrooms of a magazine that has drive and enthusiasm and confidence because everybody knows where they are going and, most of all, who is in charge.

My excuse for getting Shana out of the way was that, after a year of trying, I had finally got permission from Mahoney to cut the magazine's page size down from the anachronistic 680-line, roughly 13x10 size, which hardly anybody used any more, to the standard 429-line, roughly 8x11 size, and to cut the circulation from 8.5 million to 7.5 million. The costs were killing us and we knew we had to go down. We would save a mint in paper and printing costs. I was surprised to find out that we would save something like $60,000 a year just in ink. I'd been fighting for the changes for months. "It could be our salvation," I kept telling Mahoney, "and it will be good for the advertisers. They're making almost all their plates in the 8x11 size now, and the lower cost per thousand will make it easier for them to use *McCall's*."

The great man finally admitted to me, late one night, that he couldn't let me change the page size yet because the McCall Printing Company at Dayton had a profitable contract to print the *Ladies' Home Journal* and he had promised Ed Downe, whose Downe Communications Inc. owned the *Journal*, that *McCall's* would wait until the *Journal* was ready so both magazines could make the change at the same time. My last big pitch was to go with the January 1971 issue, and, ironically, I was in Dayton the night David called to tell me no, not yet. "Eddie told me 'John Carter wants more time to study all the assumptions,'" David said. "But," he went on in his inimitably warm style, "Eddie doesn't think it will take long. Mostly, they want to gear up to make a big PR plus out of it. Anyway, January is out. Maybe February."

I was a big boy and I understood the realities of the printing company contract, so I didn't bother to make a flag-waving speech about the *Journal* being my competition. "David," I said in my most measured tone, "I don't want it to be any later than February. That's the best month of the year, except September, to make a change like this, and if we wait until September, we may be dead."

When I got to my office in New York in the morning, I sat down at my priceless assistant Susan Huberman's typewriter and created a press release. I took the elevator down to the tenth floor and laid a copy on Mahoney's desk and other copies on the desks of his principal lieutenants, Garry Bewkes, Joe Gamache and Orhan Sadik-Kahn. I wrote it at what you might call cold heat:

> John Mack Carter, president and publisher of *Ladies' Home Journal*, a division of Downe Communications Inc., announced yesterday that *McCall's* magazine, a division of The McCall Publishing Company, was abandoning its plan to adopt the standard or 429-line page size effective with the January 1971 issue.
>
> Mr. Carter said that he and Charles Aikman, president of The McCall Printing Company, felt that the move was not in their best interests at this time. He did, however, hold out the hope that the move might be made by *McCall's* at some future date to be determined by the *Journal*.
>
> Business circles also noted with interest an announcement yesterday by the Ford Motor Company that Chevrolet would postpone the debut of its new mini-car, the Vega, until Ford is ready with its competitive Pinto.

Mahoney laughed, Bewkes laughed and Sadik-Khan laughed. Joe Gamache called me up, screaming, "You can't send that out to the papers! You'll ruin us!"

What I got out of it was Mahoney's agreement that he would tell Downe it was February and that that was it. If they weren't ready then, it was their problem. "Thank you, David," I said wearily.

I told Shana what we were doing and said I wanted her to spend her time from now on thinking about that first 8x11 issue and the ones that were going to follow it, talk to every writer and photographer and artist she knew, and fill up sheets of paper with ideas that would bowl over the people. "Stay away from the magazine," I said. "Leave Pat alone. She'll run it. You think." I encouraged her to stay home a lot, to travel, to be the original lady who takes people to lunch. "We have Pat now. Bob Stein will help, Warren Erhardt will help, McKinney will help and Al Grossman will help. What we need from you is the heart and soul of the new magazine."

It worked for a while. She stayed out of everybody's hair. "I think it may be okay," Pat said one day. "Actually, she may see that she can do us more good this way and have a better time herself. Anyway, I hope so."

"Me, too," I said. But I should have known better. The Elizabeth Regina in Shana couldn't stand taking second place. "I propose to resume command of this ship," she announced in a chilly memo to me.

With Pat here, I believe we will be able to function in the manner all of us have been hoping for.

For practical purposes, this means that I will assume full editorial responsibility for the January issue. Editorial control will have to come back to this office. I feel that it is particularly important that these priorities begin operating before the February issue. That, and subsequent, issues will never work if they are the product of Group Journalism. All editorial decisions must pass over one desk, or through one head, if a magazine is to have one clear personality.

. . . My editorial involvement in the September-through-December issues has diminished far below the level I had intended when I voluntarily stepped away in order to work on February and beyond. . . . What I mean, Fitz, is this: stories are scheduled, pieces are bought, art work is ordered, stuff is set in type, people appear on the masthead, layouts are approved—without even a ritual nod in here. I have the pervasive and accurate impression that people are trying to fog stuff past me and into print, and while that is often a favor and a relief of editorial burdens, it is often, and increasingly, a mistake. These four issues are filled with stuff I've never seen and/or don't want. Other material that I have seen, and do want, mysteriously vanishes forever.

Please, please do not take this either as paranoia or as bitching. I know I relinquished control . . . but as of next week, or as of the January issue if you prefer to think of it that way, we must revert to the previous system so far as editorial authority is concerned. I hope it isn't necessary to add that consultation and advice from management, and particularly from the experienced and patient Bob Stein, will continue to be invaluable to us. . . . But everybody must be made to understand who is now and henceforth in charge here.

Shana signed that memo, "Thanks, Ex-Token." No more love.

I didn't have to do much soul-searching. I couldn't go back on my deal with Pat, which was that she would be in charge of the magazine without question, that she would be paid at Shana's level and that as her contribution to the cause she would choke down the appearance of Shana's name above hers on the masthead. We called Shana the editor and Pat the editorial director. But the whole staff, and that small part of the world that cared, knew that Patricia Theresa Carbine was in charge of the magazine—and that couldn't change.

"Take it easy," I counseled Shana. "Bring in great stories and great writers. Write some great pieces yourself. That will make you Lady McCall's. But leave Pat alone. Run no meetings, approve no layouts, hire no people and fire no people. All of that is Pat's racket."

She didn't like it much, but, curiously, she didn't make a fuss, either. She even wrote me a letter from the Irish retreat to which she had fled to rest and recover, and it began with a peacemaker. "Dearest Fitz," she wrote. "From this lovely vantage point, our troubles of the last year seem worth it, and I can look forward to our next year with composure and keen anticipation. Since this was not precisely my mood when staggering out of New York City, I thought I should let you know. Ireland can take only partial credit for this. Mostly, it's knowing that the man who is sitting where you are is you. Love, Shana."

We got along for a few months more, but it didn't work. I suppose it couldn't work. Shana wouldn't stay out of things, and, remembering the past and all the heads in the basket, few people were willing to risk challenging her. "We can only have one boss," Pat said simply. "I know," I said.

It was Showdown Time at the OK Corral. Just before I went to confront the lioness in her den and tell her she had to stay out of the office, I got an omen in the inter-office mail. "I have at last figured out what my title around here should be," Shana said: " 'Once and Future Editor.' "

I went downstairs armed with a copy of my *aide-mémoire* of the meeting we'd had a few months before. Intended for Mahoney as well as for me, it had been written right after the meeting and it said:

Shana will turn over the management of the magazine to Bob Stein now, to Pat Carbine later.

She will leave the Oct.-Nov.-Dec.-Jan. issues to Bob and later Pat to worry about while she devotes her time to working with Clive Irving on ideas, designs, etc. for the standard-size magazine.

She will do what she can to help out on public relations.

She will do her own personal best to convince Pat Carbine that she (Shana) will do everything she can to make sure Pat is able to function without question or argument as the editor responsible for getting the magazine out.

She isn't sure what she would like the new editor to be called. She agrees it was her idea to call her "Editor" while she took the title of "Editor-in-Chief" but clearly now she feels that's a kicked-upstairs switch and she doesn't like it so much. She wants time to think it over.

The scene in Shana's office might have been written by Edward Albee. There is no way I could re-create that hour, nor do I want to. Shana began by being nostalgic, full of remember-whens and

God-how-hard-we-trieds, moved on to threatening me with all kinds of legal actions and assaults by her newspaper and magazine friends on *McCall's* reputation, my reputation and Mahoney's reputation, and finished up in a tear-streaked, throat-choked, impotent rage that ended with her picking up the first book she could lay her hands on and throwing it at me. She missed, or I ducked, or both, but it would have been all right with her if she had hit me. She wanted her magazine back, she wanted her reputation back, she wanted her dreams back and, I knew, she wanted her throne back. I had given it to her and now I was taking it away. I was the Devil Incarnate.

It seemed like hours later, but it was probably less than an hour, when she calmed down enough to ask me coldly if I intended to honor her contract, which ran until April 1972. I said of course we would. I said David and I would like her to move over to the NSI offices on Park Avenue and work out of there as a corporate ambassador to women. She could travel around the country and report on what women were thinking and doing; she could write reports, make a few speeches, do question-and-answer appearances before women's groups and help everybody, from the Hunt-Wesson people to *McCall's* and *Redbook*, find out what women were up to. She didn't like that much, but she didn't say anything. Finally, she got up and, in a characteristic gesture of acceptance, smoothed her skirt elaborately. "Will you come to my apartment tomorrow morning and sign some pieces of paper about all this?" she asked. "I'll have my lawyer there."

I went to her apartment with our lawyer and we signed everything she wanted us to sign. Whatever she wanted, within reason, was all right with me, and it didn't take long. She offered coffee, even drinks, but I just wanted to leave and she knew it. She walked me to the door of the apartment that we had found for her and rebuilt to her specifications and decorated the way she wanted it, sometimes even twice over when she changed her mind about a room. She stood up straight, all five feet three of her, and looked at me without blinking. "Well, Fitz," she said, "there isn't anything left to fight about now except who gets the picture over the mantel."

Chapter 14

NORTON SIMON'S willingness to let me start my own book-publishing company had almost as much to do with my saying yes to him as my eagerness to escape Nelson and my willingness to make some money. But from the day Norton made up his mind to back away from the business, the book company was dead. It was just that it took me a while to find it out.

There aren't many things harder to do than to start a new book company. It's hard even if you have a lot of your own money to put into it. I thought we had a chance because we had not only Norton's money, in the shape of the McCall Publishing Company's assets and cash flow, but also his sponsorship. That meant we could use all the muscle the company had with authors, agents, printers, photographers and artists. I didn't want this to be my Road Not Taken. It was the first job I asked Bob Stein to help me with and he responded like a retired fireman given a brand-new, shiny, red American La-France to drive. He hired Byron Dobell, who was looking for something interesting to do after leaving *Esquire*, to help him put together a staff and, not least, a first list of books. Naomi Burton, who had retired from Doubleday, had been earning nickels and dimes scouting for them and she agreed to scout for us for a modest salary.

Bob had some interesting books under way by the middle of 1969. He and Byron made a deal with *Esquire* to do *Smiling Through the Apocalypse*, *Esquire*'s portrait of the chaotic 1960s as seen by the likes of Gore Vidal, Norman Mailer, Tom Wolfe, William Styron, James Baldwin, Gay Talese, William Burroughs and Jean Genet. The *Esquire* book sold pretty well, but, with almost a thousand pages, printing it cost too much to allow us to make a profit. It did, however, enable us to publish one of the great magazine titles of the decade: " 'Joe,' Said Marilyn Monroe, Just Back from Korea, 'You Never Heard Such Cheering.' 'Yes, I Have,' Joe DiMaggio Answered.' "

Naomi, who had been Tom Merton's agent and was with Bob Giroux one of his executors, got us *Merton on Peace*. Father Merton's book put together all of his writings in the last ten years of his life on war, peace and non-violence. Naomi, who had known him as a civilian, so to speak, and had been one of the few people allowed to visit him at the Abbey of Gethsemane in Tennessee—she always smuggled a bottle of bourbon in with the papers in her briefcase—brought back from one of her trips a book that richly deserves reprinting today.

"Not only non-Christians," Father Merton wrote, "but even Christians themselves tend to dismiss the Gospel ethic of non-violence and love as 'sentimental.' As a matter of fact, the mere suggestion that Christ counseled non-violent resistance to evil is enough to invite scathing ridicule. . . . It is . . . a serious error to imagine that because the West was once largely Christian, the cause of the Western nations is now to be identified, without further qualification, with the cause of God."

Bob drew on his *Redbook* experience to sign up two books by longtime *Redbook* contributors: one by Dr. Benjamin Spock, *Decent and Indecent*, on contemporary social values, and a partial autobiography by Margaret Mead, *Blackberry Winter*. Our hopes that the new book company would be helped by its connection with the magazines proved to have some basis in reality. Norman Cousins had been working with Arnold Palmer on a how-to book called *Situation Golf*, which had been contracted by Simon & Schuster, and he acted with commendable speed to divert the book to us when S&S insisted on renegotiating the deal with Palmer to pay him a lower royalty on the ground that he wasn't getting the little white ball into the cup quite so readily as he used to. We sold 22,000 copies of it, and the Literary Guild sold 10,000 in the first two months after publication. We picked up another book with sports roots when we bought a book of poems, *Over the Rim*, by Tom Meschery, the star forward of the Seattle Super-Sonics. Meschery's book, which I'm glad I still have a copy of, gave us these two un-forgettable portraits:

To Bill Russell:

> I have never seen
> an eagle with a beard
> but if there is
> in some strange
> corner of the world
> and the Hindu
> belief is true,
> you will return
> and beat your wings
> violently
> over my grave.

To Red Auerbach:

> who can be
> indifferent?
> not that
> mad man
> over there—
> an owl's
> scream away
> from death.

The book company got a potent shot of adrenaline when the firm of Goodman and Sopkin said a reluctant goodbye to the Literary Guild we had all worked so hard to build and walked two blocks down Park Avenue to join us. That meant, with Vilma Bergane, Stan Donaldson, Jane Pasanen, Paula Diamond, Bob Gales and now Irv and Charlie, we had a solid core of major-league book-publishing experience. Lots of long-established houses had less.

Irv came on as vice-president of the McCall Publishing Company and general manager of the book division. Bob Stein, who was already beginning to be needed as the Dutch boy with his finger in the *McCall's* magazine dike, became senior vice-president of the company. More than ever, I was glad I hadn't sent him home with a fat check and nothing to do.

Irv came up with a big winner in Tommy Thompson's *Hearts*, the story of the Texas heart doctors Denton Cooley and Michael DeBakey. He paid $35,000 for it and promptly got $30,000 for it as a Book-of-the-Month Club alternate and a $100,000 floor from Fawcett Books as the first step in the paperback auction. Charlie produced a genuine Sopkin in *Report from Engine Co. 82* by Dennis Smith, which also became a Book-of-the-Month Club alternate and ran for weeks on the *Times* best-seller list. Charlie read a letter to the editor in the *Times* one morning that argued with something the paper had printed about Yeats. The letter was signed "Fireman Dennis Smith, Engine Co. 82." Charlie had to meet this literary fireman, and he did, and the more he talked to him, the more he knew there was a book in him. Furthermore, this fireman wasn't going to need a ghost. He was an English major from NYU and he was Irish and writing came as naturally to him as talking, which he was also pretty good at. Another profit-maker was Princess Luciana Pignatelli's *The Beautiful People's Beauty Book*, which cost Irv $3,000 and earned a $30,000 advance from Bantam Books for paperback rights. "It's a straightforward approach to narcissism," the Princess' husband said proudly. Laura Conway's mystery *The Night of the Party* got $8,000 from Bantam, and BOMC put up a $7,500 advance for *The Redbook Cookbook*.

I thought we were doing pretty well. Unfortunately, a book that we never published—and, indeed, was never written—exploded the first land mine underneath us. Mahoney almost had a stroke when he read in one of our reports that we had agreed to pay an advance of $150,000 to Orson Welles for the autobiography the *enfant terri-ble* of the movies had been threatening for years to write. "How the hell can you agree to pay $150,000 for a book that hasn't even been written yet?" he wanted to know, reasonably enough for somebody who hadn't been raised in the madhouse of publishing. David was used to counting the number of cases of Johnnie Walker that were unloaded for him on the docks of New York and multiplying that figure by his budgeted profit and coming up with a number that carried no risk whatsoever. When he weighed Welles' reputation for sobriety, industry, and punctuality, the only thing he could see in our venture was risk, risk, and more risk. "Jesus," he complained to me, "if you're going to buy a ticket on a long shot like that, can't you at least go to the five-dollar window?"

The political animal in David responded with a lot more enthusi-asm to my itch to go after the book of memoirs Lady Bird Johnson was widely reported to be ready to write. Politics always contended neck-and-neck with money as David's first love. He never enjoyed a *McCall's* problem more than the one we faced when Jackie Onas-sis cried foul because we had bought from the artist Aaron Shikler publication rights to thirteen magnificent paintings he had done of her and her children. I didn't know what she was mad about, be-cause we had asked her permission before we dealt with the artist and she had offered no objection. Now that we were ready to pub-lish them, she was mad. Mahoney swung into action. He dispatched one of my assistants, a beautiful former model, Anne Close, to have lunch at the White House with Bill Safire, who had undertaken to smooth things over. But Mahoney's instinct to involve the White House paid off and we ran the pictures without incident. We even sold a lot of copies of the issue, the second in the standard size and the second with Pat Carbine's name on the masthead. I needed David's approval of an $800,000 offer to Lady Bird for combined magazine and book rights to her memoirs, and, with no questions at all and only a few jokes about how come I never offered that kind of money to a Republican, David said yes.

Bob Stein had something of an in with Lady Bird because he had given Lynda Bird a job while he was still editing *McCall's* and she had worked there, Secret Service protectors and all, for a year. She was going out a lot with George Hamilton that year, and Lady Bird didn't like it at all. She didn't think Hamilton was even a good actor, much less in other respects a suitable candidate for her elder daughter's hand. She enlisted Bob's help in trying to talk Lynda out of too deep a commitment and she was lastingly grateful for Bob's sympathetic help. So when we made our offer, she took it seriously and even invited us to come down to the ranch for a weekend to talk it over.

It was a weekend to remember. Lyndon Johnson had been out of office only five months and had been virtually invisible to the outside world. We didn't know quite what, if anything, to expect of him, but Bob said, "Look, we're going to see *her*. We may not see him at all. Not to worry."

This is the way I described the weekend to my son, who was then a war-protesting student at Northwestern:

The trip Bob Stein, the man who is running our book company, and I made Friday and Saturday to the LBJ Ranch was something else. Riding the range in a Lincoln Continental (black) with Him at the wheel is an experience approached only by doing the same thing in a Lincoln Continental (white) with Her at the wheel. We did both, rounding up white-faced Herefords with the man and looking at endless acres of wildflowers with the lady.

We got to Austin at about 7:30 Friday evening and were met by a Secret Service man Bob had known at *McCall's* who drove us out to the ranch. Lynda Bird, her husband Chuck Robb, and their baby were the only other people there. We had a warm Texas-style greeting from Mrs. Johnson on the porch—I forgot to say you have to get past two Secret Service outposts before you penetrate the inner ranch—and then Mr. Johnson, Lynda and Chuck had a drink with us. He made the drinks, gin and tonic, very effete Eastern, no bourbon and branch water. Then into a Southern dinner, pieces of chuck steak done and done and done, as if in a Dutch oven, and served with brown gravy. I remember lots of hot corn bread, too, and hot peach cobbler with heavy cream for dessert. Each course at each meal comes with a running commentary from the head of the house giving its origin—sometimes down to the name of the cow they slaughtered for the beef.

The Man talks easily, spends most of his time playing with Lynda's baby girl Lucinda, and questioning the men who work on the ranch about whether or not they "*com*bined" the oats on the South Forty and did they remember to dig the post holes for the new fence along the river (that's the Pedernales) which runs right through the ranch and nearby Johnson City— a collection of gas stations, two restaurants, an LBJ Souvenir Shop, and an auctioneer's set-up some five or six miles down the road. He gave us one three-quarters-of-an-hour lecture on Vietnam and said nobody will ever know, or believe, the secret things he tried to do to end the war. He also said it was Dean Rusk, the great Hawk, who wanted the bombing to end and who finally persuaded him last March to end it. And he said he thinks Nixon will end it because everybody wants it ended and now it's like a pregnant woman going through her seventh or eighth month. You know it's almost over, and you know it's got to be over before much longer, you just don't know when.

Mrs. Johnson not only talks easily, and a lot, and with a much juicier Southern accent than he does, but charmingly and inter- estingly. She is informal, wears slacks and sweaters most of the time, and just lets her hair hang the way it happens to hang. I guess. Maybe it takes some artful Mr. Kenneth hours to achieve that careless look. Anyway, she looks and acts friendly and manages to make you feel as though she really is glad you're there. Of course, we were only trying to persuade her to take our $800,000, so there was no particular reason for her not to be friendly to us. She never did commit herself, incidentally, being, I guess, altogether too smart a businesswoman for that, but I left with the impression that she would decide soon—and that we had a chance. I'd like very much to do her book. I think it's going to be a good one, and specifically much more interesting and readable than his, which is going to be handicapped by the inevitable need of an ex-President to justify his administration even if it takes a thousand footnotes.

Neither of the Johnsons said much of anything about the Abe Fortas Supreme Court resignation, except for the barest reference to the sadness of it all. The head of the ranch Secret Service detail drove us to the airport Saturday afternoon and said neither he nor any of the men who worked with him ever had been bothered by any Johnson controversy as much as they were by their feeling that the old man must have known about the whole Wolfson bit when he was trying to make Fortas the Chief Justice but went ahead with it anyway. Who was it who said that all power corrupts and absolute power corrupts absolutely? [I looked it up. It was Lord Acton.]

We slept Friday night at a guest cottage called The Cedar House near the main house, with all the comforts including a bathroom with each bedroom and a package of Air Force One playing cards on an end table in the living room. We resisted the temptation to walk off with them. The matchbooks, which were somewhat coyly labeled The President's House, we did take. Well, you never can tell when you're going to need a match. We woke up Saturday morning to a magnificent sunny day (the clouds came out for good about an hour later) and walked along the river for a while, alternately ducking bulls that looked murderous and Secret Service men who looked merely skeptical, but were equipped with our names, ranks and serial numbers and were coolly polite to the guests. We were standing in front of the house, looking at a fancy swimming pool, when we heard a loud thumping on one of the windows on the ground floor. It was Mr. Johnson, in his pajamas, waving at us to come in. So we went over to the door, which he held open, and there he was standing with the baby in his arms. Mrs. Johnson was sitting on the couch reading the newspapers in her nightgown. How homey can you get? Later we had a big ranch breakfast, mostly thick homegrown bacon ("That ain't no cash-and-carry bacon," Mr. Johnson said, pushing the bacon). Lots more corn bread, this time toasted, and poached eggs for us New Yorkers. Mister President had a small steak. So much for the homegrown bacon.

Lynda, incidentally, treats the old man to a real West Point cadet response whenever he calls her. She clicks her heels, throws back her shoulders, and says, "Yes, *sir*," in a loud voice and with a heavy emphasis on the *sir*. I don't know whether she's putting him on, or the other people. Probably half and half. Young Chuck Robb is vigorously and militarily polite to him, as is proper for an ex-Marine Corps captain, but he gets even by mimicking him behind his back and by looking pained when he gets too grandfatherly with the kid.

The ritual tours of the ranch in those Continentals, which both He and She drive like armored tanks over the open pastureland, took up most of the morning, and then we sat on the patio behind the house and had a long discussion of the book with both of them. After a while he asked me, abruptly, "What do you think of the chances of *my* book?" He seemed a little hurt that we had been going on for so long about hers without even mentioning his. I told him I thought it would sell pretty well and would sell even better than that if he really opened up on his feelings about the war. He went on pretty strongly about what he wanted to write, maybe for half an hour or so, but what the hell, I thought, fair is fair.

Around the ranch The Man wears gray cotton pants and a gray cotton shirt, like a New York City probationary patrolman.

Speaking of New York, we talked before dinner about the New York City primary campaign. He wanted to know if Norman Mailer and Jimmy Breslin were serious about running and if we thought Wagner had a chance. "I never knew him when he wasn't for the folk," he said, "although I have to say he always looked as though he needed to send his clothes to the dry cleaner's."

He drove us down the 6,300-foot airstrip alongside the ranch house and complained bitterly about all the stories he'd read that said the government had built it for him. "They didn't build nothing," he said. "I paid $29,000 for it back before I was the Vice-President. It's long enough to land almost anything, even a DC-9, but it isn't solid enough to handle a 727 or a 707." He keeps a twin-engine Jetstar and a Bell helicopter in his hangar. The man who flies the airplanes also runs the farm machinery.

Mostly, Mama calls him "Darlin'" and "Angel," and he calls her "Bird."

He was cutting up the New York *Times* once, and said, ". . . that is, if you still consider the *Times* a good newspaper. . . . The trouble with the *Times* is that if you don't call in Scotty Reston before you do something, they kill you for a month."

He bought the ranch for $19,000 in 1951. He quoted what one rich lady from Houston said when she first came out for a party and he asked her what she thought of it. She tried to duck the question, but when he insisted, she said, "If you really want to know, if I owned it, I'd run a bulldozer right through it." Thinking back on all the the work they've done on it, he said, gloomily, "She was probably right. It sure would have been cheaper."

Lady Bird said once, when we were driving around the ranch and she was showing us the 80 acres of wildflowers she managed to keep Him and his crew from using for cattle feed, that "Nightfall never caught us in Washington on the day Congress adjourned. We lit out for here right away."

He and Bird apologized for the looks of one particularly scrawny herd of cattle. (The big herd is just magnificent, and when groups of kids or tourists are being brought to the house, as was the case this Sunday, LBJ makes the hired men walk the cattle up to the front and side lawns and scatter them carelessly around as props.) "We had more grass than we could eat," he said, putting himself in with the cattle, "so we got these, thinking we could fatten them up and sell them." "I hope we didn't pay too much for them," Bird said. And he said, "A hundred dollars a head. The others, the whitefaces, go for a thousand a head. But look at the difference. All of them white-faces are layin' down now, at the middle of the mornin', takin' it easy. They're full. They been full for years. Them other critters is out there hustlin'. They're still hungry."

Our last lunch was set up by a pitcher of Bloody Marys, very good and very cold, with a lot of coarsely ground pepper on top that made you thirsty enough to drink more Bloody Marys. The food was fried slices of ham, string beans cooked Soul style for hours and hours in their own juice, more hot corn bread and a great cold vegetable salad, and fresh peaches sliced and buried under what the President called "local cream."

Well, we sure got enough to eat. Then, with flight time an hour and a half away and Austin about sixty miles away, we got up and left just as a group of directors of the LBJ Corporation (the famous television station) arrived, looking for all the world as if they had been sent over by Central Casting to play the conniving Texas ranchers getting ready to foreclose on the little sharecroppers' mortgages.

I was hotly embarrassed when, while Mister President was beginning his business meeting, he answered the phone and came out to tell me it was for me. "London," he said. It turned out to be Byron Dobell, saying he hated to bother me at the Ranch but he was trying to nail down a new Stephen Vizinczey book and he had to say yes or no right now. I said yes.

We got warm handshakes and goodbyes, a car from the fleet in the yard and the top Secret Service man to drive it (which he did at ninety miles an hour all the way) and we said goodbye to the Ranch. I may never do anything quite like it again—unless we get the book, and then . . . my God, I hadn't thought of that.

The only really bad thing that happened to us was after we checked in at the airport and asked the man at the counter where we could find the bar. "Not in the State of Texas," he said, shaking his head sadly. "It's a dry state. Only packaged goods are sold here."

Wouldn't you know?

We didn't get Lady Bird's book, but we did get the magazine rights and our November and December 1970 issues were enriched by fat excerpts. Lady Bird wrote as if she were sitting next to you, talking to you. She gave a homey touch to the gravest matters and the most important events, and she made you feel you knew, as she did, the people you read about every day on the front page and saw and heard every night on the six-o'clock news. Her account of the President's growing conviction that he shouldn't run again, and their many conversations about it, provided a new insight into his decision. But it was a personal revelation, of universal interest, that stayed with me.

"I went to sleep satisfied and happy to be at Camp David," Lady Bird wrote. "Now that the time grows short, I count the days that are left at the White House, and I want to use them carefully and spend them lovingly. Churchill's words go over and over in my mind: 'So little done, so much yet to do.' And one of the oddest things is that as the result of the wedding which will happen tomorrow on a Greek island, I feel strangely free. No shadow walks beside me down the halls of the White House or here at Camp David. I wonder what it would have been like if we had entered this life unaccompanied by that shadow."

We had a warm, lively dinner party in New York for Lady Bird to celebrate the magazine's publication of the excerpts from the book. Mahoney shared an apartment in the Waldorf Towers with John Kluge, the Metromedia man, and David talked Kluge into letting us use it for the event. John may have regretted saying yes, because the only person who was inconvenienced by the dinner, and in fact was implored to leave her room because we had to use it as a cloakroom, was Kluge's friend Gina Lollobrigida. But Miss Lollobrigida graciously resigned herself to our gentle prods and left without having to be carried out. Some wonderfully interesting people turned out for our party, which consisted of a dinner for sixteen and a larger reception afterward. Mary and Walter Cronkite came, Margaret Truman and Clifton Daniel, Mary Lasker, Adele Simpson, David Merrick, Liz Carpenter, Alistair Cooke and William S. Paley.

Walking into the living room after dinner to make sure everything was properly set up for the reception, I found my friend John Sargent picking up ashtrays and wiping them out. "That's very good of you, John," I said, and he laughed. "Anything for a friend," he said. The friend wasn't me; it was our public-relations director, who was in charge of the party. John was being a good date.

The book division didn't single-handedly bring down the company. If *McCall's* had been able to generate the kind of profits *Redbook* did—under publisher Vittorini and editor Sey Chassler—some $3.5 million a year, the chances are Mahoney would have been more patient with it. Certainly, Norton would have been. But David was trying to make good in a big way and he didn't want the lake of red ink in which our new enterprise was wobbling. We had expected to lose about $400,000 in our first year, but our overhead was ferociously expensive and we were losing more like $1 million. That did not make David happy.

His first move was a daring one that I thought was going to give me instant access to my goal. David met me on the elevator one morning in May 1970 and said, "Come on into my office. I've got some good news for you." When we sat down, he said, "I bought Simon & Schuster for you last night."

My first thought was: Whatever happened to small talk? But I had no reason to deny David the impish Irish delight on his face. "I'll take it," I said. "I didn't know you even knew Leon Shimkin."

"I don't," David admitted. "Never met him. But Orhan has. He set it up and I clinched it on the phone with Shimkin last night. What kind of a guy is he?"

"He's not your type," I said, "although he does like to drink." The world's champion consumer of Canada Dry ginger ale laughed. "He's a businessman," I said, "not a publisher, but he's always had enough brains to let his editors do what they know how to do as long as it doesn't cost too much money. He's a little bit like my old friend Irving Manheimer. If you do twice as much work as you should have to do for the kind of money he pays you, you'll get along fine with him. He's been sick a lot, off and on the last few years, and the word is he doesn't always remember things. As much as he loves to run the company and be a big man in publishing, he's probably about ready to get out. It's a hell of a good company. If you're getting it for a fair price, you're buying a good thing. With at least three good people, Dick Snyder, Sy Turk and Michael Korda. And you're not only getting Simon & Schuster, which is one of the three or four best and most aggressive trade publishing companies around even if it isn't one of the biggest, but you're getting Pocket Books, too. Pocket was the first American paperback house and it's still one of the top five. What's it costing you?"

"Twenty-three point five," David said. "They did thirty-seven million in sales last year and made a million one."

I said, "It's a steal. Take it and run."

I think David began to wonder what he was getting into when the New York *Times* began its story about the merger on the next morning's front page. He called me down to his office again. "Look at this," he said, and it was easy to see he was more disturbed than proud. "I buy a company for $100 million and I'm lucky to get a couple of lines on the business page, but I pay $23 million for this little publishing company and it's all over the front page."

"It's a highly visible business," I said. "Everybody talks about it. It's mixed up with all the other newsy businesses that aren't really businesses at all, they're part of the country's fun and games. You could probably buy the Mets for a lot less than you're going to give Shimkin, and that would get you bigger headlines than this. You've got to get used to it if you're going to stay in this business." I thought I'd cheer him up and needle him a little at the same time. "Firing the president of Hunt-Wesson would interest the business page, but firing the president of the McCall Publishing Company would make headlines." He laughed.

But David didn't laugh the next morning when the *Wall Street Journal*'s "Heard on the Street" column on the inside back page quoted an Argus Research analyst as saying it was a dumb acquisition that couldn't help Mahoney's billion-dollar company and was only going to deepen his unprofitable involvement in a business that was a lot more trouble than it was worth. That was bad enough, but when NSI stock went down a point in that day's trading I didn't even try to make David laugh. Those stock numbers were his life's blood. "I'll bet the woman who wrote that," David complained to me, "is twenty-four years old and a year out of Vassar. But she took $15 million off the value of my company in a couple of minutes on the phone."

Well, it probably took more than a couple of minutes. The young woman had a lot to say: "Norton Simon," she began, "may be enthusiastic about its recently announced agreement to acquire Simon & Schuster, but at least several analysts view the proposed acquisition of the New York-based publishing concern in a negative light. I'm pulling my 'buy' recommendation because I think they're placing increased emphasis on what I believe is a less viable business than their food and beverage operations." The analyst went on to say that the printing and publishing sectors hadn't been among the company's strong points. She cited, in particular, the long-term decline in the number of paid advertising pages in *McCall's* and the labor problems in terms of a turnover in top management and difficulties with the union at the McCall Printing Company plant. "This acquisition," she said, "may hurt the company's ability to command a higher price-earnings multiple." Oh, those MBAs.

I wondered what Shana thought about all that.

I didn't have to wait long to find out what David thought about it. Right on the heels of the *Journal*'s blast, he was hit by a Merrill Lynch wire flash suggesting that because investors were already down on conglomerates, they would probably be less than enthusiastic about the NSI conglomerate taking on still another acquisition so far removed from its core businesses. The bulletin ended with the chilling comment, "NSI is in a near and intermediate term downtrend. There is no sign of a bottom as yet and we believe the stock will need considerable time to stabilize and undergo a re-accumulation phase. Support is indicated in the upper 20's while resistance to rallies will be encountered initially in the upper 30's." Wow.

David never even met Shimkin. He waited a few days to allow for an investigation that never investigated and then he called off the merger. Asked why, he said, laying on every ounce of his famous charm and transparent candor, "Public disclosure rules require the announcement of preliminary merger negotiations often before you have an opportunity to determine whether the merger makes sense for both parties. On close investigation Simon & Schuster did not fit our requirements. It takes courage to walk away from a deal."

Come on, David, I thought. It would have taken courage to stay with this one, but it would have been worth it. But, as Omar Khayyám, translated by Edward FitzGerald, said, the moving finger, having writ, moves on. The S&S deal was dead and so was the McCall Publishing Company. Not just the book company, the whole company. Mahoney wanted out. He wanted to get back to the world he knew, where you could buy a $100 million company in a cozy vacuum and not have to put up with a lot of pushy questions.

The headlines "MCCALL'S CUTS 18 FROM BOOK UNIT IN ECONOMY MOVE" and "NORTON SIMON INC. QUITTING PUBLISHING BUSINESS," which ran in the *Times* six months apart, were both accurate, but the second one, in June 1971, was more accurate. By then David had decided to close down the book company entirely, sell the *Saturday Review* immediately, because he had a buyer for it, and look around for buyers for *McCall's* and *Redbook*.

David could handle a breakup like that without batting an eye. He had taken all the courses they had to offer in a tough school. There was a time when Norton and Gus Levy of Goldman, Sachs, Norton's chief financial adviser, conceived a plan to spin off the Publishing Company from NSI by offering one share in a new and separate McCall Publishing Company for $1 a share to each holder of a share of NSI stock. "Most of our stock," Norton explained enthusiastically to David, "is held by institutions, and they won't touch the Publishing Company stock at any price. We'll buy whatever nobody wants and we'll control the company for practically nothing."

Mahoney worried. "How can I sell that to the stockholders?" he said. "I can't get up there at the annual meeting and tell them a deal like that is good for them."

"Sure you can," Norton said cheerfully. "It's no worse than a death in the family."

The *Review* divestiture, which is a high-class word for dumping, was bound to be a Shakespearean tragicomedy, because it involved Norman Cousins. He was outraged when David began negotiating with the giant forest-products company Boise Cascade, and even more outraged when, after that sale fell through, David listened seriously to two of the minority participants in the deal, Nicholas Charney and John Veronis, who had planned to run the magazine with Boise Cascade's money. Norman insisted David had always told him that he could have first option to buy the magazine back if NSI decided to sell it. "If," Mahoney said calmly, "you meet the price." When Norman insisted the price was much too high, David, with equal calm, went ahead with Charney and Veronis, irreverently known in the trade as the Gold Dust Twins. With David's blessing, I began to think about what I might do next.

The Book-of-the-Month Club had been a possibility since the middle of 1970 when Axel Rosin, the president and the husband of one of the two owners of the controlling stock—the family of founder Harry Scherman owned 60 percent of the stock, the public 40 percent—suggested to me that I ought to join his company. I didn't think I should walk away from all of the good people who were beating their brains out with me to make *McCall's* work, so I said no. But things were different now. My only responsibility was to help Mahoney liquidate his publishing properties in ways most advantageous to the people who were running them, and then I could go. The Book-of-the-Month Club looked like Heaven.

The first thing I did was to sell Axel the Cook Book Club our book company had started after Irv and Charlie got there. Vilma Bergane and Stan Donaldson went with it, so they were taken care of. Then Charney and Veronis said they wanted the book company along with the *Review*, so that took care of Irv and Charlie. Mahoney was willing to keep *McCall's* and *Redbook* going until somebody made a good offer for them, separately or as a team. David asked me to help him find a president for the reduced publishing company, and I tried. The man I wanted was John Mack Carter, who was, I was sure, deeply disenchanted with his job running the *Ladies' Home Journal* for Downe Communications.

I reported to Mahoney after my first state luncheon with Carter: "We ate at La Seine, on East 58th Street, very expensive, and John began telling me over his second Bloody Mary how bad things looked at Downe. He's clearly interested in the possibility we have in mind. He's eager to look into any attractive out and, as he said, there aren't that many around that would be exactly right for him. This one is. He has a contract that expires at the end of the year and he has stalled all suggestions that they put together a new one. He owns some stock options but he thinks his chances of making any money out of them are slim. He isn't sanguine about the company's prospects, and in fact he thinks their accounting is so creative it puts the fiction in his magazine to shame. So he's interested. . . . He will be very expensive . . . but he will be worth it."

Carter went to *Good Housekeeping* instead, which turned out to be as good for him as it was for Hearst. There isn't anybody who does what John does any better than he does it. Garry Bewkes, Mahoney's troubleshooter, who had been holding down the fort at the Printing Company, took over control of the Publishing Company after I said goodbye to my friends. All I had to do then was sign a whole lot of papers and be on my way to the Book-of-the-Month Club.

The paper-signing accidentally gave me a ringside seat at the close of the *Saturday Review* deal. David was on the telephone with John Veronis when he called me into his office, and then he answered a call from Cousins. It was clear, from the side of the conversation I heard, that Norman was still pressing his right to a first option. "But, Norman," David said with only a touch of impatience, "you've got it. I told you what they're paying. Match it right now and it's yours." After a minute of listening silently and shaking his head frequently, David hung up with a short goodbye. "He doesn't want me to sell him the magazine," he said to me, "he wants me to give it to him."

"Well," I said, "he's used to having it given to him."

Which was true. It was the De Golyer family of Texas, the heirs of Norman's great patron of decades before, who had left control of the magazine to him as an outright gift. No wonder he was reluctant to pay the kind of money Mahoney wanted for it.

When the papers were signed and I had officially given up the last two and a half years of my contract in exchange for NSI buying back my stock options and paying me the profit they had earned along with my deferred compensation, I shook hands with my friend and sometime adversary. David frowned when I handed over the unused tickets to our box at the Metropolitan Opera. "You know I hate the opera," he said.

"I know," I told him, "but some of your advertisers don't. Believe me, they'll get used."

"We'll have to have lunch once in a while," he said. "Where are you going to be?"

"Right over there," I said, pointing out of David's front window in 277 Park to the Bankers Trust Building at 280 Park, "just catty-cornered across the street."

"No kidding?" he said. "Weren't you right here in this building, 277, when you first said no to Norton?"

"Sure," I said.

He shook his head. "You mean we moved you from 277 to 230 and now you're moving from 230 to 280?"

I said that was it.

"Jesus Christ," David said, "you work a very narrow territory."

When I got down to the street, I took a cab up Third Avenue to P. J. Moriarty's and sat by myself at the bar, contemplating my world. I thought about Mahoney with friendliness and about Norton with a wistful longing for what might have been, and I thought about Shana the way you think about a lover you've lost. It had been such a good idea. When I cleaned out my desk for the last time, I'd found a letter Ralph Graves had written Shana. I read it, looking, I suppose for something that would tell me where I had gone wrong. "Joan Didion," Ralph told her, "beats you by a ratio of 10–1 on dependable, on-time, finished delivery. But how lucky *Life* was to have you, undependable, unfinished, intransigent . . . marvelously prejudiced . . . it's what makes you good as writer,

253

columnist or editor." Well, Ralph, I thought, you were at least two thirds right. I watched the little Lionel cars shake and rattle around the rickety track up by the ceiling and I wondered if Shana could make that railroad run on time.

Arthur Schlesinger came in and sat down at his regular table near the front door facing the whole room and opened his *Daily News*. Tim mixed him a martini just like mine, as dry as the Sahara, and carried it over to him. Neither one of them said anything except good afternoon. It was going to be good to be back in the book business.

Chapter 15

WALKING through the concourse at Grand Central Terminal and up Park Avenue to 48th Street, I thought about a walk I had taken in Boston with Arthur Thornhill, Sr., back in the mid-'60s.

Arthur had invited me to make my first visit to his Georgian offices on Beacon Hill and had promised me lunch at Locke-Ober's with Edwin O'Connor. I had met Ed once before, at dinner with Pat Knopf, but I was looking forward to seeing him on his own turf. I had no idea how interesting it would turn out to be. After lunch Ed insisted that we take a long walk to look at a townhouse he was thinking of buying even over Arthur's objection that it was not only a heavy investment but would "cost the earth" to keep up. On the way, we passed James Michael Curley's old house, which the author of *The Last Hurrah* dutifully pointed out to us, and that reminded him of a story. "I was passing here one day," he said, "and Himself came rushing down the steps to a car. I'd been hoping I'd run into him because I wanted to apologize for all the nasty things that had been said in the reviews about how I'd made his son look like a moron. So I did—apologize to him, I mean. I told him I'd never intended to hurt his son, and anyway, after all, it was only a novel. 'Think nothing of it,' he told me, 'he was lucky to be mentioned.' "

Well, I thought as I turned in the side door of the building on my way to the first day of work at the Book-of-the-Month Club, you always told Kevin the book business was a lot better than the magazine business. As the old joke goes, you won't be making much money, but you'll have a lot of fun. The money part was accurate enough. Axel Rosin had said he didn't want to upset the other people on the staff, so he was paying me exactly $1,500 a year more than I had been making when I left Doubleday at the end of 1968. A far cry from my *McCall's* pay. But for a while I didn't even have much fun.

My joyously attractive assistant, Susan Huberman, had even less. It was bad enough that we had left the splendor of a three-room suite, complete with bathroom and bar, overlooking all of Park Avenue, for a tiny closet of an office for me and a desk out in the hall for her, but she was even criticized for wearing jeans to the office. "We don't do that here," Harry Brown, the dour—and, as it proved later, delightful—treasurer of the company, told her when he first saw her. "Jeans are not worn here."

"Well," Susan said, "you'd better tell Ed. He likes them."

Anybody who didn't like the sight of Susan Huberman in a pair of tight-fitting jeans was sadly lacking in an appreciation of the aesthetic. In the end, Susan and her jeans had no more enthusiastic admirer than Harry Brown. He just thought he had to defend the old traditions.

The other Harry Brown I came to know and love was in his element at one of the first meetings I attended. The subject was the name of a new business the club was launching to sell original lithographic prints in limited, numbered editions. The working name for it was the Atelier Society, but that had been challenged by another company that was using the word "Atelier," and the general feeling was that we might as well avoid any legal problems by picking another name. Carl Connellan, who had been brought in from the Collector's Guild to run the new venture, favored Fine Arts 260. I wondered why 260. "The exact number doesn't matter," Carl explained in his rapid-fire Irish brogue. "It's just to show that the number is finite. It can be any number, except that it shouldn't be too big or it will turn people off. They want to feel they're getting one of a few."

"Well," I suggested, "why not 280? At least that's the number of our building. It would have something to do with us."

Harry interrupted. "If I understand correctly," he said in his formal European manner, "that the exact number has no significance except to limit the number of prints we will press, it might be better for us if we moved to 100 Park Avenue."

Another time he looked on with interest as I unwrapped a Swiss chalet that predicted the weather by having the woman pop out of the door if the forecast was good and the man come out if the forecast was bad. "In the old country," Harry observed, "on a good day the man comes out."

Harry was a good friend to my daughter, Eileen, while she was president of her Dharma Center on West 19th Street. He helped the group incorporate and did all their legal and accounting work for nothing, which was important because they didn't have any money. "We don't have any rich patrons," Eileen told him when she was thanking him for all he had done. "In our group, you're affluent if you have a job." Only one of the men, she explained, could be counted on to have some money in his wallet and that was because he worked for the *Reader's Digest*. "They pay good salaries," Eileen confided to Harry. "Yes," Harry said, "they do. And if they ever find out what he's up to, he'll be out of a job in five minutes."

Harry probably helped, but it didn't take me long to convince myself that, money or no money, office or no office, this place was right for me. It was a joy working again with books, talking about books, drawing up lists of books, reading books and, better still, book manuscripts—long before they were published. It was more exciting having lunch with book people even if the restaurants were the same. I was doing what I liked best and in the place where I had always dreamed of doing it. When the Literary Guild was sticking firecrackers up the Book-of-the-Month Club's regal tail, I used to dream that it would all end with Harry Scherman calling me up and saying, "Hey, you belong over here. Why don't we have lunch and talk about it?"

Sitting in my corner cubicle looking out at Susan's jeans, I was reminded of a Sunday we had spent with Laura and Milton Runyon in a little English town called Virginia Water, visiting Milton's friend Bill Warwick, the captain of the new, still un-launched *Queen Elizabeth II*. When we arrived in our rented Rolls Royce, Captain Warwick took us out into his garden, pointed across the rolling fields toward Windsor Castle, and said, "That's where She lives." Then he directed our chauffeur to his "local," his favorite Virginia Water pub, where we were to have a martini before going on to dinner. When we parked in front of the pub, the captain, a big, broad, brusque man with a great guardsman's mustache that had helped make him a celebrity on the telly, told the three women we would carry drinks out to them and asked what they wanted. When he had their orders, he shut the car door and led Milton and me into the pub, which could easily have served as a backdrop for a scene in "Masterpiece Theatre." Following him obediently into the bar, I was surprised to see a dozen or more women in the room, some with and some without male escorts. It all seemed, as one would expect on a Sunday afternoon in Virginia Water, entirely respectable. Curious, I asked the Captain innocently why we had left our ladies in the car. "They belong there," he said empirically.

And I, I knew, belonged at the Book-of-the-Month Club.

Liby, incidentally, has always insisted that she didn't in the least mind being left in the car that day. "It's the only time in my life," she says, "I'll ever be served a martini in a Rolls Royce by the captain of the *Queen E. Two*."

The extended quiet time of my first six months at the Club probably owed as much to a piece that ran in *Advertising Age* as it did to Axel's natural reluctance to upset the applecart. "FITZGERALD MAY TAKE TOP BOOK-OF-THE-MONTH POST," the headline said. "According to informed sources," the story reported, "Edward E. Fitzgerald, 51, president, McCall Publishing Co. (*McCall's* and *Redbook*), is resigning and will become president of the Book-of-

the-Month Club. A spokesman for Norton Simon Inc., the publisher's parent company, said 'no comment' when queried about the
report. Mr. Fitzgerald, whose career has included stints at Literary
Guild of America and Doubleday & Co., could not be reached for
comment. Nor could Axel Rosin, B.O.M.C. president since 1960."

That was exactly what Axel didn't want. He wanted time for me
to become absorbed by and into the company. Even the sainted
Harry Brown asked him "What's he doing here if he isn't going
to be the president?" But Axel didn't want to hurry, and *Ad Age*
slowed him up even more.

At least two good things came out of my unexpected vacation
without much pay. The first was that we got a good book because
I read Roger Kahn's *The Boys of Summer* and pushed hard to have
it presented to the judges as a strong candidate for a main selection. Ralph Thompson, who as editor was in charge of passing
books on to the judges, didn't mind adding it to the judges' chores
in what was a light month anyway. Astonishingly to me, considering that John Hutchens was the only baseball buff on the four-man
board of judges—which hadn't yet picked up Wilfrid Sheed or
Mordecai Richler, both of whom know a suicide squeeze when
they see it—they picked it.

The senior woman reader at the Club, Elizabeth Easton, a de-
lightfully proper and altogether literary lover of the printed word,
called it "a baseball book that entrances a lady who doesn't know
a bunt from a line drive. . . . I was amused and moved and delighted
by the whole book, and I never thought I would be. . . . Roger
Kahn knows how to write." Another reader contributed the fact
that "Roger Kahn's father thought up questions for 'Information
Please,' an old radio program," apparently forgetting that the
quirky stars of that early excursion into trivia were Oscar Levant,
Franklin P. Adams, John Kieran and the dean of the Book-of-the-
Month Club's judges, Clifton Fadiman.

So a month after I had signed a contract to work for the club, I
had helped find it a main selection. The fact that it was a book of
rare humanity beautifully written by an old friend made it so satis-
fying an event that it almost completely took my mind off my

implacable boredom. It even helped me get through a painful goodbye to Susan Huberman, who, once she had helped me move into a more comfortable office, took off for the Bonnier's store on Madison Avenue, where she was going to manage an Italian shoe department. "They may not let you wear jeans there," I said. "Then I'll be back," she said with her mischievous laugh. But she never came back. Proving what a small world publishing is, she sold a pair of shoes to a *Ms.* magazine person a few months after Pat Carbine had left *McCall's* to join Gloria Steinem in becoming the Founding Foremothers of the magazine. "Tell Pat Carbine that Susan Huberman said hello," she told her customer. Pat did more than say hello. She called Susan that afternoon, took her out to lunch and hired her as her assistant.

But Susan was around long enough to share my pleasure and Roger's joy in the startling success of *The Boys of Summer*, the first sports book ever to become a Book of the Month. "I see the boys of summer in their ruin," Dylan Thomas had written, and Roger not only knew a good title when he saw one but he knew when he had come upon a faultless précis of the book he wanted to write. He never had any doubt about the title and only the standard doubts of a normally neurotic author about the book. When he worried about our plan to offer it to our members between the middle of January and the middle of February, he asked me if the book wouldn't do better during the baseball season or at least the spring training season. "I can't think of a question argued more frequently or more fruitlessly," I said, "than the question of when to publish. I'm convinced that winners are always published at the right time. Except in rare circumstances, it doesn't make a damn bit of difference. And in the case of your book, we can't have it both ways and argue that it isn't a baseball book but a book about people and at the same time worry that it has to be published at the beginning of the baseball season. The wintertime is a pretty good time to sell books, and you have to remember that you don't sell books to middle-aged Dodger fans; you sell them to book readers.

"Christmas," I said, "is always an interesting problem because you can't laugh off the big holiday sales. But they're more important for a book that doesn't quite make it than they are for one that really makes it. If *The Boys of Summer* is as good as we think it is, it will be selling like mad at Christmas, and if you weren't so goddam wordy, it would be in a lot of Christmas stockings."

A facsimile copy of the *Book-of-the-Month Club News* that presented *The Boys of Summer* in the spring of 1972 would be a matchless gift for any young person so interested in language that it might, like the life of the religious to some, seem an ill-paid but necessary career. "Happy the man who can make his living out of his passion," Paul Horgan, the distinguished author, wrote in the first sentence of his review, "assuming," he added, "both to be legitimate."

Harold Rosenthal, playing the part of the gruff elder statesman, gave Roger a short course in press-box etiquette. Harold didn't bother to tell the kid there was no cheering in the press box; he assumed even a boy from St. Mark's Place in Brooklyn would know that. But he did tell him, "Now, listen, if you're gonna cover this club, there are a few things you better learn right away. First, don't use words like wow. Second, when you get excited, you talk too fast. Third, get your hair cut. This is no place for a Jewish musician."

Red Smith, introducing the author to a presumably bemused world, said a whole lot in two paragraphs:

His mother taught English literature and composition at Thomas Jefferson High, and Roger learned from her that his early fondness for John Keats was not a shameful thing, though perhaps rather quaint. His father taught history at Thomas Jefferson and framed the questions for "Information, Please," one of the first and probably the most popular of panel quiz shows on radio. Gordon Kahn taught his son that it was permissible to attend a baseball game and a concert on the same day and enjoy both, and that when Joe DiMaggio was at bat intelligent left fielders played deep.

Incompatibility with organic chemistry led Roger from the Bronx campus of New York University to the *Herald Tri-*

bune. There he earned $24 a week as a night copy boy sub-
servient to editors, rewrite men, copyreaders, reporters, secretaries and the head copy boy. With few exceptions, copy boys
travel one of two roads. The good ones become members of
the staff. The others quit the newspaper business for television
and become network vice presidents.

My second good thing was QPB, officially known as Quality
Paperback Book Club. I would have come up with it sooner or later
because it had been on my mind for years—Goodman and I must
have talked about it over a hundred lunches during the Doubleday
days—but it happened a lot faster because I didn't think I ought to
sit in the office all day just reading books. And I got mad when
Axel proposed to publish a memorandum appointing me the un-
disputed czar of such lesser BOMC ventures as Fine Arts 260, the
Dolphin Book Club, the Cook Book Club and, God forbid, Erica
Wilson's Creative Needlework Society. So, driven by the guilty
compulsion to do something to earn my keep, I slowly put together
the paperback book club of my dreams. The notes and the charts
and the memos I slaved over joined together the pieces of what is
essentially the same QPB (at first we called it Quality Paperback
Book Service) that celebrated its eleventh anniversary in January
1985.

I almost helped the company paint itself red for embarrassment
in the famous Clifford Irving–Howard Hughes caper. The first I
heard of it was when I got a telephone call on December 7 from
Charlie Sopkin. Charlie had just heard that McGraw-Hill and *Life*
magazine were going to announce that afternoon that an autobiography of the billionaire recluse would be serialized by *Life* and
then published in book form by McGraw-Hill, with a paperback
edition coming later from Dell.

I should have paid more attention to the fact that it was the anniversary of Pearl Harbor Day.

I also should have paid more attention to the announcement, when
it came, that Clifford Irving, the writer who was putting the book

together, had last been seen as the author of a book called *Fake* about the art forger Elmyr de Hory.

Beverly Jane Loo, who was handling subsidiary rights for Mc-Graw-Hill, took John Hutchens and me to lunch on December 9 to talk about the book. The executives of the Hughes Tool Company already had hollered that the book was a hoax—the joke quickly went around the gossipy book trade that it was going to be retitled "Fake II"—and Beverly told us all of the reasons McGraw-Hill and *Life* were sure it was the real thing. It was a good lunch. I had Dover sole and Beverly picked up the tab.

The book was set in galleys, and as more and more people got to read it, selected anecdotes from it were choice bits savored at publishing lunches and cocktail parties. If you were one of the relatively few who actually had read the book, you could, as they say, dine out on it every night in the week.

You could, for instance, tell this one. "When we made *The Outlaw*, the censors drove me crazy. In one scene Jane Russell had to climb in bed with Billy the Kid (Jack Beutel) because he was sick and needed to be kept warm. She was Doc Holliday's girl, and when Doc (Walter Huston) came in and saw them, he didn't like it. Billy had loaned Doc his horse, so he tried to smooth things over by saying, 'You borrowed my horse, so I borrowed your girl.' But the head censor, Joe Breen, said that line was too suggestive and he made me change it to 'Tit for tat.' "

Or you could quote the author talking about his interest in the science of cryogenics—freezing dead bodies and putting them in a vault against the day when science will know how to bring them back to life. "I know what everybody's going to say. They're going to say, 'That's just like Howard Hughes. If he can't take it with him, he isn't going to go.' "

Then, on January 7, Richard Hannah, Hughes' public-relations man, arranged the strangest press conference anyone could remember. For two and a half hours Hughes, or somebody who said he was Hughes, talked from Paradise Island in the Bahamas to seven newspaper, wire-service and television reporters, all of whom had known him before he went underground. He denied that he had ever met Clifford Irving, he said the so-called autobiography was a fake and the reporters unanimously agreed that the voice they had heard over the telephone was the voice of Howard Hughes.

How come no television camera on him to prove it was him? What do you want to do, spoil this with proof?

McGraw-Hill and *Life* remained calm. In fact, they moved up their publication dates to capitalize on the blizzard of publicity. Harold McGraw, Jr., went on television and waved the checks his company had given Irving to give Hughes. (No, of course they didn't mail them; this was Howard Hughes they were dealing with, and everything had to be secret and passwordy and very hush-hush between Irving and Hughes.) The checks were endorsed by H. R. Hughes and the endorsements had been held good by the Chase Manhattan Bank and Crédit Suisse in Zurich, where the monies ($650,000 in all) had been deposited. McGraw-Hill also had a long handwritten letter signed by Hughes authorizing them to proceed forthwith with publication, and their handwriting experts had compared the letter and signature with known Hughes signatures on official documents and pronounced them the same.

So who had put the money in the bank if, as Hughes and his lieutenants insisted, he hadn't?

The Swiss bank began writing the next chapter by letting it out that the H. R. Hughes checks had been deposited by a woman who identified herself as Helga R. Hughes. Mike Wallace of CBS, who had read the manuscript to prepare for an interview with Irving on "60 Minutes," thought Helga might be a Hughes girlfriend mentioned briefly in the book. That might mean she simply was acting for Hughes.

"Just so long as it wasn't Mrs. Irving," the trade said in a kind of a nervous joke.

Shoulder-length hair became very important when the Swiss bank's fuller description of the lady depositor included that point. The *Daily News* ran a front-page picture of the attractive Edith Sommer Irving, the author's fourth wife, and the caption carefully called attention to her shoulder-length hair.

On January 28 the world knew not only that the checks had been deposited by Mrs. Irving but also that she had withdrawn the money in Swiss francs and redeposited it, or most of it, in another bank across the street.

And, oh, the questions.

"How could he possibly think he could get away with it?"

And the jokes.

"He's too dumb to invent such a crazy, complicated plot and too smart to think he could pull it off."

And the new characters on stage—lawyers, assistant district attorneys, Postal Service inspectors, a Democratic candidate for U.S. Senator from New Mexico, a Danish folk-singer and a blonde scuba diver.

But no longer any hurry to publish the manuscript, no certainty at McGraw-Hill or *Life*, just the kind of feeling you had when you were a kid and couldn't wait to read today's installment of Dick Tracy.

And one last trade joke that was true. On the first floor of the new McGraw-Hill Building on Sixth Avenue was a branch of the Irving Trust Company.

One good thing came out of this near-miss. While I was at the Jerusalem Book Fair in 1983, the hot story—and the hottest book, if there was a book—was the Adolf Hitler diaries. When the pressure was put on me to pre-empt them, I thought back to the Clifford Irving time and to the lesson we had all learned that nothing that good can be real. "Not for me," I said firmly. "No way."

Axel's first move to bring me into the whole business instead of just part of it was to suggest that I sit in on the judges' meetings whenever either he or Warren was away. Sensibly, he thought we shouldn't overpower the judges by having three members of management at the table with five judges. (Paul Horgan had retired and Sheed and Richler had come aboard.) Besides, if there were eight of us, we might have to escalate from two bottles of Sherry-Lehmann's best French wines to three. I went to a couple of meetings and then began to find reasons why I couldn't make it. I don't think I went to more than half a dozen of them in the thirteen years

I worked at the Club. Liby always says it's just that I won't go to any meeting at which I can't have the last word.

His second step was to make me a member of the board of directors. I was now openly a part of the company. And what a company. There can't have been many like it. Ever since Harry Scherman started the Club in 1926 with advertisements in literary publications like the *New Yorker*, the *National Geographic*, the *American Mercury*, the *Atlantic Monthly*, *Harper's* and the *New York Times Book Review*, the Book-of-the-Month Club has been recognized as quickly for its high standards as for its conspicuous commercial success. Lewis M. Smith, Jr., who worked on the account at Wunderman, Ricotta & Kline as well as at the Club itself, contends that the first Harry Scherman headlines, repeated over and over in those first ads sixty years ago, said it all. "You Can Now Subscribe to the Best New Books," the first one said, followed by the equally descriptive "Handed to you by the Postman—the Outstanding Book Each Month!" Despite the inevitable jibes about the Club packaging culture on an assembly line, few serious critics would dispute that the level of the more than 350 million books it has sent out to its members has been extraordinarily high. Authors whose works have been distributed by the Book-of-the-Month Club have won scores of Nobel and Pulitzer prizes. Many of the books would have been read by a far smaller public if it hadn't been for the appreciative membership of the Club. Anyone whose library is built exclusively of Book-of-the-Month Club titles owns an admirable balance of worthwhile reading, ranging from the fiction of Thomas Mann, Katherine Anne Porter and E. L. Doctorow to the nonfiction of Winston Churchill, Bruce Catton and William Manchester. The Book-of-the-Month Club helped put William L. Shirer's *The Rise and Fall of the Third Reich* and Rachel Carson's *Silent Spring* in hundreds of thousands of American homes and helped find an audience for John Irving's *The World According to Garp* and Alice Walker's *The Color Purple*.

Harry Scherman shipped 4,750 copies of the club's first selection, Sylvia Townsend Warner's *Lolly Willowes*. I was impressed to see, in my first year with the Club, that the highest-priced selection BOMC had ever had, *The Tree Where Man Was Born* by Peter Matthiessen and Eliot Porter, entirely sold out its first printing of 125,000 copies despite its $19.95 price and forced us to charter a TWA 747 to bring over 25,000 more copies from Italy to satisfy the members' demand. I was even more astounded when Alexander Solzhenitsyn's *Gulag Archipelago* sold 264,000 copies the first month it was offered.

"They're Hertz," we used to say at the Literary Guild, "and we're Avis." It felt good to be Hertz.

The Book-of-the-Month Club is so much the dominant club in the business that all the book-club jokes are made about it. Nobody ever heard a joke about the Literary Guild, but there is an inexhaustible supply of them about BOMC.

The Art Buchwald joke has been done and done, but nobody does it better than Buchwald, who says he tried for years to get out of the Book-of-the-Month Club but he has finally given up. "It's impossible," he says. "I kept writing them letters saying I didn't want any more of their books and would they please just take my name off the list. But they kept sending me IBM cards billing me for the books I'd told them I didn't want. I finally got so mad I bent, folded and mutilated the card and sent it back to them. I figured that would do it for sure. But the next month I got another card with the message, 'If you do that once more, we will send you the entire Encyclopaedia Britannica.' "

Then there is the Helen Hokinson cartoon that we run ourselves in an ad once a year. That's the one in which the suburban matron is shaking hands with the town librarian. "I'm afraid it's goodbye, Miss MacDonald. I'm joining the Book-of-the-Month Club."

The National Lampoon invented the Half-a-Book-of-the-Month Club. "You can receive half of a great best-seller every month," they said. "These books are half as easy to read and half as easy to afford. Why not start your membership today by choosing any 8 half books for just $1?" Some of the titles they offered in their spoof ad were "How to Feel Good About Feeling Bad," "Creative Hypertension," "The Complete Book of Black Lesbian Running" and "Painless Foreplay."

Another cartoon has one with-it young woman telling her equally funky friend, "Oh, God, he belongs to the Book-of-the-Month Club. I mean, how can you reach somebody like that?"

My own favorite is the scene in *Same Time, Next Year* in which Doris tells her once-a-year lover, George, that she's really trying to improve herself, to get to be a more interesting person. "I've even joined the Book-of-the-Month Club," she says proudly.

"Good for you," George says.

"Listen," Doris says defensively, "you don't know the half of it. Sometimes I even take the alternate selections."

"I'm really proud of you, honey," George says admiringly.

But that night, for the first time in their complicated relationship, the sex doesn't work so well, and in the morning George looks at her lying ravishingly naked in bed and shakes his head sadly. "You know something, honey?" he says. "I liked you better before you joined the Book-of-the-Month Club."

The people who work for the Club even have their own family stories, sometimes stealing them right out of the correspondence files.

One woman wrote that instead of the main selection offered in the *Book-of-the-Month Club News* that month, she would like to have a book on "How to Raise Mink Coats." Another member wanted to know if it was possible for the Club to have his copy of Jane Austen's *Pride and Prejudice* autographed by the author. Then there are always the people who complain that the book the Club sent them that month is too obscene, too unspeakably filthy to be kept in the house. "As soon as I've finished it," the letter says in one form or another, "I'm going to burn it." And another constant is the lame reply of the member who is asked why his Club history shows a long record of returning each selection two weeks after receiving it. "We can't continue to spend so much money sending you books that you're going to return two weeks later," the Club's form letter says firmly. "Well, I don't know what else I can do," the injured member responds, "I'm reading them as fast as I can."

But being with Hertz didn't, as I had once thought it would, make life a bowl of cherries with whipped cream on top. I ran into two heavy problems right away. One of them was that the war between the book clubs was at least as furious as ever; I had just changed sides. The other was that now I had to worry about an independent editorial board: the celebrated judges, equipped by Harry Scherman with the singular authority to choose the Book of the Month. I couldn't, as I had at the Guild, do it all by myself.

The first thing I did was organize a determined Book-of-the-Month Club assault on the array of books that the judges either weren't interested in at all or had considered but rejected. I wanted them as alternates, but it turned out to be anything but easy to buy them. Nelson had equipped his lieutenants with the charge to go after them and the money to pay for them—up to a point. That meant we had to pay a lot more money for them, in advances against royalties, than we wanted to. Nelson didn't want to give all that money to publishers, authors and agents, either, but he wanted to keep the Guild in the fight. It was the best thing that ever happened to the author. Overnight, books that might have commanded a $5,000 advance when only one club was pursuing them became objects of great price. First, the two clubs bid their way past the $25,000 bumper, then got into a brand-new ball game when the Guild decided to pick two books a month, in first a thirteen-month and then a fourteen-month year, with the option to send its members as many as four special selections also under negative option. The Guild paid a minimum of $35,000 each, and frequently ten or even twenty times that much, for the few books we both contended for vigorously. The cost of having a seat at the book-club blackjack table had gone out of sight.

I took myself out of the early auction rounds by persuading one of the best editors I knew to give up the joys of freelance writing and go back to work. I knew the Book-of-the-Month Club had to have a knowledgeable, bold editor to direct our tactics in the battle for the books, and I thought I ought to start by talking to my old friend Goodman. I asked Irv to have lunch with me and tried the classic head-hunter's technique. When we were finishing off the Valpolicella, I told him about my problem and asked if he knew an editor I might go after. The rules of the game dictate that at this point your luncheon companion says, "What about me?" But Irv didn't. He thought hard, interrupting the thinking process every now and then to tell me how happy he and Charlie Sopkin were with the Charney-Veronis *Saturday Review*. That was definitely within the rules; he was letting me know, without injury to my enthusiasm, that he wasn't interested and that he didn't think Charlie would be interested, either.

"What about Al?" I asked him.

Irv, my friend of more than twenty years, charter member of the *Sport* magazine mafia, said, "Al who?"

When I said Al Silverman, Irv said, "No way. He likes what he's doing too much. That's why I didn't think you meant him. He loves the magazine, he's writing books on the side, he's making a lot of money and he's happy. He'd never do it."

So the next day I made a lunch date with Al Silverman and he said yes. He was working on a book, *Foster and Laurie*, about two cops who had been senselessly murdered on the Lower East Side of New York, and he agreed to show up for work as soon as he had finished it. He's running the company now, and the only thing he misses about *Sport* is the tickets to the World Series and the Super Bowl.

The next member of the old mafia to join us was Jack Newcombe, who had been relieved of steady employment by the death of *Life* in 1972. I was having a before-lunch drink at the Berkshire when somebody tapped me on the shoulder. It was Newk. He had been holed up in Carlisle, Pennsylvania, writing a book on Jim Thorpe and the Carlisle Indians. "It's called *The Best of the Athletic Boys*, if you'll forgive the plug," Jack said, "but it's finished and now I need a job, so I'm going over to talk to the people at Time-Life Books."

"You ought to talk to Al, too," I said. "He needs an assistant." A couple of weeks later Newcombe was that assistant, which, I suppose, is why Sam Vaughan of Doubleday calls publishing "The Accidental Profession."

The team of Silverman and Newcombe fought the skirmishes and the pitched battles with the Guild over the telephone, at cocktail parties, at theater and dinner parties and especially at lunch. Their lunch tabs were substantial, but they were pebbles on the Montauk beaches compared with the unearned advances we were forced to choke down because of the Guild's relentless counter-bidding. Sometimes it seemed they wanted to take books away from us even at ruinous prices, although they did have the advantage of owning their own printing plant, which meant part of the money they had to spend stayed with them.

They had an even bigger edge, if one of dubious principle, when it came to a Doubleday book. In their rare exchanges with the press they despised, a luxury that can be indulged in by a privately held company that doesn't have to tell anybody anything if it doesn't want to, the Doubleday people were fond of making pious protestations that book-club rights to Doubleday books were offered to all contenders in arm's-length transactions. Well, that was true when it suited them for it to be true. But when we wanted to send copies of Sara Davidson's novel *Loose Change* to the judges for consideration as a main selection, Doubleday's subsidiary-rights department calmly told us the Guild had already bought it.

"Without letting us bid?"

"You had a copy of it," they said without shame.

"Doesn't it bother you that your author may have been done out of more than $100,000?" we wanted to know.

"She has a book-club selection," they said.

That's what Doubleday means by an arm's-length transaction. They did the same thing with Patty Hearst's book. We had a copy of it and we had people reading it when Al got a call from Doubleday saying the Guild had made an offer for it—it couldn't have cost much, it was an intra-company call—and we had until three o'clock that afternoon to make a counter-bid. "One bid," the caller said, "is all you're allowed." There was no mention of whether or not the Guild would be given a chance to top our bid. The question seemed too ridiculous to ask. Al refused to play. "We won't bid at all under those conditions," he said. "You're seriously impairing our relationship and we think you're perilously close to violating the law." Al is a gentleman. When I called Time Inc.'s counsel and asked if he thought Doubleday's action was in restraint of trade, the head of the law department told me simply, "I'd love to represent the author in a case like this."

Those were only warmups. The debris really hit the fan when Bill Safire, the language maven, wrote a novel, *Full Disclosure*, for Doubleday in 1977. Bill was represented by the self-confessed best lawyer-agent in the business, Mort Janklow, and Doubleday's cavalier notion of arm's length didn't get very far with him. It did in the end prevail, however, which may indicate that Dwight Gooden had better not take on Nelson in an arm-wrestling duel unless he has the baseball commissioner on his side. Safire, who despite the fact that Doubleday is his publisher, has always been partial to the Book-of-the-Month Club, and Janklow coveted a BOMC selection for Bill's novel about an incapacitated but sexually active President. Mort gave me a major pitch in behalf of the book and saw to it that I had an early Xerox copy to read. When he called to ask what I thought of it, I gave him an honest answer. "Nobody is going to accuse it of being great fiction," I said, "but it's entertaining and it has all the touches of White House verisimilitude you would expect from Safire. I like it."

"Well?" Mort wanted to know. "You going to take it?"

"We'll certainly try for it at least as an alternate," I told him, "but we won't know about a selection until the judges have their next meeting." I looked at the calendar on my desk. "That's next Tuesday."

But the next morning the Doubleday rights people told us that *Full Disclosure* was no longer available because the Guild had taken it as a selection. No money was mentioned, just the fact that they had sold it to the Guild. The Davidson and Hearst scams had made me mad enough, but this one lit a bonfire. I knew from our time together at *McCall's* that Anne Close, who had been the BOMC's personnel manager for a few years, was a longtime Safire friend. It was Safire's recommendation to Mahoney that had inspired David to send her to me at *McCall's*. I talked to Anne, told her what had happened and asked her to make sure Bill knew what Doubleday was doing. She did, and he didn't, and he didn't like it, and the next voice I heard was Mort Janklow's. "They can't do that," Mort said heatedly. "I'm a lawyer, for God's sake. Do you think I'd give them a book without an approval clause? They can't sell the book-club rights or the paperback rights or any other kind of rights without my approval. Are you still willing to consider the book as a selection?"

"Sure," I said. "That's why I asked Anne to call Bill."

"Then go right ahead and consider it," Mort said. "I'll take care of Doubleday."

The judges duly met and chose the book. We offered Doubleday an advance of $150,000 for it, knowing from the information Janklow had thoughtfully provided us that that was more than Doubleday had proposed to pay for it in their nifty scheme to side-step competitive bidding. The rights people across the street noted the bid and, by now obviously aware that this was a hot potato being baked by the master chefs in the executive suite, said nothing beyond a non-committal "We'll get back to you." They never did. This one was out of their hands for good.

For a couple of days I talked to Janklow morning, noon and night. Doubleday, stonily accepting Mort's claim to approval rights, topped our bid. Mort asked me for more and I obliged him. Doubleday topped that. I topped that. It went on like that, a silent war, nobody at Doubleday talking to us and Janklow talking to both of us. Finally, I told Mort I'd had enough. It was getting to be ridiculous. Doubleday's bid stood at $250,000. Mort's satisfaction was unrestrained. He was so happy he was even willing to quit fighting for still more money. He called me at home at five minutes before midnight and said, in the secretive tones of a Guy Burgess speaking from London to the head of the KGB in Moscow, "I'm ready to exercise my right of approval to give the book to the Book-of-the-Month Club. I know you don't want to bid any more money and I don't blame you. All I need is for you to top their bid by something, anything, and I'll sell you the book."

"Okay," I said wearily. "We'll give you $255,000."

"You have just bought a book," lawyer Janklow said. "Congratulations, and thank you. You've done Bill a good turn."

I just hoped the book would sell well enough to justify all this

commotion and all that money. But I never got a chance to find out.
The next morning Mort was on the phone again. "I'm in Nelson
Doubleday's office," he said in his conspiratorial voice. "I mean, I'm
right outside it. This is the first time I've been allowed to talk to
him, and he's really hot. He has their company lawyer in there with
him and they told me they're willing to go to court over the propo-
sition that we have the right of approval but not the right to sell.
What Nelson said specifically was 'If you want a book-club selection, you're going to have to take the Literary Guild. We will never
sell this book to the Book-of-the-Month Club. Take it or leave it.' "
Mort was quiet for a few seconds. "Well," he asked me, "what do
I do now?"

"Sell them the fucking book," I said. "Bill worked too hard on it
to be screwed out of all that money. Let them have it. At least you're
getting three times as much money as they wanted to give you."

"Thanks," Mort said, and he went back inside and sold Nelson
the book. Some arm. Some length.

A couple of weeks later Bill and Mort took Anne and me to the
Four Seasons Grill Room, that greenhouse of publishing deal-
planting, and bought us a splendid lunch. A few months later I got
a copy of *Full Disclosure* in the mail at home. "To Ed Fitzgerald,"
the author had written in it, "with profound gratitude."

BOMC's war with the Guild hasn't reached such heights of personal vindictiveness since the Safire affair. It has simply been expensive. They made us pay $305,000 for William Styron's *Sophie's
Choice* and $625,000 for William Manchester's *American Caesar*.
We made them pay $725,000 for Arthur Schlesinger's *Robert Ken-
nedy: His Life and Times*.

Students of the book-club war may find it puzzling that the two
clubs should fire their biggest guns at each other when, mostly, they
mine quite different literary territories. The fierce bidding struggles
come when the Guild feels it has got to have a big new book that's a
cinch to attract tremendous review attention and probably domi-
nate the best-seller lists for months. They can't rely only on Sidney
Sheldon, John Jakes, Jackie Collins and Judith Krantz. That's when,
as they did with the Schlesinger book, they move in on the Book-

of-the-Month Club's turf and try to make off with a book that will function as a loss-leader in their advertising. And that's when some lucky author gets a chance to buy a block of IBM or a summer house on the Vineyard.

Al Silverman's first bid for *Robert Kennedy* was $150,000, meant to test the waters and find out how seriously the Guild might pursue it. Very seriously, it turned out. When I saw Al an hour or so after he made his first pass at the book, the Guild was up to $325,000. Al went to $355,000. Sometimes the odd $5,000 steals a book for the Book-of-the-Month Club because beyond a stipulated point the approval of the Doubleday brass is required and they're not always around; they could, if it's a nice day, be in the owner's box at Shea Stadium. But the $5,000 nudge didn't work in this case. The Guild stayed in the contest through the $400,000s and through the $500,000s, and when Al and I met after lunch they were up to an impressive $655,000.

I told Al it was time for us to get out of the auction. The money was getting to be insane. "Tell Houghton Mifflin," I said, "we'll give them $705,000 on condition they accept it then and there. If they won't, we'll quit." They wouldn't, we quit and the Guild bought Arthur's book for $725,000, at that time—March 1978—the highest price ever paid for book-club rights. I was satisfied that we were right to let the Guild win. We owned John le Carré's *The Honourable Schoolboy*, James Michener's *Chesapeake*, William Manchester's *American Caesar*, Mario Puzo's *Fools Die* and *The Stories of John Cheever*. What the hell, I figured, we can't buy every book that's published.

If the book-club war were to end now, which it won't, the Gettysburg of the conflict would have to be the savage duel fought for James Michener's *The Covenant* in June 1980. *Chesapeake*, like *Centennial* before it, had been a smash hit. The reviewers don't think much of Michener, but they get their books for nothing. The people Out There who pay for their books love him. So, even though they were nervous about the book's African locale, both book clubs wanted *The Covenant* desperately. They wanted it even more when Random House's Milly Marmur, the doyenne of the subsidiary-rights business, told the contenders that she wanted to package the new book with Michener's much-talked-about work in progress, a novel about Texas, and sell both books at once. She didn't have to tell us she didn't want to hear any number that didn't start with a million dollars.

Al's first bid, put in at two o'clock on the afternoon of June 4, 1980, was $375,000. Fifty-five minutes later the Guild had shot up to $1,425,000 and Milly was thinking about what kind of champagne she ought to take home for dinner. Al cautiously went to $1,500,000 and the Guild took exactly three minutes to throw $1,525,000 at Milly. We took two minutes to go to $1,700,000, the number I'd decided hours before was our limit. I didn't think *The Covenant*, Michener or no Michener, would do all that well, and I thought we were once again beginning to treat money like confetti. At three thirty-five p.m. the Guild took the book, or books, with an uncontested bid of $1,750,000.

I was reminded of Robert Southey's appropriate lines:

> "And everybody praised the Duke,
> Who this great fight did win."
> "But what good came of it at last?"
> Quoth little Peterkin.
> "Why, that I cannot tell," said he;
> "But 'twas a famous victory."

When the Guild brought out *The Covenant* not only in one of its dreary 5½x8¼ editions, printed on cheap paper by rubber plates, the kind of book that John O'Donnell had said at Chasen's was better-looking than Knopf's, but also in two volumes because their immutable page size was too small to fit it all into one, I couldn't believe that Michener had allowed his book to be brutalized that way. I decided to ask him why he had done it. Maybe, I thought, I would learn something. So I wrote him:

Dear Mr. Michener:
  I think the notion of writing this letter is outrageous, which is why I've finally decided to do it anyway.

Yesterday, these many months after the celebrated auction of book club rights to your novel, *The Covenant*, I was handed the Literary Guild edition of the work. It would help me a lot to better understand the business I work in if you would tell me candidly what you think of the look and the feel of this two-volume, rubber-plate edition of your book. I'm quite serious in saying that I have no motive in asking for this generous expression of your opinion except to make more complete my perspective of what is important in transferring an author's work to the printed page and the bound book. And, of course, into the hands of the reader.

As you well know, the Book-of-the-Month Club makes books that are the same as the trade publisher's. It's what we have always done with earlier James Michener novels. Is what we do, at considerable cost, important or not important to the author? I'm asking you a serious question and I will be grateful to you if you will take the time and trouble to tell me what you think.

With best wishes,
Ed Fitzgerald.

The only thing I took away from that letter and Michener's confidential reply was a renewed conviction that the Book-of-the-Month Club should keep on making its books for its members, not for the publisher. If, I concluded, a book like *The Covenant* can be condemned by a publisher like Random House to a sleazy edition for a difference of less than 3 percent in the advance, and ignore the pride and taste of the author in the bargain, we'd better not make them for the publisher. The members are more reliable.

Chapter 16

"Bᴏᴏᴋs are a delightful society," William Gladstone said. "If you go into a room filled with books, even without taking them down from their shelves, they seem to speak to you, to welcome you."

If you're a book-lover, that's how you feel when you walk into the Book-of-the-Month Club's board room. The walls are lined from floor to ceiling with old BOMC selections and featured alternates, and the simple beige pillars allow the hanging of portraits of Harry Scherman and three of his five original judges, Heywood Broun, Dorothy Canfield Fisher and William Allen White. Beige wallpaper and beige carpeting lend a soft look that makes you want to sit right down and read a good book.

More talking than reading is done there. It is where the judges meet fifteen times a year—the Book-of-the-Month Club has invented three months of its own, Spring, Midsummer and Fall—to pick the main selection, and it is where the author of the Book of the Month is honored at a lunch for a dozen or so people chosen by him and his publisher. It is also where important company meetings are held, but, as one who would quickly choose a five-mile hike over a meeting, I will say nothing about them except to quote the inscription on the mallet Megan McKernan of the Club gave me when I retired:

"The usefulness of any meeting is in inverse proportion to its attendance." Amen.

It's hard to say who puts on the better show, the authors or the judges, but the authors probably would win because their numbers guarantee them a wider range and make it less likely that they will repeat their favorite stories. And although the judges can lay claim to a considerable amount of distinction within the world of publishing, they are not the celebrities that some of the authors are. Henry Kissinger, for instance. Whatever your measure of Dr. Kissinger's career and contributions may be, there can't be any disputing his celebrity rank. For the first of his two appearances as a Book-of-the-Month Club luncheon guest, the Nobel Peace Prize winner drew far and away the biggest crowd of curious company employees, most of whom are women, to line the halls as he entered and left. More than John Irving, more than Philip Roth when he arrived with his friend Claire Bloom, more even than Liv Ullmann.

Kissinger was the only author guest whose office called us in advance of the luncheon to warn us that "Dr. Kissinger never talks at these events. We thought you ought to know so there won't be any confusion." His spokesperson also told us the former Secretary of State would be accompanied by two bodyguards who would have to be given seats in inconspicuous corners from where they could at all times keep the door to the room and their employer in full view. We took care of the physical arrangements and even politely overruled the spokesperson, who said we didn't have to worry about feeding the private army, and we waited for the non-speaking Mr. Secretary to arrive.

The luncheon was set for twelve thirty. Kissinger walked into the board room at twelve thirty sharp, smiling warmly and greeting everybody. He sat down to join the circle having drinks, began telling stories and never shut up until he left at two thirty and shook hands with dozens of our people on his way to the elevator.

At his second luncheon, when *Years of Upheaval* joined *The White House Years* as a main selection, he was just as talkative, much to everybody's delight. There have been few more gifted raconteurs in that room. Dr. Kissinger can do a lot more than assure

279

you that he doesn't wish to run for President, that he is only interested in hereditary office. At the second luncheon he even gave Liby, who sat in on her only author luncheon that day, advice on what we should be sure to see on the trip we were about to take to China, a country I understood he and Richard Nixon had discovered. Our French chef from the Bronx, Steve Bierman, fed the good doctor royally. Kissinger talked through everything.

I wondered what he might have said if I had shown him the mountain of letters we had received protesting our use of his book. One of the most bitterly eloquent said, "Henry Kissinger is a war criminal and a constant, practiced, vicious liar. I will not remain a member of an organization that assists his further ambitions as you have chosen to do. Do not send me the current selection, cancel my membership, and give my accumulated Book-Dividend credits to the Cambodian people, if you can find any."

Presumably he had already read Barbara Tuchman's report on the book in the *Times Book Review*. "Why," she asked, "is he trying in this book to make himself appear something he is not, to wear a Roman toga, as it were, over a coat of mail?"

My own exercise in integrity was to leave Seymour Hersh's book *The Price of Power: Kissinger in the Nixon White House* exactly where it had been displayed for a week, on the ledge that circles the room in the middle of the bookshelves. Leaving it there was probably more an act of defiance of our new parent Time Inc.'s corporate posture of idolatry toward Kissinger than anything else. *Time* magazine's piece on the book in the issue of June 13, 1983, had provoked the only argument I can remember having with Henry Grunwald, the editor-in-chief.

"You didn't even review the book," I complained to Henry on one of the company's jets flying back from Washington.

"Sure we did," he said in his mild manner, "you must have missed it."

"If you mean the news story you ran on it, the one with all that personal opinion in it, I did read it. But that wasn't a book review. It wasn't even signed. The book reviews, Henry, are in the back of the book, aren't they? This was a news story, on page fifteen, right next to a story about the Air Canada DC-9 that caught fire and made an emergency landing at Cincinnati with twenty-three dead people in the cabin. You call that a book review? Did you read it?"

"Yes, I read it," Henry said. He thought for a while and then he said, "Maybe you're right."

Time's article, run in the news section under the headline "Scattershots," with the subhead "A new book attacks Kissinger," made no bones about whose side it was on:

> . . . Reporter Hersh sets out, metaphorically, to massacre Kissinger. . . . Perhaps the nastiest of Hersh's charges is the assertion that during the 1968 presidential campaign, Kissinger secretly supplied the Nixon camp with inside information about the Paris peace talks, then being conducted by the Johnson Administration. At the same time, Hersh claims, Kissinger was also offering to turn over damaging files on Nixon that had been compiled by the Rockefeller campaign staff, for whom Kissinger had worked, to Zbigniew Brzezinski, then Hubert Humphrey's foreign policy coordinator. Kissinger has written in his memoirs that he was approached by both campaigns for advice. But Hersh, quoting some former Nixon campaign officials, paints Kissinger as a double-dealing job seeker. . . . Hersh's book is less the work of a historian, or neutral journalist, than of a prosecutor. . . .

We carried our adversary relationship with our parents over the Hersh-Kissinger duel to another medium when Al Silverman and his programming assistant, Robert Riger, invited Hersh to appear as a guest on our cable-television show, "First Edition." With the camera on him, the man who won the 1970 Pulitzer Prize for his reporting on My Lai rose to rhetorical heights which might have benefited from some editing. Kissinger, he said in a torrent of condemnation, "has to spend his nights counting maimed and burned Vietnamese, Laotian, Thai, Bengalese and Chilean babies."

But it is a fact that in our board room Kissinger was as witty as he was wise, as courteous as he was masterful. Whether he is a wicked sorcerer or a humanistic philosopher, he captivated us. It would be easy to say that the worst rogues are always the most charming people, but you can't altogether dislike a man who, after *Time* ran a portrait of him on its cover, got up at a dinner in his honor and said he wanted to thank "the man who posed for my portrait."

Isaac Bashevis Singer and his wife, Alma, gave us a memorable moment when I congratulated the author on his Nobel Prize for Literature and his sixteen honorary degrees. I was proud of myself for having had the foresight to look them up. But Mr. Singer looked up from his dessert and said, briefly, "Nineteen." He was promptly one-upped by Mrs. Singer, who observed that "The honorary degrees are cheap but the frames are very expensive."

Joyce Maynard, who wrote *Baby Love*, became the only author guest to ask me if I had enough influence with the Book-of-the-Month Club computer to help her break through its unforgiving bars and regain membership in the club. This twenty-six-year-old New Hampshire woman had published her autobiography when she was nineteen and had managed to talk her way into an extended series of interviews with the literary hermit J. D. Salinger when she was a senior in high school. But she had met her match in our IBM 4300. It refused adamantly to let her in, she told us over the tiny lamb chops she wouldn't eat because she is a vegetarian and the roast potatoes she wouldn't eat because they were served on the same platter with the lamb chops. "I'm on your hit list of bad credit risks," she confessed proudly. "I got a lot of books from you and I didn't pay for them. I guess the computer got mad."

"Okay," I told her, "I'll tell the people who talk to the computer to tell it to let you back in."

"Well," Joyce said, "you'll probably have to clear not only Joyce Maynard but Joyce Bethel, too, that's my married name, and Maynard Joyce, which I also used. I ripped you off three different times."

Joyce, I decided, was very much a child of her time. But I was forgiving. I told her we'd let her back in anyway. We'd just add up her entire bad-debt history, I said, and deduct it from her royalties for *Baby Love*.

Abba Eban's wife, Suzy, came to lunch with him wearing a gold pendant that had a little square opening in which I could plainly read the word "NO." I was curious, but I didn't say anything about it until we were having dessert and I noticed that it said "YES." That was too much for me, so I asked her about it. "Well," she said with an irresistible smile, "when I got here I thought No, but after a while I decided it was a definite Yes."

The Ambassador himself was, as advertised, no slouch as a talker. He told us that he had finally bludgeoned Defense Minister Chaim Herzog into clearing his book for publication by appealing to him "as one author to another. I guess I flattered him into it." He also congratulated us on our wisdom "in choosing my book as a main selection and making Moshe Dayan's book only an alternative." But his best line was a foray into American politics. Undiplomatically dismissing Richard Nixon as a non- as well as an anti-intellectual, he said in a caustic summing up, "Nixon was elected by every city and town in your country that doesn't have a bookstore."

John Kenneth Galbraith was a major-league storyteller, right up there with Henry Kissinger. He talked entertainingly about his days as an editor on *Fortune*. "The magazine was good in those days," he said, "because Harry Luce thought the quality of the writing was more important than any political viewpoints the writers might express. So he got together a bunch of crypto-socialists like Dwight MacDonald, Archibald MacLeish and me, whose political views revolted him but whom he had the good sense to leave alone to do what they knew how to do, write." One of Galbraith's recollections was of an interviewer asking James Thurber why so many prominent American writers—Faulkner, Fitzgerald and Hemingway, for instance—were hard drinkers. "Jim thought it over for a few minutes," he said, "and then delivered his opinion. 'Well,' he said, 'they wrote all those books and they made all that money and they could afford to buy liquor by the case.'"

John Fowles was another author whose wife made a lasting impression on me. Arthur Thornhill, Fowles' publisher, was upset because the *Times* had just that morning printed an unflattering review of *Daniel Martin*, and, like a good publisher, he was trying to make John feel better about it. "I don't know where he got off

saying the book was 'occasionally tedious,' " Arthur said righteously. "He was way off the mark with that one." Elizabeth Fowles
wasn't in that immediate conversation group, but she was close
enough to hear what Arthur had said, and she walked right up to
her husband, took his arm affectionately and said, "Oh, come now,
John, you know perfectly well it's tedious."

Arthur C. Clarke was delighted to see on our shelves a copy of his
incredibly prescient 1952 novel *An Exploration of Space*, and paid
us back by telling us stories of his days as a struggling writer living
in New York's legendary Chelsea Hotel, the Edwardian building
that had been home to writers from Mark Twain and O. Henry to
Thomas Wolfe, Dylan Thomas and Brendan Behan. "The thing I
liked the most about the place," Clarke said, "was the sign by the
elevator in the lobby: 'Please Remove Your Own Dead.' "

I don't know what it says about today's writers, but most of them
left the serious drinking to their publishers and stuck to white wine
or Perrier. One who didn't was Joseph Alsop, the author of *FDR:
A Centenary Remembrance*. Mr. Alsop, who was a distant cousin
to the President, shared his subject's recorded fondness for an occasional strong drink and became the only author who ever left one of
our celebrations without the leather-bound copy of the book that
we give each author of a Book of the Month. For a time there was
some question about whether he would be leaving at all.

Drink also played a part in one non-appearance. The judges had
taken *Voyage: A Novel of 1896* by Sterling Hayden, the sometime
movie actor perhaps more famous for his marriage to Madeleine
Carroll (who later was married to *Time*'s Andrew Heiskell) and for
his bouts of intemperance than for his acting career—although he
did give at least one memorable performance in *Dr. Strangelove*.
But Sterling couldn't make his luncheon because he was between
rounds in his biggest fight, which, he said, he was winning "with
the assistance of lithium, vitamins and a touch of common sense."
He also said something perceptive, I thought, when he confessed to
being so set up by his novel's selection by the Book-of-the-Month
Club that he couldn't understand why it didn't immediately estab-

lish itself on top of the New York *Times* best-seller list. "How susceptible to flattery we all are," he said.

Lew Smith wanted me to enliven our lunch with Nixon's man John Ehrlichman by saying "It's a pleasure to welcome an author with convictions," but I resisted the temptation. We never did get to meet Bob Haldeman, Nixon's other man, who acknowledged our leather-bound copy of his book in a pleasant note written on a sheet of plain paper mailed, with no return address, from Lompoc, California. Another presidential assistant who made us worry about his future safety was Hamilton Jordan. He was so unrestrained in his praise of the word processor that had helped him write his book that he was moved to say, in the presence of the dazzlingly attractive lady, "If I had to choose between my word processor and my wife, I'm afraid the processor would come out first." We wondered what he got for dinner that night.

We collected a drinking story of a different kind from Paul Nagel, author of *Descent from Glory*, the story of the four generations that followed John Adams. He asked our waiter, before lunch, for "a Bloody Shame," a request that was new to most of us. Even our editor, Gloria Norris (now a judge), who has been to her share of publishing parties, was surprised. "What's that?" she asked. Mr. Nagel, a man of impeccable manners, said, "It's tomato juice with a little Worcestershire and a little pepper." "You mean a Virgin Mary," Gloria said. "I suppose so," Nagel admitted, "but my High Episcopalian sensibilities cannot confront that term."

John Irving gave us an insight into the thought processes of the writer who has defied the odds and struck it rich practicing his craft. When *The Hotel New Hampshire* was published, he showed up for lunch wearing a pair of Adidas sneakers and admitting that he had run down Park and Lexington Avenues "to keep in some kind of shape." Gloria wondered if he was worn out from the ritual tour of the talk shows and he said, "No, it's not so bad. It's a lot better than working, and, thank God, I don't have to do that anymore." John's presence in the office created a great deal of breathlessness among our young women. When he walked down the hall to shake hands with Lorraine Shanley and talk a little about QPB, he could have been Robert Redford stocking up in the neighborhood Food Emporium.

David Cornwell (John le Carré) hasn't been to see us in a long time. He's always on some exotic island spending all the money George Smiley has made for him. But he does keep in touch. He was glad I had fallen in love with Charlie, the irresistibly appealing actress "of uncertain distinction" who plays the star part of the double agent in *The Little Drummer Girl*, and he felt so guilty "after Bob [Gottlieb] fleeced you for that perfectly disgraceful advance" that he promised to fix me up with a date with her. We paid him the money, but he hasn't come through with Charlie yet. Maybe he's writing a sequel.

Robert Daley, the man his father had said wasn't going to write tripe, brought his collaborator, Detective Robert Leuci, with him to celebrate our selection of their book, *Prince of the City*. Detective Leuci, we learned, is not only a cop "who knew too much," as it said on the jacket of his book, but also a cop who loves to read. He had been a member of the Book-of-the-Month Club for years, he said. He has a sense of humor, too. Al told him that he'd been to the publisher's party for his book and was impressed to see that, despite Leuci's reputation as a Benedict Arnold, the place was crawling with cops. "Yeah," Leuci said, "they'll go anywhere for a free drink. When I put the invitation up on the bulletin board, I didn't think anybody would come. But I should have known."

Judith Guest, the *Ordinary People* and *Second Heaven* author, was one of my favorites. She told us that when Viking took *Ordinary People*, the famous book that came in "over the transom," she practically swooned over the $1,500 check that came with its acceptance. "It's great, honey," her husband told her. "I'll put it in the bank tomorrow."

"But that wasn't what I had in mind," Judy said. "I put it in a brand-new bank account of my own. It was my money and I was going to hang on to it. But then, when the Book-of-the-Month Club took the book, and there was a big paperback sale, and Robert Redford decided to make a movie out of it, and the big checks started to come in, I handed all the money over to my husband and told him to take care of it."

Then there was James Michener, who shared with us a piece of publishing advice he got from Nat Wartels, the elder statesman of the whole business. "Go to every bookstore you can," Nat told him, "and sign every book in the store. Then they can't send them back."

There was no end to the pleasures of getting to know authors as people. John Updike told me he loved to play with QPB golf balls because the distinctive logotype printed on the balls made it easy for him to recognize his ball even in the rough and totally did away with "those nasty disputes with golfers coming down the other fairway claiming that your ball is theirs." William Buckley loved it when we took the first of his Blackford Oakes espionage novels, *Saving the Queen*, but he sold the next one to Doubleday, his publisher, for their Literary Guild. "Oh, well," I said when I saw him next, "we'll just have to console ourselves that in this one Blackie makes out with a Hungarian commoner, but we had the one in which he laid the Queen of England." Bill Sheed didn't seem to mind my telling the Time Inc. people in one of my reports that my favorite scene in his memoir of Clare Boothe Luce was the one in which Harry protested her wildly enthusiastic shopping in Tiffany's and Clare said, "Damn it, Harry, are we rich or aren't we?"

One author I've never met, and it's probably better that way, is Mayor Edward I. Koch of New York. I asked Gloria Norris to buy his book "if you can get it for very little money," and she did—$1,000, about a dollar an insult. Gloria agreed with me that because of the intense interest in the problems of America's big cities, it had a chance of selling a few copies even outside the city of New York, and besides it was bitchily funny. Maybe, because we gave him so little money, we should have invited the mayor to lunch. Later, though, he got enough money from us in royalties to buy lunch at every Chinese restaurant in New York.

Umberto Eco taught us that money isn't as important to an author as recognition. Lorraine Shanley put up a $1,500 advance for *The Name of the Rose* and Professor Eco was so grateful he walked unannounced into our offices and shook hands with everybody in sight.

James Carroll and his wife, Alexandra, taught us a different kind of lesson. When we had lunch with him at the time *Mortal Friends* was published, he told us that he had been a priest. "I thought," I said, "priests only married nuns." "I," Alexandra said, "was a nun."

Julia Child told us she wouldn't eat in the Cleveland hotel into which her publisher kept booking her. "Thank God," she said, "there's a McDonald's next door."

Our friend Bill Safire, who liked us as much for the book we didn't use as he did for the two books we did, gave me advice on what to watch for in the next presidential campaign. "Going into the primaries," he said, "we may have the first husband-and-wife team in history fighting it out for the Republican nomination. You're going to have to watch every week to see who's leading, Bob Dole or Elizabeth Dole."

"You're missing a good line there," I said. "If you're going to write that, you ought to tell people to keep an eye on who's on top."

"Abe Rosenthal," Bill said, "would never print it."

But it was Maxine Hong Kingston, the author of two touching memoirs of her family, *Woman Warrior* and *China Men*, who told us everything there is to know about writing your own life.

"Are your books," somebody asked her, "fiction or nonfiction?"

Mrs. Kingston didn't answer right away, but then she said, "I won't say. It's the way I remember it. It's the way it should have been. It's the way I wish it was."

The Book-of-the-Month Club's judges may not be as celebrated as its authors, but they are every bit as interesting. There are now six of them: Clifton Fadiman, the dean, John Hutchens, Wilfrid Sheed, Canada's Mordecai Richler, David Willis McCullough and the reformed editor, Gloria Norris. Gloria is only the fourth woman ever to wield a vote in this deliberative body, her predecessors having been Dorothy Canfield Fisher and Amy Loveman way back in the beginning, then Lucy Rosenthal in the '70s. Actually, the judges don't vote. They just talk about the books they have been asked to read, and when a consensus thrusts itself upon them, they agree to make the book a selection. They drink a little vodka or Scotch or Perrier before lunch, a little good wine with lunch, and have never been known to raise their voices in passion. Their discourse is thoughtful and friendly. Their comments, however, can be very much to the point.

Kip Fadiman has called Norman Mailer "a Belushi with brains." He has also said that "psychoanalysis is strictly a Jewish science," and in the same vein that "there is a Wailing Wall at the end of every street in Brownsville."

When Mordecai Richler was asked if he could describe the sociopolitical attitudes of an important woman writer whose new book was being considered by the board, he said briefly, "Sure. She's a Fascist." Speaking from the depths of personal experience, Mordecai also said, "To be a Jew and a Canadian is to emerge from the ghetto twice."

Mordecai can take it as well as give it. He was able to laugh when a Canadian film-maker responded to Mordecai's charge that the movie business in Canada suffered from "unbelievable bad taste larded with greed" by saying, "I love his book anyway. I buy it every time he writes it."

Three of the judges are intensely interested in baseball, and since Al and I are former reporters of the men who played the game when the grass was green, there was at least one other subject besides politics that could be talked about before lunch. Well, religion made it one day in 1984 when the *Times* led off an editorial on Archbishop John J. O'Connor's running feud with Governor Mario M. Cuomo about abortion by saying, " 'You did not talk religion to him,' wrote the novelist Wilfrid Sheed about his Roman Catholic father, 'unless you were serious enough to break a sweat.' " That's understandable because Frank Sheed was the head of the Catholic publishing house Sheed & Ward, and Maisie Ward was Bill's mother. Religion was a serious matter in that family.

Baseball isn't exactly a religion with Bill, but it is a serious interest and he, Mordecai and John Hutchens like to talk about it almost as much as they like to watch it. That's how I collected one of my two all-time favorite baseball race stories. The first was Rachel Robinson telling how Jackie used to come home from the ball park some afternoons so frustrated that he would take a pail of golf balls out behind the house and, as tired as he was, hit them one after another into the nearby woods. "Yeah," Jackie said, "they were white." I got into the second one by telling Bill, Mordecai and John about Frank Frisch, the old Fordham Flash, standing in our living room and showing Kevin how to hold a bat properly. When he finally put down the bat and picked up his glass, Frank discoursed generally on baseball. "The game went to hell when they brought in all those college kids," he said disgustedly, conveniently forgetting that in 1919 he had gone straight from the Fordham campus to the infield at the Polo Grounds. "They don't even talk right anymore. You watch. Somebody hits a fly ball out to center field and the center fielder runs in and yells, 'I *have* it, I *have* it!' Can you imagine a major-league ballplayer calling for a ball like that? 'I *got* it!' he should be yelling. 'I *got* it!' "

"Today," the literary Bill Sheed, Oxford '54, said thoughtfully, "he'd run in for the ball and yell, 'Yo lo tengo!' "

The kind of people the judges are can be determined even by the reasons some brilliantly qualified authors have had for not being judges. Paul Horgan quit because he couldn't do justice to the work and at the same time keep up with his teaching responsibilities at Wesleyan. A distinguished woman writer regretfully said no to an appointment because she didn't see how she could do her own work, fulfill the responsibilities of a judge and still have time for her husband and children. She knew, she said, she could hire nannies and a cook, but she hadn't had children in order to have them raised by others.

For the making of a judge there is no formula. About the only thing the present ones, with the exception of Ms. Norris, have in common is a perplexing love of Havana cigars. Because Mordecai can bring them in from Canada, the judges are spoiled regularly by the real thing. They live in constant fear that the Canadian customs will shut off their supply, but it hasn't happened yet. "I did ask a customs man once what they do with the cigars they confiscate," Mordecai said, "and I was relieved when he told me, 'Sir, we destroy them, one by one.' "

Chapter 17

H<small>ARRY</small> B<small>ROWN</small> told me once that nobody since Harry
Scherman, who invented the whole thing, had made enough
of a difference in the Book-of-the-Month Club to be sure of being remembered for it. "You've got a chance," he said, "because of QPB."

More to the point, QPB has made a difference. The Book-of-the-
Month Club will never be the same as it was before its paperback
baby took dead aim at shaking up not only its conservative parent
but the whole book business. Even though a lot of people, inside
and outside the company, thought we were cannibalizing ourselves,
there was a great big hole in the book-distribution system just waiting for QPB. By the beginning of the 1970s we had raised a generation of young people who think paperback. They dismiss the
expensive hardcover book as a showy waste of money, proportion-
ately as bad an investment as a mink coat or a Mercedes-Benz. What
counts to them is what's in the book and how much satisfaction it
will give them. But they love books too much to settle for the small,
cheaply made mass-market paperbacks, which are all right for reading on jet planes but not for building a home library. For that, it was
obvious, they wanted paperbound books made like the hardcover
ones, with the same type size and the same good paper, but bound
in handsome paper covers and costing a lot less money.

Voilà, QPB. We gave the college kids what they wanted.

In the beginning, when we had no staff and Vilma Bergane and Al Silverman were my only assistants in this Manhattan Project of the book business, my models for what I was trying to do were my own kids, then twenty-six and twenty-four, respectively. Eileen, the older, was heavy on Eastern thought and philosophy. Kevin must have read every book ever written on the assassination of John F. Kennedy. Both were hotly sympathetic to the Civil Rights movement and Kevin in particular thought Black Liberation was the way for our beleaguered brethren to go. His gas mask from the Days of Rage in Chicago is still in our attic. And Eileen's room at McGill University in Montreal was home to a black cat named Stokely.

When they were home, they and their friends debated the cosmic issues of the times so heatedly they almost drowned out the music that never stopped. Crosby, Stills and Nash, The Electric Flag, Seals and Crofts, Supersession, the Mamas and the Papas and The Grateful Dead provided a never ending counterpoint to the between-semesters arguments. So did the kings and queens of the folk-singers, Woody Guthrie and his son, Arlo (who even got the kids to memorize the endless verses to "Alice's Restaurant"), Pete Seeger, Joan Baez, Bob Dylan, Leadbelly, Judy Collins, Odetta and Buffy Sainte-Marie. Sometimes, but not often, they stopped talking for the Beatles. Once they got Liby to take them to hear The Who do the rock opera *Tommy* at the Metropolitan Opera House.

These kids did not listen to bad music or read bad books. I was convinced that somewhere in their educated, opinionated, eclectic tastes there had to be a book club. It was for them that we put together QPB, although not only for them. We were sure there were lots of older hard-core readers who had the same kind of adventurous minds, restless readers who would rather read the *Evergreen Review* than subscribe to *Time*, who thought the Literary Guild was for people who wanted something to read while they watched television, and who would gladly go to the guillotine before they would pick up a copy of the *Reader's Digest*.

Right from the beginning we went after our target intellectuals with no holds barred. If we thought a book would turn off the people we wanted to reach, it didn't get on the list, no matter how many copies it had sold or how famous its author was. We made no concessions. We were convinced there was no point in enrolling in the club people who didn't want the kind of books we would offer them later on, which isn't a bad principle for any book club to live with.

Kenneth Clark's *The Nude* got us off to a smashing start. A Princeton/Bollingen book, beautifully printed in rotogravure on expensive paper, and at 7½x10 inches exactly the same page size as the original, it dramatized the message that QPB was like no book club anyone had ever seen. The members' price, $5.50, was plainly a steal for what they were getting. We hadn't yet come up with the kind of catchy, provocative advertising that Lord, Geller, Federico & Einstein gave us a couple of years later, with its eye-catching caricatures of literary figures like Sigmund Freud, Virginia Woolf, Scott Fitzgerald and John Updike, and its headlines like "The first Book Club for Smart People Who Aren't Rich," but we got the message across through the books.

The Alternate Selection in the first issue of the club's publication, *QPB Review*, was Lawrence Durrell's *Alexandria Quartet*, all four volumes in a boxed set for $6.95. A triple alternate offered Albert Camus' *The Plague*, *The Fall* and *The Stranger* for $5.55. Like the readers we hoped to attract, we struck out in all directions. We offered *Good Cheap Food*, *Vagabonding in America*, *Great Songs of the Sixties*, *The History and Practice of Magic* and *The Art of Tantra*, with 151 illustrations. We had Kenneth Clark's most famous book, *Civilisation*, and *The Woodstock Craftsman's Manual*. We had the illustrated text of Erich von Stroheim's film classic *Greed*. We offered Thomas Pynchon's *Gravity's Rainbow*, *Ulysses* and *Finnegans Wake*, and *Getting Clear—Body Work for Women*.

We pointed out that more than 7,000 new paperbacks were published every year, and that if ours were books of the kind you found yourself looking for fruitlessly in store after store, we would find them for you and save you money, too. We promised to offer our books at the best discounts we could manage off the publisher's trade paperback, if there was one, and right from the beginning we did our own "QPB Exclusive" editions of books that weren't available anywhere else in paperback editions the same size as the hardcover. We offered publishers royalties almost as high as BOMC's—8 percent of the club price for books we sold to members and half that much, 4 percent, for books we distributed as premiums or bonus books.

The bonus-book plan we devised for QPB was, we thought, sure to appeal to the readers we were after. Every book they bought would earn them bonus points, pegged to the price of the book, and with a minimum of six points they could choose a bonus book for nothing except the shipping charge. The first issue of the *Review* told, as it does today, how many bonus points were given with each book listed and how many points were needed to obtain it free. Most of the books could be had for six points, some more expensive ones for twelve points, and a handful of high-priced books, like the four-volume *The World of Mathematics*, *Greed* and *The Art of Tantra*, all heavily illustrated, were fixed at eighteen points.

Like conventional book clubs, we started with a minimum number of purchases, but it didn't take long to see that the people we wanted most were the ones most likely to be put off by what they saw as a punishing requirement. I went back to my typewriter and came up with a "Let's Try Each Other for Six Months" proposal. It was disarmingly simple. It said that you have no obligation to buy any given number of books, but that if you don't buy at least one in six months we'll throw you out. It worked so well we even had T-shirts made that said "Let's Try Each Other for Six Months." I've never been sure what it says about the relationship between physical makeup and mental, but over the years we've shipped about twice as many Large shirts as Medium and almost twice as many Medium as Small. What mattered was that the offer worked.

QPB lost more than $2 million before it began to show a profit, but it was obvious after two years that it was here to stay. The members responded to our advertisements in such numbers that the enrollment cost was happily low; they stayed in longer than members of most book clubs did, they bought a lot of books and they paid their bills. That was a relief because the skeptics had thought that by deliberately shaping our appeal to the interests, and for that matter the prejudices, of the young, we were letting ourselves in for the kind of casual ripping-off that carefree Joyce Maynard had practiced on the Book-of-the-Month Club. It didn't happen. It has never happened.

We didn't push the membership growth too hard. We advertised at a steady pace and kept trying to find new places to advertise. But we never risked bringing in a flood of members who would really rather be somewhere else. There was no hurry; what was important was to do it right.

The new advertising did it right. "New Hope for the Hard-Core Reader," it promised, and "How to Be Well-Read Even If You Aren't Well-Heeled." One that is still used when the club has the right books for it is "QPB Makes History."

In the beginning I had thought that the irreverent tone of the QPB ads might cause me trouble with the Old Guard. This was long before BOMC's merger with Time Inc. and the average age of the members of the board of directors was probably over seventy. They were already worried about our robbing Peter to pay Paul and I feared their appetite for sabotage might grow in a hurry if they thought QPB was kicking mud on the Book-of-the-Month Club's reputation for good taste. I've always been convinced the new club would never have been allowed to get off the ground in the form it did, taking on the Book-of-the-Month Club as well as the Literary Guild in ads that were aggressively adversarial, if I hadn't had Bernardine Scherman on my side. Mrs. Scherman was a smart bookseller and a tough competitor, and when I first told the board of directors what I was up to, she did everything but clap her hands and shout hallelujah. Up until then I'd had a quiet disagreement going with the Old Guard. They wanted to ease into paperbacks with a catalog—that's how we got into the early use of the word "Service"—offering only to help BOMC members find whatever titles they wanted. I was fighting for a real book club, out there on its own, competing openly with the big Club. Bernardine won my battle for me in a matter of minutes. "Let's go over to your office," she said to me when the board meeting was over, "I want to hear more about this."

When I had given her the whole story, she was ready to become a consulting editor on the spot. "Don't waste any time," she urged me. "Hurry up and get your ads out. If we don't do it"—and she pointed across the street—"they will."

A few months later Bernardine was dead, but she had given QPB the crucial push it had needed. She shut off, and shut up, the snipers.

There was an understandable amount of grumbling when QPB's losses reached that $2 million point, but it was never serious. Both Kathy and Axel Rosin were staunch supporters of the club, and because they held total control of the company, their backing was all I needed. They knew the soundness of the argument that if we didn't do it somebody else would, and they were competitors, too. We all felt good when it began to be clear that we were winning our bet. The members kept coming in and the club's revenues began steadily to catch up to its expenses, and the coverage in the press was so admiring I might have written it myself.

We brought in some help in the unique person of David R. Godine, the young and moderately wealthy head of the Boston publishing house that bears his name. David had the kind of personality and temperament and fondness for battle that we needed, and he helped us a lot for a while, but it was a foregone conclusion that no job would satisfy him the way running his own house did, and that he would leave, and he did. We were lucky we had Lorraine Shanley, a young woman with little experience but a lot of talent, to take over. In an amazingly short time Lorraine put it all together and she has been running the club ever since. "The average QPB member," she once said to me, "is me." That means the average QPB member is in her early thirties, has curly blond hair, lively eyes that give her a cheerfully quizzical expression that makes you sure nobody but you and she understands the point of it all, and a wry sense of humor that is, as she is, quintessentially QPB.

Lorraine is running a lot more than QPB now. She's the executive vice-president and editor-in-chief of the whole company. But as long as Lorraine is within shouting distance, nothing bad is going to happen to the book club that people who don't join book clubs join. Susan Weinberg, who learned about the club working with me, and Marty Asher, a fine editor, are looking after it full-time and are the managers who pushed it over the half-million level early in 1985. If Ms. Shanley doesn't buy the champagne when they get to 750,000, I will. "Go to Hell with QPB" was an effective headline to use with *Dante's Inferno*, but there is no chance that QPB is going to go to hell.

If QPB could survive Three Mile Island, it can survive anything. When the accident struck the reactor on the little island just outside Harrisburg, the newspaper stories were datelined Middletown, Pennsylvania, which is the post office QPB used when it was launched. All of the post offices in the area—including Camp Hill, which is the one the Book-of-the-Month Club uses—flow into and out of the Harrisburg office, but not everybody in the world knows that. Some people—not many, but some—were afraid to open QPB book packages with the Middletown postmark for fear they might be radioactive. The Pennsylvania Bureau of Radiation Protection said emphatically there was no chance of that happening, but in those March 1979 days official credibility was not high. It took a while before everybody forgot about the problem.

QPB celebrated its tenth anniversary with a bang and will surely have many more than half a million members by the time it is fifteen years old.

More letters may be written by more authors saying, as John Cheever said when he thanked us for sending him a copy of the QPB edition of his collected stories, that they have never seen such a handsome paperback book.

It's interesting that the Book-of-the-Month Club has used—and so has the enemy in the high-rent district across the street—more and more soft-cover books in the last few years. "But nobody," Lorraine Shanley says thoughtfully, "has said anything about BOMC cannibalizing QPB."

It may come to that.

Chapter 18

I F the words of the prophets are written on the subway walls, they can also be printed on buttons. At the publication party for *The Boys of Summer*, Irving Rudd, who used to be the publicity man for the Dodgers, wore a big button saying "KEEP THE DODGERS IN BROOKLYN." Unswerving Irving, which is what his two million friends call him, appreciates a little irony. "When You Sell It, You Sell It" isn't so much irony as it is fact, but it ought to be printed on buttons so that everybody who is thinking of selling the old candy store to a conglomerate might be reminded forcefully that if you do it, things aren't ever going to be the same again.

With further apologies to Simon and Garfunkel, the one sound you aren't going to hear anymore once you turn over the keys to the comptroller or treasurer or chief financial officer of the big company is the Sound of Silence. You will hear from them.

I'm convinced that in Time Inc. we found the best possible home for the Book-of-the-Month Club; we were lucky enough to fall among people who wanted to make money but who cared deeply about how they made it. But in working our way through almost a dozen offers, we narrowly escaped a few disasters, and even after we had what turned out to be the best possible deal, there was no way of stifling an occasional stab of nostalgia for the good old days when we were on our own and could spend all our time working instead of writing reports explaining why we were doing what we were doing.

Axel's investment bankers had convinced him that the company had to be sold to protect his two daughters from ultimately having to give a ton of money unnecessarily to the Internal Revenue Service. Once that decision was made, the question was not "if" but "to whom."

There was no shortage of suitors. Felix Rohatyn, the Lazard Frères financial wizard who in his role of chairman of the Municipal Assistance Corporation had been busy saving New York City from bankruptcy, sorted them out and tried to spare us the bother of talking to the ones he considered poor match-ups. Time Inc. had expressed guarded interest off and on for a couple of years, but when Axel's intentions became known, others soon clamored more loudly than Time. CBS and American Express were at the top of the list. Axel had said unselfishly that he wouldn't sell the company to anybody I thought would make me and the other key employees unhappy, so I paid a lot of attention to what went on. My early favorite was American Express, not just because they had so much money they could buy us as though we really were a neighborhood candy store, but also because they weren't in the publishing business, didn't know anything about it and would probably leave us alone.

Axel and I had a friendly lunch with Howard Clark, the chairman, and Bill Morton, the president, in their private dining room with its heart-catching view of New York Harbor. The food was delicious and we learned a lot about how much money they made off their "float"—the money they held that belonged to people who had bought American Express traveler's checks and hadn't used them yet. We thought they were the kind of people we could get along with and we left feeling good about the possibility. They had made it clear that the price we had in mind was all right with them, so that didn't seem to be a problem.

What turned out to be a problem was the cadre of MBAs and CPAs they assigned to look into our business. The numbers people were friendly enough when they took me to lunch and made arrangements to spend a week in our offices going over our books. They even seemed awed that Felix Rohatyn was our man on the deal. I had the feeling that they wanted us in the family. But when they showed up at 280 Park Avenue, they treated us like job applicants whose reputation was none too good. I was amused when they behaved as though they thought Axel was trying to sell them a worn-out Rolls Royce that might not make it back from the gas station, but I got really mad when they implied that Harry Brown was showing them a creative set of books and hiding the real ones in the safe. I told Axel I didn't think we'd be happy with this company, and he agreed. We told the posse we would rather talk to their sheriffs and we never heard from any of them again. Felix said he would pursue it if we wanted him to, but we said we'd rather not. It was written in the newspapers a few times that we rejected American Express, but that was an exaggeration. The truth was that we rejected each other.

We had another *de luxe* meal with Ed Carter, chairman of Carter, Hawley, Hale, who had told Felix he would like to talk to us about buying the company. There was nothing backward about Mr. Carter. He made it clear right away that he was interested in our company not for itself but for what it might do for him. His retail empire included Waldenbooks, one of the two (the other is B. Dalton & Co., owned by Dayton-Hudson) giant bookstore chains in the country. He didn't ask Axel any questions, but he dug extensively into my background, probably on the assumption that I was the one who would be working for him. He knew both Norton Simon and David Mahoney and obviously had asked them about me. He seemed especially interested that I hadn't gone to college. "You did this all on your own?" he said. That surprised me. "Haven't we all?" I said, and I could have bitten my tongue because I realized that not all of us had. But he was ready with his next question. He wanted to know how many copies of our main selections we printed. "About 125,000 to 175,000," I said. "If it's a book by a very big author, maybe 200,000. Books like *All the President's Men*, *Tinker, Tailor, Soldier, Spy*, Schlesinger's *The Imperial Presidency* and Ed Doctorow's *Ragtime* have been on the high side."

"Why *Ragtime*?"

"Because it had had so much pre-publication publicity, including the fact that Bantam was paying a mint for the paperback rights. That always helps our sale."

"How many copies do you print of books that aren't selections?"

"Anywhere from 5,000, sometimes even fewer, to 50,000. Some books that don't make it as selections are obvious winners anyway. David Halberstam's *The Best and the Brightest*, for instance. Germaine Greer's *The Female Eunuch*. I told a couple of our judges that I thought *The Best and the Brightest* wasn't the Book of the Month, it was the Book of the Year. We print what we think we're going to need. We can always go back for more, but it isn't so easy to get rid of the ones you print and don't sell."

"What do you do with them?" Carter wanted to know.

"We remainder them—that is, we sell them to companies that specialize in selling overstock books in department stores and discount bookstores for anywhere from thirty-nine cents to four ninety-five."

"What do you get for them?"

"It depends on how salable the remainder house thinks the author or the subject is. Sometimes I think they buy them—and sell them, for that matter—by the pound. Big art books sell very well. Big novels, especially by authors like Michener or Mailer, do well. Biographies are usually pretty good. Special-interest books or books that are very literary don't do well at all."

"Well, what I'm wondering is this: on the selections, with those big print runs, you could easily add enough for Waldenbooks, couldn't you, and on the remainders Waldenbooks could just take most of them off your hands. That would help you, wouldn't it?"

I laughed. "It would help put us in jail," I said. "There's a law against that in this country. We're allowed to sell books only to people who are bona-fide members of the book club. So using our printings to supply Waldenbooks would be absolutely illegal, and anyway the publishers would have a collective fit. We'd be taking a big piece of their market away from them. Remainders are different. We can sell them to anybody so long as we offer them to everybody and especially offer them first, at manufacturing cost, to the publisher."

Mr. Carter's interest in us lasted as long as it took to finish our coffee and tea.

Quaker Oats took me to lunch and I still don't have any idea why they wanted to include us in their diversification program. For them, I thought, we would be diversification with a capital D.

Dick Snyder, Simon & Schuster's energetic president, told me regularly that his bosses, Gulf & Western, would love to have us and would pay a good price, maybe more than anybody else would.

Bertelsmann, the German book-club colossus, never got tired of putting out feelers. I had known some of their executives since Doubleday and they would remind me every now and then that they were still interested. When I told one of their top men that Axel wanted a tax-free exchange of stock and wasn't interested in selling to a foreign company, he said quickly that the deal could be done for cash. "But the taxes would kill him," I said. "Not," he said, "if there was enough cash."

Finally, Bertelsmann gave up on us and started their own American book club, using the same door-to-door technique that was so effective in Europe, but it never got anywhere and they killed it in 1984. Their abortive venture reminded me of the time Doubleday tried door-to-door solicitation and we hired an experienced Avon manager to run it for us. The morning she sent out her first team, she called me just before lunchtime to tell me one of her agents had been arrested in Syosset, Long Island, for soliciting without a license.

Ed Booher of McGraw-Hill called to say that another German publishing titan, Dieter von Holtzbrinck, whose empire included Deutscher Bucherbund, had asked him to intercede with us in their behalf. "They are interested," Ed said, "in getting together with you in any way possible—a complete takeover, a merger, a joint venture, whatever." Nothing came of that, either. Axel wanted the ownership of the company, which we all considered an American institution, to be kept in America.

The Pritzker family of Chicago let me know through Ray Eyes, who had been running *McCall's* for them since they bought it from

David Mahoney, that they would like to talk to us. The Times-Mirror Company said we should call them any time we wanted to talk. One publishing visionary proposed a three-way merger of one of the country's biggest paperback companies, a distinguished trade publishing house and us. Axel and I thought that one might not get past the anti-trust watchdogs at the Department of Justice, and we were sure it would inevitably hurt our relations with the other trade publishers. So we said no.

CBS made the first big move on us early in 1974. Felix, who knows everybody, was a friend of William S. Paley, and Paley asked Felix to bring us to lunch for a serious talk. It was serious, all right. Paley, whose name, the old story says, "is on every door at CBS," offered Axel a price that was a little bit more than we had set in our minds. The trouble was, he told us flat out that he intended to put us together with the Columbia Record Club in what would be a mail-order marriage of two companies he considered eminently compatible. "They can help you a lot," he told us regally. "They know everything there is to know about mail order."

Axel politely said nothing and I decided that was what I was there for. "But, sir," I said, "we're not really a mail-order company. We don't publish books ourselves, but we're actually more of a publishing company. That's the way we see ourselves and that's the way the people in the publishing business see us."

"You can do it better," Paley said imperturbably, "if you're in with the Columbia Record Club. You can spend your money more efficiently. You'll get bigger faster."

No matter how many times I interrupted him to say "But, sir," he sailed serenely along on his predetermined course. He was going to put us in bed with the Columbia Record Club and that was that. It didn't bother him when I said we thought the lowest-common-denominator approach of the record club's advertising was exactly the opposite of the way we promoted our club. If anything, he made it plain that he thought the way we were doing it was the wrong way. Much later than we had wanted to leave, we extricated ourselves politely at three o'clock and got into the chairman's private elevator.

"Well?" I asked Axel as we descended swiftly.

"You first," he said.

"No," I said.

"That's correct," Axel said, and when we got back to the office we got Felix on the telephone and told New York's most celebrated deal-maker that this was one deal he wasn't going to make. Felix said no for us, and later he told us that Paley was surprised. "Didn't I offer them everything they wanted?" he asked. "No," Felix told him. "You offered them money, but you didn't tell them they could run their business the way they want to run it. You blew the deal."

"At least," I told Axel, "we've seen another one of the great private dining rooms of New York."

Paley didn't give up entirely. John Purcell, a CBS division vice-president, took me to lunch—at Lutèce, no less, and in his own chauffeured Cadillac, to give me a taste of what the CBS world was like—and said we could be in his division and stay completely apart from the record club. He followed that up with a friendly note telling me he had ordered several of our books at home last night and had felt a couple of twinges about our venerable institution. He said it was one thing if we decided not to sell, but if we did, he was convinced there was no better place for us than CBS. But Axel, bless him, ended it. "Money," he said, "isn't everything."

The next time we sat down to talk about it, I had a suggestion for Axel. "Why don't we ask Felix to sound out Time Inc.?" I asked. "That's our kind of publishing company. They would understand us. I'll bet we could be happy there." Axel was willing and he had a preliminary lunch with Andrew Heiskell, Time's chairman and chief executive officer. Then Felix talked with Heiskell and we were invited to meet all of the Time hierarchy at dinner in the Library Suite of the St. Regis on March 8, presumably to shake hands on the deal.

The Book-of-the-Month Club was represented by Axel, Harry Brown and me, with support from Felix Rohatyn. Along with Heiskell their side lined up Jim Shepley, their president; Arthur Temple, the colorful chairman of Temple-Eastex, the forest-products company that had merged with Time a few years before and in the process had made Temple the biggest single stockholder in the company; Hedley Donovan, the editor-in-chief; Dick Mc-Keough, the chief financial officer; and Joan Manley, the group vice-president for books, the wonder woman who had climbed from being a secretary at Doubleday to running Time-Life Books and Little, Brown along with half a dozen other Time-Life interests in the book business. She was going to be our boss, which seemed to me to be a very good thing indeed.

Andrew Heiskell, then and now one of the most impressive and most interesting men I've ever met, talked about Time's philosophy of management and emphasized that we would be expected to run our own business. "If we can help you, we'll help," he said, "but we will not interfere. That's not our style."

Temple spoke with the forcefulness of a born entrepreneur and followed Heiskell's lead in promising us autonomy. Hedley Donovan told us how important quality and responsibility were to Time's publications and said the reason they wanted us was because they knew we shared their ideals.

Joan Manley, just off the airplane from Paris and emotionally up for an occasion that obviously meant a lot to her, ended the speaking if not the drinking part of the evening by throwing her arms enthusiastically around Axel and saying, "All that's left now is for you to marry me."

When we went home that night, Axel, Harry and I thought we were married.

It was a stunning shock when Felix called the next morning to tell us that, despite last night's euphoria and despite the fact that he had earlier made it clear to our crosstown friends how much per share we wanted for the company, the offer they had just made to him was five dollars less than our price. We were disheartened. It wouldn't be fair to the public shareholders to sell the company for a figure drastically lower than we could get somewhere else. "Anyway," I said, "if that's all they think we're worth, they can't think very highly of us."

Nothing happened for weeks. Time never called Felix and never called us. There was no "Hey, why don't we talk this over?" Just silence. "Maybe they're just waiting us out," I said to Axel. "They will have a long wait," he said. We didn't even hear anything from Joan Manley. I hoped she hadn't bought a wedding dress.

The only bright spot I can remember from those days came when some friends of mine in England—John Letts, who had worked for a while for the Doubleday-Smith partnership, and Halfdan Lynner, who had been with the George Weidenfeld firm—talked to us tentatively about the Book-of-the-Month Club acquiring the Folio Society, a book club selling fine editions of classics. "I don't know," I told Axel and Harry, "it reminds me of Phil Glatfelter's story." Glatfelter, whose Spring Grove, Pennsylvania, paper mill supplied most of the BOMC's book paper, had almost sold his company to Weyerhauser, one of the giants of the industry, but had changed his mind and then decided with his brother that maybe they ought to expand their product line by acquiring the Bergstrom company in Wisconsin. "Well, I don't know," Phil's mother had said when he told her about the Bergstrom idea, "first you're selling, then you're buying. Do you boys know what you're doing?"

Kathy and Axel Rosin were in Europe when Felix and I got together in late June and talked about Felix's hunch that Andrew Heiskell was willing to talk again. "Good," I said, not willing to get too excited about it. A week later Heiskell said he was interested, and at our price. "Can we do this deal," which is how investment bankers, even ones who went to Middlebury, talk, "even with Axel in Europe?" Felix asked me between meetings of the Municipal Assistance Corporation. "Sure we can," I said. "If they want to pay our price, we can make a deal by three o'clock this afternoon."

We didn't do it quite that fast, but we did it quickly. The *Times* ran a story on the merger on July 6 and the same day I got a telegram from Joan Manley saying, "I'm delighted. I'm sure our union will be joyous and fruitful." Maybe, I thought, Joan *had* bought a wedding dress.

None of the reporters who called or came to the office could get me to give an unequivocal answer to their questions about independence of management. I brought out the Manheimer adage, I said we're selling it and they're buying it, and I said we wouldn't be selling it to them if we didn't think we had a good chance of being left alone to run the business the way we always had. "What if they tell you you have to buy, or not buy, a certain book?" one reporter asked me. "They won't," I said. "But what if they do?" he persisted. "They'll have to get somebody else to do it," I said. But it never happened. The Book-of-the-Month Club had found the right home.

When Heiskell made his first tour of our offices, with Pat Lenahan, the erudite if Irish publisher of *Fortune*, who was going to join our board of directors, they stopped and stared at a group of artifacts Eileen had given me. They all had something to do with her interest in Tibetan Buddhism. There was a mandala, which is an aid to meditation, a medal her Dharma Center's Lama had given her for me, and a God's Eye she had woven "to ward off evil spirits." Heiskell and Lenahan, both unusually tall men, had to bend over to inspect the items. "Your daughter is a Buddhist?" Pat asked me.

"Yes," I said, "she takes it very seriously."

"Don't I remember that her name is Eileen?" he asked.

"Yes."

"And you mean Eileen Fitzgerald is a Buddhist?"

"Yes, she is," I said. "In fact, she's the president of her Dharma Center."

Returned to his full height, Pat looked Heiskell in the eye and said, "Well, Andrew, it's better than being a Protestant."

I knew there was no way we could go wrong with men like these. Or women like Joan. Not to mention Joan's astonishingly versatile assistant, Betsy Wiegers, whose husband, George, helped Time's investment bankers, Lehman Brothers, put together the merger. Betsy and George threw a splendid party to celebrate the merger, and that made us officially members of the family. This time the knot stayed tied. Joan didn't wear a wedding dress, but we were married anyway.

The party was a great success and so was the merger. Nobody could have asked for better people to work with—Heiskell, Shepley, Temple, McKeough, Manley and Dick Munro, the heir apparent to Heiskell. The closest any of them ever came to involving themselves in the nuts and bolts of our business was when Clifford Grum, who is now back in Texas running the spun-off Temple-Eastex company, called me the morning after our loss of *The Covenant* to the Guild. "I just want to offer my condolences, Ed," he said. "I know how much you wanted the Michener book. But I do want to remind you of one thing: you still have all that money."

You could never get mad at people like that. When Heiskell turned over the company to Munro, he said, "All of us know, or should, that in promoting people one of the dangers is replication, choosing people like ourselves. In Dick's case I can honestly say that I personally am untainted by replication. He is a man with absolutely no interest in food or drink, who confuses Château Margaux with Château Gallo, or for that matter with cream soda. He breakfasts at the Dorset on Philadelphia scrapple, thinking it's whole-wheat toast."

Our bosses didn't even get mad at me when I said some nice things about Ariel Sharon when he was suing *Time* for $50 million. Liby and I and Marc Jaffe of Villard Books, who wanted to do a book with him, had had a fascinating three-hour lunch with Sharon and his wife, Lily, at their thousand-acre farm in the Negev, where they raise a thousand sheep and grow enough melons to be Israel's single largest exporter of the fruit. "Your sheep live pretty well," I said to the general, "the farm comes out to an acre per sheep." Mrs. Sharon laughed. "They should be that lucky," she said.

Sharon was interested in Marc's idea for a book. He wanted to tell his side of the Lebanon story—"I was made the sacrifice," he said— and he was tired of farming. "I'm probably the only man in the Cabinet who can get up on a tractor," Sharon said, "but I'd like to do something else now."

The general opened a bottle of Israeli wine to go with the lunch of fish, chicken, asparagus, potatoes and carrots. He reached for the plate of rolls, but Mrs. Sharon yanked them away from him. When we left, Mrs. Sharon said, "Arik"—which is what everybody who knows him calls him—"let's pose together," and Liby took pictures of them. The last thing I can remember Mrs. Sharon saying, as we shook hands in front of the Israeli soldiers guarding the house, was a regretful "He used to be a hero."

The only sad thing about the merger, for me, was that I had to give up that kind of involvement in the world of books and the people who make them when I reached the mandatory retirement age. Time Inc. may not subscribe to Shakespeare's dictum, "When the age is in, the wit is out," but they're not taking any chances. Pat Lenahan had warned me, in his typical fashion, what would happen when the time came. "When you're sixty-five," Pat said, "you're out on your ass." Fair enough. For seven years it was an exhilarating ride and the Book-of-the-Month Club had had its wish: to be left alone to do what it thought was right.

Benjamin Franklin said that for a man who cares more about the spiritual than the financial rewards he can claim from his work, there are only two professions worth entering: politics and journalism. I didn't need Franklin to convince me it was journalism that I wanted. Missy Lyon's typewriter had convinced me. That first by-line when I was twelve years old had convinced me. Smelling the wet ink on the newspapers coming off the presses had convinced me.

In the end I made enough money to live the way I wanted to live, but that wasn't what made me do it or what kept me at it. My reward was seeing my column in print, seeing a magazine I had laid out sitting on the rack of the big Union News stand on the lower level of Grand Central Terminal, holding my first book in my hands and feeling the cloth binding and the glossy dust jacket, looking guiltily but with lively satisfaction at the file cards with my book titles and their Dewey Decimal System numbers on them in the New York Public Library.

Shana Alexander made a nervous appearance at the Lotus Club a few months after I had moved to the Book-of-the-Month Club and she had begun to write a column, "My Turn," for *Newsweek*. She called me out of the blue and asked if I would go to the luncheon and lend her some moral support. "I told them I won't make a speech," she said, "I'll just sit with them and answer questions. But that's bad enough. I wish you'd come." So I did, and she was good. But what interested me most was the way the question period ended.

"Mrs. Alexander," one of the members said, "you've worked on *Flair*, you've had a column in *Life*, you've been the editor-in-chief of *McCall's* and now you're writing a column for *Newsweek*. I'm wondering, if somebody was willing to give you five million dollars to do whatever you wanted to do next, what would you do?"

Shana looked him boldly in the eye. "That's easy," she said. "I'd take the five million and run like hell for Australia."

I don't agree with Shana. If somebody wanted to turn me loose with that much money, I would start a book company. I would become the original publisher in soft covers of the kind of books QPB uses. I would give it one more shot.

As the foolish Master Constable said to Borachio in *Much Ado About Nothing*, "Thou wilt be condemned into everlasting redemption for this."